T0144186

TRAINING
LAW
ENFORCEMENT
OFFICERS

TRAINING
LAW
ENFORCEMENT
OFFICERS

RICK D. GIOVENGO, PhD

Human Performance Consulting
Brunswick, Georgia, USA

CRC Press
Taylor & Francis Group
Boca Raton London New York

CRC Press is an imprint of the
Taylor & Francis Group, an **informa** business

CRC Press
Taylor & Francis Group
6000 Broken Sound Parkway NW, Suite 300
Boca Raton, FL 33487-2742

© 2017 by Taylor & Francis Group, LLC
CRC Press is an imprint of Taylor & Francis Group, an Informa business

No claim to original U.S. Government works

Printed on acid-free paper
Version Date: 20160322

International Standard Book Number-13: 978-1-4987-6883-2 (Hardback)

Library of Congress Cataloging-in-Publication Data

Names: Giovengo, Rick D., author.
Title: Training law enforcement officers / Rick D. Giovengo.
Description: Boca Raton, FL : CRC Press, 2017. | Includes bibliographical references and index.
Identifiers: LCCN 2016007216 | ISBN 9781498768832
Subjects: LCSH: Police training--United States. | Law enforcement--United States.
Classification: LCC HV8142 .G56 2016 | DDC 363.2068/3--dc23
LC record available at http://lccn.loc.gov/2016007216

**Visit the Taylor & Francis Web site at
http://www.taylorandfrancis.com**

**and the CRC Press Web site at
http://www.crcpress.com**

Printed and bound in the United States of America by Publishers Graphics, LLC on sustainably sourced paper.

"Blessed are the peacemakers, for they will be called children of God." (Matthew 5:9, New International Version)

Dedicated to those officers who put on the badge every day and do what they are trained to do.

Contents

Foreword

Law enforcement training is at a critical juncture. Almost a daily an officer makes a mistake, and it usually ends up being headline news. Almost all of these mistakes are related to the officer's training, or lack thereof. I cringe whenever I watch a video of an officer doing something wrong, especially because I know that an incident could have been prevented if only the officer had been properly trained. That is the primary reason for writing this book. This book aims to assist officers to perform better.

It all started when I was giving a presentation to a group of individuals about the Federal Law Enforcement Training Accreditation (FLETA) Standards. At the end of the presentation, I asked if there were any questions or comments. One lady basically stated the standards are a "how to" manage an academy or develop a law enforcement training program. I thought to myself, "Well that's true." Being a FLETA assessor has given me the opportunity to see how various law enforcement academies and programs conduct their business, both good and bad. What an opportunity!

This thought caused me to reflect on the various training I had during my life, from the US Marines, to the Illinois State Police Academy, to my training as a Federal Agent, to the various advanced trainings, to my own experience as the person responsible for administering both basic and advanced training programs for my own agency. I thought of the great training programs (along with the not so great ones) I had personally been through. I thought about myself being responsible for my own agency's training programs, and how there was no "how to" policy or procedures when I arrived. Everything done before my arrival was fly-by-your-seat training. We were pulling working agents out of the field and putting them in front of students. This was good and bad as you can imagine. The good thing was these were working agents that had a firm understanding of what they were talking about because they were doing it. The bad thing was there was no standardization of how the material was presented. There were no lesson plans, some instructors had some materials, some had lots of materials, some had nothing at all, and none had any formalized training on how to instruct.

It was even worse regarding in-service training. Our mandated 40-hour yearly in-service training was to update, reinforce, or improve the field agent's skill sets. This was the agency's most costly training event because every agent had to be brought in from all over the country to one centralized location. The Level 1 feedback from these yearly events was telling. The training branch would get comments such as "You brought me in from Alaska to hear someone talk about the meetings they attended. Really?" "You owe me 40 hours of my life back" and "Couldn't you just put this on a CD and send it to me?" I tried to leverage this Level 1 data to get upper management to understand how we were failing. Instead, I was told, "The agents always need something to complain about."

The more I learned, the more I knew this was a broken system that needed fixing. But upper management did not understand why we needed any changes. Their argument was nothing was broken—this had all worked before, why change? When I tried to argue about possible litigation if there was an incident, they retorted that they had never been sued before regarding training, so why change now?

I realized I had to figure this stuff out on my own. From that experience, I recognized there was a disconnect from the managers I worked for, the hiring process, the field supervisors, the trainees, and all their concepts and perspectives of what training meant. They all had their own ideas of what entailed "training."

The hiring process did not understand the training process. The upper-level supervisors did not understand the training process; they just wanted boots on the ground as soon as possible—"Just get them through training, and make sure no one fails," I was told. The field supervisors thought the new agents coming out of training had all the tools to do the job and wanted the new agents to hit the ground running, and the trainees looked at training as just something they had to get through, hopefully with as little effort as possible. I realized that this whole process was failing. We were putting agents in the field who were not prepared to do the job. To exacerbate the problem, there were no support systems in place to help them succeed once they arrived at their workplace.

At first, this was just going to be a book about outlining the process of training, but the more I wrote, the more I researched. I started to ask myself questions on what goes on in the brain when a person is going through training: How is the brain functioning when officers are placed in high-pressure situations? How did they perform? How can we help them perform better?

I further realized the training process has to be linked with the hiring process. The managers of the agency needed to understand how important training is for their long-term investment. Training is not just something you go through to get a certificate. The officers need to be held accountable for what they have been trained. I found that an officer's training does not end when they graduate—it continues. The officers need to be given more opportunities to develop their new skills once they hit the field. I realized that supervisors need to be included during the design and development of a training program, along with subject-matter experts and star performers. All aspects of training have a need for a multitude of stakeholders, not independent silos. I made a lot of mistakes during this learning process.

During my time spent in and around law enforcement training (and being a former law enforcement officer myself), I have noticed a paradigm shift on how officers are trained. I have noticed that almost all law enforcement training now revolves around the officer's perspective. The officer's perspective is important; however, it is not the only perspective; there is also the citizens' perspective, along with that of the public, and this is where problems arise—the clash of perspectives. Law enforcement is not an easy profession; it is a messy one. Law enforcement is not an exact science; it is a dynamic science. Everyone involved—the public, the officers, and the managers—needs to realize there are a multitude of variables that arise when a law enforcement officer interacts with members of the public. It is like walking a tightrope; it can end in success, or it can end in tragedy. Unfortunately, not many success stories make the headlines, tragedies almost always do.

I have also seen military tactics leak their way into law enforcement training. This becomes a dangerous proposition. Many military tactics are used when dealing with a foreign enemy, not a civilian population; a population that has constitutional rights. Some military tactics and equipment are good, but only in specific situations. Training is an organic, ever-evolving process. However, as persons responsible for training, we need to ensure that we do not get caught up in the "shiny object" syndrome. Law enforcement officers are often drawn to new techniques, new processes, or the latest gadgets with no real thought given to whether the agency can benefit from them or to public perception. You will find in this book a substantial discussion of how important analysis is when it comes to training. A thorough analysis will be able to help decide the *who*, *what*, *when*, and *how* of training.

When taking on a project of this magnitude, chances are, one will be indebted to and thankful for the help of many people. First, I would like to thank all my friends at the US Coast Guard's Maritime Law Enforcement Academy (MLEA). The staff at the MLEA are some of the best professionals with whom I have the honor of working. A good portion of this book is attributed to what I learned while working at the MLEA as their FLETA Accreditation Manager. The US Coast Guard knows training better than any other organization I have come across, and this is coming from a former US Marine. I would especially like to thank my former commanding officer at the MLEA, Paul Baker. Paul is a true intellect regarding training, and he took some of his precious time to read my book from cover to cover and provided useful insights and suggestions.

I would also like to thank my numerous friends in the Federal Law Enforcement Training Accreditation community. From 2001 to present day, they have been providing guidance to some of the best practices in the law enforcement profession. From my novice days, people in the FLETA community gave me ideas and suggestions regarding training. These people are the unsung heroes of training.

I am grateful to Mr. Ari Vidali, CEO of Envisage Corporation. I met Ari when he came into my office in 2002 selling his little known Acadis (it was not called that during that time) Learning Management System (LMS). Though my agency had no interest in buying his product, I knew he was on to something special; now, Acadis is one of the most widely used LMSs in law enforcement. Ari assisted me in writing the chapter on LMS. Although he has never been a law enforcement officer or a law enforcement trainer, his astute understanding of law enforcement training systems shows what an intelligent person he truly is.

I am likewise thankful to Ms. Tonya Lopez from the Federal Law Enforcement Training Center, who reviewed the curriculum development portion of the book and provided much needed insight regarding curriculum development.

Finally, I am indebted to my friends and family. I am grateful to senior special agent Steve Stoinski who has continually provided words of support during the worst and best of times. I would also like to express my gratitude to my best friend and former field training officer (to whom I was assigned when I was a new state officer), Tim "Buz" Henrichs. Buz taught me some of the best law enforcement skills after I had graduated from the State Police Academy. He showed me where the rubber meets the road. Lastly, I am grateful to my wonderful wife and true best friend, Keren, for I have truly been blessed by having a spouse as supporting as she, and to my son, Matthew, whose maturity is far before his time. Both had to put up with "Dad's on the computer again." Thanks to all.

Author

Dr. Rick D. Giovengo is an organizational psychologist with 28 years of law enforcement experience as both a state law enforcement officer and a federal agent. His specialized skills include undercover investigations, criminal investigations, personnel development, leadership coaching, and training. Dr. Giovengo designed the Covert Operator Selection School, which was considered a premier undercover school in federal law enforcement training. Dr. Giovengo was on the Federal Law Enforcement Training Accreditation Task Force during 2001–2002 and has more than 14 years of law enforcement accreditation experience. He was an adjunct instructor for the Federal Law Enforcement Leadership Institute from 2004 to 2009. Dr. Giovengo has trained law enforcement officers in Botswana, Brazil, Canada, Cambodia, and South Africa. He proudly served as a platoon sergeant in the US Marine Corps.

Introduction

1

Training—The act, process, or method of one that trains; the skill, knowledge, or experience acquired by one that trains.

Law Enforcement—The generic name for the activities of the agencies responsible for maintaining public order and enforcing the law, particularly the activities of prevention, detection, and investigation of crime and the apprehension of criminals.

Law Enforcement Officer—An employee of a law enforcement agency who is an officer sworn to carry out law enforcement duties. (*Merriam-Webster Dictionary*)

The first known use of the word *training* can be traced back to 1548. However, the Spartan and Roman Empires were known for their strict and harsh training regimes before 1548. The first recognized training of law enforcement officers in the United States was not until the early 1900s, stemming from widespread corruption in police departments (Chappell 2008). In fact, the first recognized formalized training for police officers was started in Berkeley, California, in 1908, soon followed by the New York City police academy in 1909 (Bopp and Schultz 1972). However, there is some evidence that New York City had some police training going back to 1853 (Palmiotto 2003). The police were quick to adapt a military model of training owing to familiarity to the model, a behaviorist method of learning. In 2006, the Bureau of Justice Statistics reported a total of 648 law enforcement training academies nationwide that trained approximately 57,000 recruits annually.

Training has evolved during the last century of law enforcement. Law enforcement training still has many facets of the basics but now has elements of more sophistication. Law enforcement training has changed from just providing basic recruit training to advanced training involving computer forensics and other forms of technology. Also, there has been an expansion of training methods now being incorporated into law enforcement training. Further, law enforcement training academies have grown to where there are some academies that have a 30-week basic training course, and yet, almost on a daily basis, law enforcement officers find themselves in trouble regarding the way they conduct their business. Avoidable failures continue in almost every realm of law enforcement. The reason is quite simple: the volume of complexity of knowledge today has exceeded our ability as providers of training to properly deliver to the officers—consistently, correctly, safely. We train longer, specialize more, use ever-advancing technologies, and still fail. Knowledge has both saved us and burdened us. We need to have more of an *understanding* of how we train. The *Interim Report of the President's Task Force on 21st Century Policing* (2015) stated the following regarding training:

> As our nation becomes more pluralistic and the scope of law enforcement's responsibilities expands, the need for more and better training has become critical. Today's line officers and leaders must meet a wide variety of challenges including international terrorism, evolving technologies, rising immigration, changing laws, new cultural mores, and a growing mental health crisis. All states, territories, and the District of Columbia should establish standards for hiring, training, and education. (p. 51)

Civil Litigation

Many officers and their departments find themselves involved in litigation, and many times this leads to the officers, as well as the department, having to pay huge sums of money as a result of lawsuits. Civil attorneys have become more astute in examining the training records of the officer(s). What were the officers taught, how were they assessed, what standards were they expected to meet, did they meet those standards? How was the training documented? This includes not only basic training and advanced training, but also in-service training. Though statistics on civil litigation against law enforcement agencies are not tracked, and are easily hidden, Gaines and Kappeler (2011) estimated that more than 30,000 civil actions have been filed against police officers each year over the past 15 years; that number is increasing every year, and the amount paid to litigants is estimated way into hundreds of millions of taxpayer dollars.

City of Canton, Ohio v. Geraldine Harris is a Supreme Court ruling in 1989 addressing law enforcement training, or failure to train. According to the Supreme Court in the *Canton* ruling, training of police is a management responsibility. The agency can be held liable if the training provided to an officer is inadequate or improper, which causes injury or violates a citizen's constitutional rights (McNamara 2006).

The Three-Prong Test

An agency should consider a three-prong test when conducting training (Figure 1.1).

The **validity** of training refers to the accuracy of training—whether or not it prepares the officer to perform a specific task at an expected level of proficiency. The best way to understand this idea is to ask yourself this

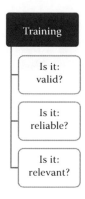

Figure 1.1 Three-prong test for training.

question: "Is the training providing the officer with the skill(s) necessary to perform in his or her *current* work environment?"

Reliability is a measure of administering the same training to different groups of officers and the results are relatively the same. Reliability is about consistency. The question you ask yourself regarding reliability is: "Can every officer we trained perform the same task in his or her *current* work environment as he (or she) was trained to do?"

Relevancy pertains to the issue of whether what is being trained is actually used in the officers' job. Are officers being trained to what is *current* with law, policy, procedure, equipment, and skills needed to perform the job *today*? The question you ask yourself here is: "Do the officers need to know this, or do the officers use this?" Even if your training is *reliable*, it may not be *valid* or *relevant*, meaning if every officer can perform the task the same in his workplace as in training does not mean it is relevant or necessary for the officer to perform his or her job.

Conditions for the Transfer of Training

There are four conditions (Figure 1.2) that need to be met to ensure the material covered during training is transferred to field work:

1. **Motivated Officers**—Officers should be motivated and ready to learn.
2. **Well-Built Curriculum**—The curriculum needs to be designed and developed to provide enhanced task to performance instruction and evaluation.
3. **Qualified Instructors**—Instructors have to be qualified to teach what they are teaching.
4. **Conducive Environment**—The training environment has to have maintained equipment and facilities that provide a safe and realistic learning venue.

Figure 1.2 Conditions for transfer of training.

All these conditions need to work in harmony with each other. Diminishing one condition reduces the transfer of training.

We have to recognize that training is just one aspect of an officer's performance. There are other variables that come into play that we will examine in more detail later in this book. However, the impact of training is a critical matter for any law enforcement agency because performance can be enhanced and training can build capacity (Intergovernmental Studies Program 2006). Further, law enforcement agencies are striving to enhance performance from personnel, and training professionals are expected to deliver results (Burke and Hutchins 2008). Law enforcement agencies have to learn to work smarter and to conduct training in a more efficient manner. The days of the "sage on the stage" instructor standing in front of the classroom are numbered as improvement in technology and training methodologies has enhanced such training modalities as collaborative, experiential, and online learning. Law enforcement instructors should learn to become facilitators of learning and not "sages on the stage." This is not to be misinterpreted in saying that instructors are going to be replaced by technology, or that simulations are going to replace real-world training models; that is not the message. The message is that law enforcement agencies should become more adaptable and progressive in how they deliver training. Everything is faster, more interconnected, and less predictable. Getting aligned with the new world is the road to longevity for any training academy or program, as well as the fulfillment to your officers. Before you conduct training, you should ask yourself, "How does this training make the officers more proficient and effective in their job?"

The Realities of Training

One reality of training is that most training will yield some predictable results (Apking and Mooney 2010). Here are some predictable outcomes of training:

1. Some officers will learn valuable information from training and apply it to their job and produce concrete results.
2. Some officers will not learn anything new or will not apply the training to their job.
3. Some officers will learn some new things and try to use their newly acquired knowledge and skills, but for some reason (i.e., lack of opportunity, time pressure, lack of initial success, lack of accountability, or lack of supervisor reinforcement), they will give up and go back to their old ways.

Another reality in training is not everything has to be trained; formal training may not be the answer, and many times it gets overused. Training law enforcement officers is an expensive enterprise. Millions of dollars are spent every year training law enforcement officers. Many times, training is ordered based on a single incident. The common answer to organizational issues is "let's conduct training" when formal training is not warranted. Elliott and Folsom (2013, p. 167) state: "Often management relies too heavily on training as a universal response to inadequate performance. Further, managers frequently confuse training with learning; losing sight of the fact that training is in large measure an attempt to standardize work."

Often, training is a "smoke screen" for problems other than skill deficiencies. There can be many other root problems leading to poor performance, such as the lack of tools necessary to do the job, poor job design, poor management, or misguided incentives. In her analysis of performance problems, Jean Marrapodi (2010) reported her findings as shown in Table 1.1.

Table 1.1   Analysis of Performance Problems

External/Environmental Conditions 85% of Performance Problems Fall into the Below Categories		
1. Expectations and feedback	2. Equipment and resources	3. Consequences and incentives
Internal/Employee Conditions 15% of the Performance Problems Fall into the Below Categories		
4. Skills and knowledge	5. Selection, assignment, capacity	6. Motives and preferences

Source: Reprinted with permission from Jean Marrapodi (2010). Front end analysis: Show me the problem. Presentation at the Learning Solutions Conference, Orlando, FL.

Why are we spending so much time and money on training when it is less than 15% of the problem? It appears we have a management problem, not a training problem. This emphasis gives us a source of many law enforcement performance issues. Harmon's (1984) Iceberg Model is a metaphor when we start addressing a possible performance issue using training as an assumed solution; we neglect to consider all of the levels of the iceberg below the surface (see Figure 1.3).

Another reality of training is the misuse of training. Some officers attend training not to improve upon or develop new skills, but instead just to get the certificate given at the end of training. Sometimes, officers are just trying to get a "ticket punched" to move up in the agency. This happens often when officers are sent to training and are not held accountable for the training they just attended. Many times, officers are just trying to improve their resumes. Sometimes, training is used as an award. Often, officers and managers look to training as just a week out of town, hopefully in some really nice location. The goal of training is not merely to obtain a certificate, it is to learn, utilize, and develop skills and knowledge to improve the mission of the agency in accomplishing its goals. Almost all of law enforcement training is paid for by taxpayer money; that money should be spent wisely.

Further, the term *training* is loosely used. Training is used for skills, and it needs to be evaluated. Many times, the term *training* is really nothing more than workshops or seminars. If it is not evaluated, it *is not* training, and often, when the budget gets tight, training is the first to take the

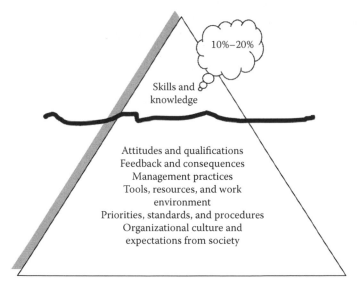

Figure 1.3 The Iceberg Model. (Adapted from Harmon, P., *Performance and Instruction*, 23(10), 27–28, 1984.)

budgetary hit. What departments have to learn is to keep their training current, efficient, effective, valid, relevant, and reliable. A butt in a seat in a classroom is an expensive endeavor, and the return on investment needs serious consideration.

Law enforcement academies have loaded up on teaching technical information, but little on how to actually police society, a society that involves people. Ask any experienced officer and he or she will tell you that it is not about what kind of weapon you carry, or car you drive, it is how you deal with people. We spend a lot of time shooting, driving, and handcuffing; albeit all of these are important, but do we teach enough on how to deal with people? Are officers mindful enough to see how their interactions affect the people with whom they are dealing? Do we spend enough time looking at the perspective of a person being policed versus being the police? We have to be careful that we do not make the task of policing society more important than the people in society.

> As a result, training programs and training simulations technologies have directed much of their focus toward improving the technical expertise of the trainees. Unfortunately, these improvements in training techniques and technologies did not really change the overall success in terms of improving performance during critical incidents. (Ken Murray 2006, pp. 23–24)

Law enforcement training academies need to shift their paradigm from a place where someone goes to train to a place that delivers training, anyplace, anywhere, anytime. Law enforcement academies need to understand an instructor is not just an instructor; an instructor is a deliverer of knowledge, a facilitator of knowledge, a researcher of knowledge, an evaluator of knowledge. All this leads to the fact that we need a different strategy for overcoming failures, one that not only builds on experience and takes advantage of the knowledge officers have, but also makes up for our inevitable human inadequacies. There is such a strategy; in fact, there are many strategies, several of which will be outlined in this book. Table 1.2 shows the difference between old school and new school paradigms.

Table 1.2 Old School, New School Paradigms

Old School	New School
Talking at us	Talking among ourselves
Control	Connection
Keynotes	Interviews
Audience	Participants
Follow the rules	Push the boundaries

70:20:10 Training

Not surprisingly, the way we learn in the workplace has dramatically changed under the pressures of evolving complexity, accelerated change, and the tidal waves of information that are constantly bombarding us. In the mid-1990s, Mike Lombardo and Bob Eichinger (1996) found in their research that roughly 70% of an employee's development comes from challenging jobs (such as law enforcement), 20% was learned from peers (both good and bad examples), which is considered informal learning, and 10% came from formal training (Figure 1.4). This coincides with the Intergovernmental Studies Program (2006) estimation that a modest "10 to 20 percent of knowledge or skills taught in training programs are effectively transferred to the workplace" (p. 1). Now, there are series of variables that can contribute to that 10% to 20% figure, such as the audience, the material, the presentation, and so on. The point of bringing this figure to light is to have you reflect on your own training programs. What percentage do you think your officers use from your training programs?

In a 2009 study, the American Society of Training and Development (ASTD) found that 41% of respondents said informal learning is occurring in their organization to a high or very high extent, and another 34% said it is occurring to a moderate extent (ASTD 2009). More than half said informal learning will increase as time progresses (ASTD 2008).

The 70:20:10 learning processes are broken down in the following:

- **Formal learning**—this is where learning objectives are set up by trainers, which provides a learning product (i.e., training program). It has structured learning objectives, activities, and feedback.
- **Informal learning**—in this case, learners set the goals and objectives of their learning. Learning is not necessarily structured in terms of effort and time (i.e., workplace).

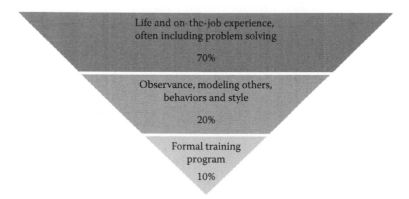

Life and on-the-job experience, often including problem solving

70%

Observance, modeling others, behaviors and style

20%

Formal training program

10%

Figure 1.4 70:20:10 training.

- **Nonformal learning**—someone in the organization who is not necessarily part of the training department (i.e., field training officer [FTO], supervisor) sets the learning objectives or tasks.

In practical terms, formal learning consists of all the products offered by the training division or academy that has learning objectives, including instructor-led classroom training, online facilitated courses, and self-paced web-based courses. Nonformal learning stems from communications from supervisors or field training officers about requirements by the organization to learn a topic, read a manual, or gain a skill. Informal learning encompasses everything else as long as it is self-directed. This includes discussions with peers, online searches, participation in communities of practice, use of job aids, requests for coaching and mentoring, book reading, blogging, reading, writing wikis, and other forms of social media (Figure 1.5).

This is not to say that formal training is a thing of the past; this is not the point whatsoever. What is being stated is having a training academy or program lasting 15 weeks or longer is going to show very little return on investment. The Bureau of Justice Statistics found in 2008 that basic recruit training for state and local agencies included more than 19 weeks (Reaves 2009). It is estimated that an agency can spend anywhere from $80,000 to $200,000 per recruit in basic training. The cognitive load factor for such an academy is way too high, and that is not counting the cost of a lengthy law enforcement academy or program. Yet over the last 20 years, we have seen an explosion in the length of time spent in law enforcement training academies. There are some academies that now have 30-week training programs; that is equivalent to 2 years of college work. We have fooled ourselves in thinking that *longer* training equates to *better* training—it does not. The US Marines can get a group of people from all walks of life, and varying educational backgrounds, and have them marching in perfect formation, performing complex tasks (like shooting a rifle from 500 meters) in as little as 12 weeks. Why? Because their training program focuses on basic tasks, based on a thorough analysis; their

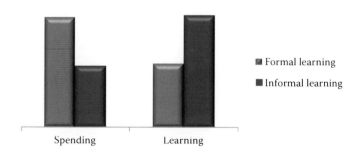

Figure 1.5 Spending/learning paradox.

concept: keep basic training simple and repetitive. Simplicity and repetition are the ultimate form of sophistication.

Longer Training ≠ Better Training

The amount of practice and real-world experience determines the level of proficiency of your officers. It should be the goal of every training program to increase the proficiency of the officers. However, this is where stakeholders of training often fail the officers. Because of budget and time constraints, we train our officers to a very *basic* level of proficiency. An officer may have received training, may have practiced, and may have even passed a *single* performance evaluation. However, with any certainty, given a real-world situation, and with no additional practice or training, will that officer perform in a proficient manner? Part of the failure lies here. If you want your officers to perform under stress, then train them under stress. Basic training alone will not help officers and agents gain mastery; it can get them to a baseline of proficiency. To keep the process going, we must look beyond formal training and transition from the academy to the workplace. If we can do this, we can positively affect training and performance (see Figure 1.6).

Here is the bottom line for increasing memory and ensuring your training carries over to the workplace: *If you have tough realistic training done in a repetitive manner, your training will carry over to field work.*

All this leads to the fact that having a robust field training program is critical to the overall training of an officer or agent. The field training program is where the skills and abilities are truly evaluated, developed, and advanced. In addition, the field training program can fill the gaps for which the academy does not have the time.

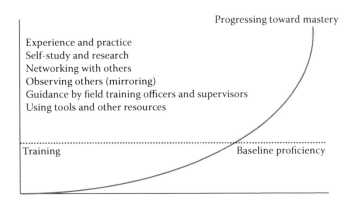

Figure 1.6 Proficiency to mastery curve.

Human Performance Technology
and Law Enforcement Training

Human performance technology (HPT) is a relatively new concept in training law enforcement officers. HPT is a systematic approach to analyzing and diagnosing human performance problems. HPT is a field of practice that has evolved largely as a result of the experience, reflection, and conceptualization of professional practitioners striving to improve human performance in the workplace. It is a relatively new field that has emerged from the coalescing of principles derived from the carefully documented practice of behavioral and cognitive psychologists, instructional technologists, training designers, organizational developers, and various human resource specialists. HPT possesses a base of research and theory but, as a rapidly evolving professional field, its practice frequently outpaces its research and theoretical foundations.

HPT grew much out of instructional systems design as a way to improve training programs. Many organizations have found that HPT improves the way they train and develop people. Throughout this book, in particular, the section on instructional system design, you will find elements of HPT. HPT is an organizational methodology; this book will mainly focus on the training aspects of HPT.

HPT *is systematic*. It is organized, rigorous, and applied in a methodical manner. Procedures exist that permit practitioners to identify performance gaps (problems or opportunities), characterize these in measurable or observable ways, analyze them, select suitable interventions, and apply these in a controlled and monitored manner.

HPT *is systemic*. It perceives identified human performance gaps as elements of systems, which in turn interface with other systems. It rejects accepting apparent causes and solutions without also examining other facets of the system. Performance is seen as the result of a number of influencing variables (selection, training, feedback, resources, management support, incentives, task interference), all of which must be analyzed before appropriate cost-effective interventions are selected and deployed.

HPT *is grounded in scientifically derived theories and the best empirical evidence available*. It seeks to achieve desired human performance through means that have been derived from scientific research, when possible, or from documented evidence, when not. It rejects enthusiastic, unsubstantiated interventions that cannot demonstrate firm theoretical foundations or valid performance results. HPT is open to new ideas and potentially valuable methods or interventions. It requires, however, that these offer systematically organized evidence to support their potential value.

HPT *is open to all means, methods, and media*. It is not limited by a set of resources or technologies that it must apply. On the contrary, HPT is

constantly searching for the most effective and efficient ways to obtain results
at the least cost.

HPT *is focused on achievements that human performers and the system
value.* It seeks bottom line results or, as Gilbert (1996, p. 17) characterizes these
valuable accomplishments, "worthy performance." The focus is not on behavior
or on one-sided winning. HPT has worthy performance as its aim, as perceived
by both the performer and the organization in which he or she performs.

HPT, therefore, is an engineering approach to attaining desired accomplishments from human performers. HP technologists are those who adopt a
systems view of performance gaps, systematically analyze both gap and system,
and design cost-effective and efficient interventions that are based on analysis
data, scientific knowledge, and documented precedents, in order to close the
gap in the most desirable manner. Analysis is a strong portion of the HPT process and here's why: Have you ever seen training segments placed into a program for no real reason? This happens a lot and causes "training creep"—that
is, an ever-expanding training program with no rhyme or reason to explain
the "creep" other than "more time is needed," or "they (the officers) really need
to know this information." A strong analysis will scientifically tell you whether
additions or expansions to your training program are really needed.

At this point, the obvious question is, "What is performance?" A better
question is, "What are the factors that influence performance?" Figure 1.7
shows the many variables that influence performance.

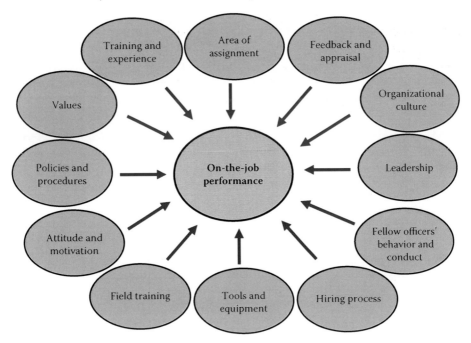

Figure 1.7 Performance factors.

Learning versus Performance

Learning: The activity or process of gaining knowledge or skill by studying, practicing, being taught, or experiencing something.
Performance: The act of doing a job or an activity.

Most people have a job in which they have to do something; that something is related to tasks that are linked to an overall performance. Is learning linked to performance? Most would say yes. But have you learned things in your life that were not linked to performance? Again, most would say yes. In fact, many of us are still waiting to use that calculus we learned in high school. The relationship between learning and performance is problematic. For one, research shows learning can occur without a change in performance; conversely, an increase in performance can fail to produce learning (Soderstrom and Bjork 2013). This is where learning and performance can part ways. In a performance, there is an end product; in learning, there may never be an end product. Performance is linked to a behavior; learning can be just a mental activity. For instance, reading a book may not change a behavior, but you can still learn something. The job of a law enforcement officer is performance related. Practically almost the entire job of a law enforcement officer is performance related.

Competent performance may enable officers to achieve success, but it does not ensure it. Consider the use of written tests based on knowledge. Often, people who pass such tests are less than successful on the job (Hale 2002 as found in Teodorescu and Binder 2004). This discrepancy may be due to the fact that while written test scores might reflect attainment of knowledge, they do not assess the actual job performance requirements—what people actually have to *do* and *produce* to be successful on the job (Hale 2002). Many written tests are not needed in a job that is almost totally performance based.

Conditions of Training

The following are some conditions of training:

1. **Primacy**—Officers retain information they learn for the first time longer than they retain information they must relearn. Unlearning incorrect procedures, or bad habits, is always more difficult than learning the correct procedures from the beginning.
2. **Readiness/Motivation**—Officers learn when they are physically, mentally, emotionally, and motivated to learn. An instructor can do everything right, the materials can be top notch, the training venue can be fantastic, but there still can be barriers to the training process.

3. **Practice**—The adage "Perfect Practice Prevents Poor Performance" holds true in training. The training also has to be meaningful to the officer.
4. **Intensity**—A vivid learning experience is learned and retained longer. When an officer experiences a bad guy role player sticking a gun in their face, they will remember that experience. Sitting in a classroom is really low on the intensity scale.
5. **Effect**—An officer learns best those things that result in satisfying consequences. Officers want to know how the training is going to benefit them immediately.
6. **Recency**—Officers retain information acquired last the easiest. The longer officers go without practicing a new concept, the easier it is for them to forget.

Both learning and training focus on performance; learning focuses on foundational preparation, and training focuses on execution (Leutner 2013). Learning, as measured by an end of instruction test, does not necessarily translate into better job performance (Clark and Wittrock 2000).

Determining Whether There Is a Need

Training primarily focuses on five moments of need:

1. **New:** When officers are being trained to do something for the first time.
2. **More:** When officers are expanding the breadth and depth of what they have been trained to do.
3. **Apply:** When officers need to act on what they have been trained to do, which includes planning what they do, remembering what they may have forgotten, or adapting their performance to a unique situation.
4. **Solve:** When problems arise, or things break down or do not work the way they were intended.
5. **Change:** When officers need to learn a new way of doing something that requires them to change skills that are deeply ingrained in their performance practice (Gottfredson and Mosher 2011).

Learner Analysis

A basic principle of any instruction is, "Know your participants." A good strategy is to collect information about your officers during the early stages of your instructional design process. As you can imagine, this process can take a fair amount of time so some people wonder why they should even bother.

You should invest the time to do a learner analysis because knowing information about your officers can affect many design choices. Here are just a few examples of how information about your officers can affect the instructional design of a course:

1. The number and location of your officers will affect your choice of training strategy (i.e., e-learning vs. instructor-led vs. on-the-job).
2. The experience and knowledge level of your officers will affect your activity choices during training.
3. The cultural mix of your officers will affect what you say and how you say it during a training session.
4. The presence of subject-matter experts in your future learner group will affect the structure of your class, as you may want to use them in some way to help teach the novices in the group.

The Power of Checklists

The "checklist" is a powerful training tool and job aid that has been around since early airplane pilots were trained. In fact, checklists are such a part of pilot culture that pilots have developed checklists that cover almost every possible scenario from getting an airplane to fly to solving problems that occur in flight. What early pilot trainers figured out is that in a complex environment, there are two extreme issues. First is the fallibility of human memory and attention, especially unexciting, routine matters that are easy to overlook under the strain of pressing events. Second is that people can lull themselves into skipping steps even when they remember them. Checklists seem to provide an answer to human inadequacies. They remind us of the minimum number of steps and make them explicit. They provide not only the possibility of verification but also a discipline of higher performance.

There is no better illustration of this than as found by author and medical doctor Atul Gawande in his fascinating book *The Checklist Manifesto— How to Get Things Right*. In his book, Dr. Gawande researched the value of a checklist in the operating room. Now, you can only imagine the resistance Dr. Gawande received when he proposed his idea to these highly competent, ego-driven doctors, that they needed a checklist to ensure they are covering all the steps in performing a surgery. Because of his findings, infection and mistakes in the operating room were greatly reduced by using simple checklists.

Checklists provide us with a kind of "cognitive net" to catch mental flaws of memory, attention, and thoroughness (Gawande 2009). In police work, there have been documented failures to properly conduct an eyewitness lineup or, in training, not double-checking to ensure there are no real live weapons in a nonlethal training area.

Another significant benefit in using checklists during training involves *data*. Where are mistakes being made? Who is making the mistakes? Why are mistakes made? A checklist provides you documented trends and tendencies not only among officers but also among instructors.

Gawande (2009) offers up some suggestions when developing checklists:

1. You have to define a clear pause point where the checklist should be used. Is it at the entry of a nonlethal training area? When firearms are checked in?
2. The checklist should not be lengthy. A rule of thumb is between 5 and 10 items. It should fit on one page.
3. The wording should be simple and exact. There should be no confusion on what the checklist is checking for.

Some instructors may find these checklists a burden, but it is not a burden; it is protecting all those involved in the training evolution, the officers, the instructors, the supervisors, the agency.

Conclusion

There are some expectations in training law enforcement officers. The first expectation is one of selflessness: As trainers, we accept responsibility for others. We place the needs and concerns of those who depend on us above our own. Second is an expectation of skill: We aim for excellence (not perfection) in our knowledge and expertise. Third is an expectation of trustworthiness: We will be responsible for our personal behaviors toward our chosen profession.

Training law enforcement officers is an expensive and arduous process. Thorough analysis will determine if there needs to be formal training conducted. The HPT model provides law enforcement academies with an efficient and effective process to train law enforcement officers. Though learning and performance can go hand and hand, there are some differences. Almost all of the tasks performed by a law enforcement officer are performance based.

This book explores the following topics: the brain, academy and program administration, training staff, training development, and training delivery. It is not necessary that you read the book from beginning to end; you can just select an area in which you are currently involved. For instance, you might be a new instructor and looking to develop your skills, in which case the chapters on training delivery would help you hone your instructor skills. Or, you might have been assigned to develop a training program so the training development chapters would then be able to help you out. This book is intended to offer comprehensive coverage of all aspects of training law enforcement officers. It is intended for you.

The Brain on Training

2

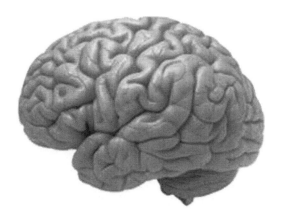

Introduction

To have a clear understanding of your role in training, and how training affects your officers, you should have some rudimentary idea of how the brain functions. That 3-lb gray squishy organ on top of our bodies has a huge impact on how an officer functions in training and in the field. Our brain can be considered the most complex organ on Earth. The good news is our understanding of how our brain functions has had some clear breakthroughs over the last 20 years.

Thanks to functional magnetic resonance imagery (*f*MRI), computed tomography scans, brain mapping, and other modern devices, we have a better understanding of how our brain functions. We have been taught many myths, which have been found to be completely wrong. For instance, many of us were taught that we only use 10% of our brain's capacity. Wrong. Brain scans using *f*MRI have found that we use many portions of our brain at any given time; it is all according to what we are experiencing at the time. Another theory that has recently been debunked is the right/left brain idea—that we each have a dominant sphere of the brain we favor. Wrong. First, the sweeping description of the two spheres of the brain misses the mark: one is logical and the other intuitive, one analytical and the other creative. The left and right halves of the brain do function in some different ways, but these differences are more subtle than is popularly believed. (For example, the left side processes small details of things you see; the right processes the overall shape.) Second, the halves of the brain do not work in isolation; rather, they always work together as a system. Your brain is not an arena for some never-ending competition, the brain's "strong" side tussling with its "weak" side. Or how about the theory that our brain cells begin to die off (and never to be regenerated) after we reach our early 20s? Wrong. While it is true that brain cells die, those cells are replaced by new brain cells; our brain is ever evolving. It is now widely believed that the brain does not stop developing until around age 25, and the brain never stops changing. Norman Doidge, MD, in his book *The Brain That Changes Itself*, puts it like this:

> The common wisdom was that after childhood the brain changed only when it began the long process of decline; that when brain cells failed to develop properly, or were injured, or died, they could not be replaced. Nor could the brain ever alter its structure and find a new way to function if part of it was damaged. The theory of the unchanging brain decreed that people who were born with brain or mental limitations, or who sustained brain damage, would be limited or damaged for life. (Doidge 2007, p. 27)

Because of the fascinating research on stroke patients, we are getting a clearer understanding that the brain can "rewire" itself and generate new neural pathways.

Basic Brain Structures

Conscious thinking involves deeply complex biological interactions in the brain among billions of neurons. Neurons—these are basic brain cells, and there are billions of these cells in our brain. Neurons have a specialized ability to manage bioelectrical information and to communicate with each other by exchanging chemical information in the form of neurotransmitters (chemicals) through connections with other neurons, known as synapses (each neuron has about 10,000 synapses). All brain functioning is the result of neurons exchanging information, and the functions we depend on emerge from large groups of neurons working together as networks. Every movement in the body is only possible because of a network of neurons. If a network of neurons supporting a brain function is repeatedly stimulated through practice and training, it will become stronger, contributing to the optimization of that brain function (more on this later in the chapter).

The prefrontal cortex (PFC) is located in the very front of the brain, just behind the forehead. The PFC is in charge of abstract thinking and thought analysis; it is also responsible for regulating behavior. This includes mediating

conflicting thoughts, making choices between right and wrong, and predicting the probable outcomes of actions or events. This brain area also governs
social control, such as suppressing emotional or sexual urges. Since the PFC
is the brain center responsible for taking in data through the body's senses
and deciding on actions, it is most strongly implicated in human qualities
such as consciousness, general intelligence, and personality.

Mind Maps (or Schemas)

Mind maps (or schemas) define the essential structure, the logic, for a particular type of experience. Our schemas differ from each other just as our
experiences do. Understanding a new idea involves creating maps in the PFC
that represent new, incoming information and connecting neurons in a map-
like fashion. Making a decision involves activating a series of maps in the
PFC and making a choice between these maps. Recalling involves searching
through the billions of maps contained in memories and bringing just the
right ones into the PFC. Memorizing encompasses holding maps in attention
in the PFC long enough to embed them in long-term memory (more on this
later).

Brain Plasticity

Brain plasticity, also known as *neuroplasticity*, refers to the changes in how
neurons and synapses interact with each other in our brain, thus affecting
our behavior, our brain processes, our thinking, and our emotions, as well as
the changes resulting from brain damage. Dr. Doidge states,

> The idea that the brain can change its own structure through thought and
> activity is, I believe, the most important alteration in our view of the brain
> since we first sketched out its basic anatomy and the workings of its basic com-
> ponent, the neuron. (Doidge 2007, p. 38)

Plasticity tells us a great deal about learning and the brain. As human
beings, we tend to learn things the same way. The idea that we are using
just 10% of our brain is just plain incorrect. Any portion of the brain that is
not being used can be taken over for processing other information. Again,
Dr. Doidge states,

> The competitive nature of plasticity affects us all. There is an endless war of
> nerves going on inside each of our brains. If we stop exercising our mental
> skills, we do not just forget them: the brain map space for those skills is turned

over to the other skills we practice instead. If you ever ask yourself, 'How often must I practice French, or guitar, or math to keep on top of it?' you are asking a question about competitive plasticity. You are asking how frequently you must practice one activity to make sure its brain map space is not lost to another. (Doidge 2007, p. 42)

Competitive plasticity explains why old training techniques are difficult to break or unlearn. When we learn a technique, it develops a brain map, and each time we repeat the technique, it claims more control of that map. However, when we learn a new technique over an old technique, a new brain map has to be rewired over the old map. That is why unlearning an old technique is often more difficult than learning a new technique. Thus, we have to be careful that we are not changing techniques for the sake of change. We must be cognizant how changes in techniques will be received by officers. There has to be an understanding that when we introduce a new technique to older officers, who have been using an old technique for many years, the older officers will need more practice time than new officers learning the technique. A new neural pathway has to be built. In terms of skills, it is clear that an activity repeated will become more glued in one area for processing. In other words, old dogs can be taught new tricks, but it just takes more patience and practice.

Our brain has developed in a way that provides more and more brain area for abilities we use all of the time. This allows the possibility that thoughts, skills, and routines can become more embedded until we can no longer change them. However, there is one overriding principle—motivation. New studies in neuroscience clearly indicate that new neurons are formed when we are motivated to learn. Brain plasticity now tackles how we understand human potential. If potential exists, we surely must be able to change it over time.

Myelin

Again, when we look at how the brain functions, we get a better understanding of how important practice is in psychomotor learning. The more we develop a skill circuit from the brain neurons to the muscle fibers, the less we are aware we are using it. Our brains are built to make psychomotor skills automatic, to store them in the subconscious portions of our memories. Our brains are building vast, intricate circuits, and we are simultaneously forgetting that we built them. This is where *myelin* steps in. As stated earlier, our brains are composed of thousands of neurons that interconnect with each other. Myelin is an electrically insulating substance that forms a layer, the myelin sheath, usually around only the axon of a neuron. The more an officer

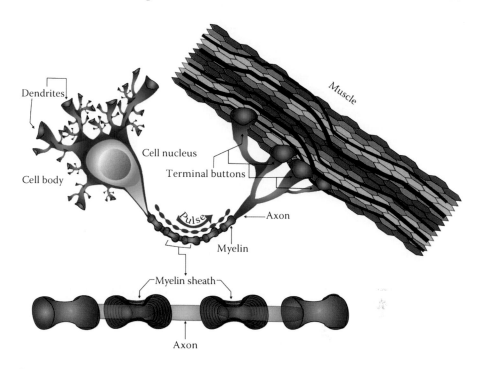

Figure 2.1 Neuron and myelin.

practices a psychomotor movement, the more myelin gets built around these circuits. The more myelin builds around a circuit, the quicker electronic pulses travel through the circuits to the muscles. In other words, neurons that fire together wire together. Therefore, each time an officer practices firing a weapon or performing a strong-arm takedown, he or she is slowly building myelin around his or her psychomotor circuits. The more practice, the more myelin, the quicker the circuits (see Figure 2.1). In other words, practice does make perfect.

Memory

Learning requires memory. Anytime there is a discussion about learning, there has to be a portion of that discussion dedicated to memory. Cognitive psychologists have spent years studying how we remember certain things, but do not remember other things; it is a very complex process. Instructors and officers need a clear understanding on how memory is a critical component of an officer functioning under pressure.

Currently, what is agreed upon is that, as humans, we have three forms of memory, *sensory memory*, *working memory* (sometimes called short-term memory), and *permanent memory* (sometimes called long-term memory).

Sensory memory is memory based on the temporary storage of information from the senses (smell, taste, etc.). Anderson (1995) describes it as follows:

> Sensory memory is capable of storing more information or less complete records of what has been encountered for brief periods of time, during which people can note relationships among the elements and encode the elements in a more permanent memory. If the information in sensory is not encoded in the brief time before it decays, it is lost. What subjects encode depends on what they are paying attention to. The environment typically offers much more information at one time than we can encode. Therefore, much of what enters our sensory system results in no permanent record. (p. 160)

Short-term or *working memory* uses information from both permanent and sensory memory; it is information we actively process. However, this information is stored for a short period (about 12 seconds without reinforcement). Working memory is the cognitive structure where conscious processing happens (Kirschner et al. 2006). Working memory has restrictions on how much information it can hold before information starts getting dumped; this is referred to as *cognitive overload*. Why is this important? What your subject-matter experts need to understand is they can sometimes overload the novice officers' working memory with too much content using new terms and lengthy lectures and unrelated anecdotes or stories (Clark 2015).

Long-term or *permanent memory* contains organizing ideas, information, processes, and skills that are in the cognitive domain. Everything that we know and understand is stored in permanent memory (Marzano and Kendall 2007). Long-term memory can store huge amounts of data and is considered the dominant structure of human cognition (Kirschner et al. 2006).

Cognitive psychologist George Miller argued in his 1956 Information Processing Theory that short-term memory can hold from five to nine "chunks" of information, and too much information given at once will likely be quickly forgotten. What is a chunk? A chunk of information is similar to a computer byte: the smallest unit of "memory" needed to encode a single character of text. Of the trillions of pieces of information we store, a chunk of neural information is comparable to a single word or object. These chunks can build upon one another. In other words, new chunks can be added to old chunks. From an instructional point of view, this can be done by adding relevancy to the material; this is sometimes referred to as "scaffolding." Scaffolding can enhance working memory function (Dehn 2011). From a psychomotor point of view, Terrace (2001) suggests making pauses during learning for the officers to "download" the material. See Figure 2.2 to get an idea on how memory flows in the brain.

High levels of stimulation or emotion will increase the ability to store information into long-term memory. Otherwise, moving information to long-term memory can be challenging. For permanent memories to form, close attention has to be paid to incoming information. You must practice

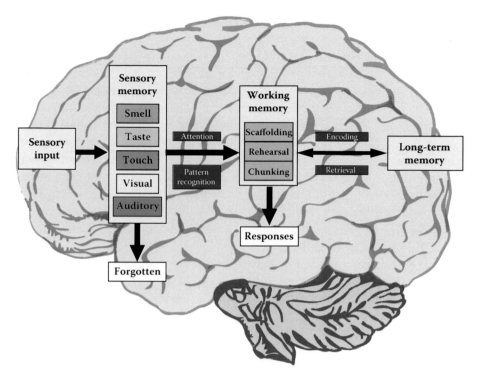

Figure 2.2 Flow of brain memory.

specific activities over and over until they become embedded in long-term memory. Research has shown that taking repeated tests (including practical evaluations) stimulates active retrieval of information from memory (Karpicke and Roediger 2008). Therefore, you must train memory.

There is research suggesting the term *muscle memory* has some relevance, that is, that some "memory" is actually stored in muscle tissues. The key to long-term memory formation is not the amount of time spent learning, but the amount of time between learning. We learn best when our brain cells are switched on and off, with short periods of learning and breaks in between. By switching your officer's brain cells "on" (during learning) and "off" again (during breaks), the officer's unconscious has time to internalize the knowledge and the repetition results in long-term memories. Research has also shown that longer breaks between teaching sessions can result in longer-lasting memories. You can enhance memory retention using the following methods:

- Provide steady relevant practice
- Create job-related problems and scenarios
- Use team projects
- Ask questions
- Be consistent

Hermann Ebbinghaus was a psychologist who gained fame for his early studies in the late 1880s on memory. Based on his own research studies, he came up with the concept of the "forgetting curve." He used his study data to create a curve that showed people will forget 90% of what they learn within 3 to 6 days unless learning is reinforced with multiple repetitions. Since then, thousands of studies have been done on spaced repetition, forgetting, memory, and so on. Will Thalheimer (2010) published a paper that argues against Ebbinghaus's global 90% statement. He points to these many subsequent studies—done in a more noteworthy way—which show that the percentage of forgetting is *highly* variable. It depends on numerous factors such as the following:

- The type of material that is being learned
- The officers' prior knowledge
- The officers' motivation to learn
- The power of the learning methods used
- The contextual cues in the learning and remembering situations
- The amount of time the learning has to be retained
- The difficulty of the retention test (Thalheimer 2010)

As mentioned earlier, basically our brains are bundles of circuits (around 100 billion neurons) connected to each other by a synapse. When we do something, our brain sends a signal through these circuits. So how do we get physical and mental processes *hardwired* into an officer's permanent memory? Here are some strategies to increase memory retention:

1. Provide frequent, spaced intervals of learning.
   a. Organize content into small chunks or groupings.
2. Provide multiple repetitions.
   a. Early repetitions may be iterations of what an officer already learned.
   b. Later repetitions should allow for greater elaborations. On the knowledge side, early repetitions may involve recall of the fact or a different presentation of the fact. Later repetitions may require the officers to apply the fact to a context of a specific setting. On the psychomotor side of things, think in terms of "Show me. Let me practice."
3. Provide immediate feedback for mistakes, and make sure officers get it right before moving forward.
   a. Provide officers with feedback at the point where they made the mistake. Require officers to correct the mistake before they can move on. This action ensures that they embed the "correct" way of responding or performing something rather than embedding incorrect responses.

b. Make sure feedback specifies exactly what the officer did wrong or offers a clear clue that the officer was successful.
c. Offer strategies, examples, and other guidance to aid in performing correctly (Clark 2015).
d. Use praise sparingly. Sometimes, praise can divert learning from the task to the learner's ego. Hattie and Yates (2014, p. 67) in their recent research state, "We know of no research finding suggesting that receiving praise itself can assist a person to learn or to increase their knowledge and understanding."

Cognitive Load Theory

Information overload erodes the quality of training. What is cognitive load and why is it important in law enforcement training? Cognitive load theory was developed by John Sweller during his studies on problem solving (Sweller 1988). He found that too much cognitive load (stuff to remember) can have damaging effects on task completion. Cognitive load depends on three factors: (1) the learning objective and its associated content, (2) the officer's prior knowledge, and (3) the instructional environment (Clark et al. 2005). Research has found many techniques that reduce cognitive load improve efficiency in the learning of complex tasks. Cognitive load theory is universal. Cognitive load applies to all types of training content and all types of multimedia presented to the officers. It is universal because it applies to instructors, instructional developers, and learners. Use of efficient instructional environments leads to faster learning and improved learning. Therefore, the general rule for achieving efficiency in learning is to minimize cognitive load in your instructional materials when learning tasks are complex.

Recent brain research proves that a large amount of cognitive material, if not soon after repeated, is forgotten. John Medina in his book *Brain Rules* (2008) found from brain research the following:

- Most cognitive material disappears within minutes if not repeated.
- Memories found in permanent memory sometimes can take weeks, months, and even years to be formed.
- The way to make permanent memory more reliable is to integrate new information gradually and repeat it in time intervals.

According to cognitive load theory, learning requires processing in working memory, and if working memory gets overloaded, learning is disrupted. Cognitive load is a helpful theory to guide the design, development, and implementation of instruction. There should be a focus on minimizing extra cognitive load by shortening, eliminating, and simplifying the amount of the learning material. Focus your training on a single concept at a time. For example, instead of training your officers in "Use of Force," conduct a series of single-concept sessions, such as "Situations Involving Level 1 Use of Force Encounters," "Situations Involving Level 2 Use of Force Encounters," and so on.

The Brain under Stress or Pressure

Many officers would like to think they can perform under high levels of pressure. However, many do not want a lot of stress in their job. What is the difference between *pressure* and *stress*? Are they one and the same? Most of us would like to be the officer who performs under pressure, but we do not want to be the officer who is stressed out. Here are some definitions to more easily differentiate the two:

> *Stress*—When an officer interprets the demands of the situation outweigh the officer's ability to respond. Getting a divorce, a significant life event, and a boss who makes their life miserable are common factors of stress. An officer may feel that he or she does not have enough money, time, or energy to deal with the situation. Stressful events transform into feelings of being overwhelmed. Stress reduction is the goal.
>
> *Pressure*—When an officer is in a situation where the consequences affect the level of success or survival. Pressure is the "do or die" situation. Pressure is performance or task related.

Everyone has some form of stress in their lives; it is just a portion of human existence we all have to deal with, and how we deal with stress affects our levels of performance. Law enforcement officers need to be able to perform under high levels of pressure sometimes. What makes it difficult to be prepared in the law enforcement profession is that job performance can go from 0 to 100 in a matter of seconds, and the public demands that officers make sound critical judgments during those moments of high pressure. Something an officer routinely does, a traffic stop for instance, can turn into a life or death situation in a matter of seconds. Law enforcement trainers need to be keenly aware of how to build training scenarios that place officers in realistic situations. Further, law enforcement trainers need to teach officers on how to perform correctly under high-pressure situations. A study completed by the Federal Law Enforcement Training Center (FLETC) on officers performing in high-pressure scenarios found that 70% of the students made poor tactical decisions, 70% were unable to correct equipment malfunctions, and 49% "failed to maintain a position of advantage during specific phases" of the scenario (FLETC 2011, p. 3-2). This type of data shows that we are not preparing officers to perform correctly when they confront real pressure situations.

Stress and pressure means there is too much electrical activity in the PFC. Remember the PFC is the area that decides where we are going to eat, what we are going to watch on TV tonight, and whether a person has a concealed weapon. The PFC is also where our judgment calls are made. However, there are other portions of our brain that work their way into our functioning; these areas are sometimes referred to as our "reptilian brain." Why? Because these portions of our brain are very similar to those found in reptiles. These subcortical portions are where more of our instinctual functions come from, sleeping, eating, sexual reproduction, and so on. One area is called the *amygdala*; it is part of the larger system called the *limbic system*. The limbic system is there to protect you; it is there to minimize danger and maximize reward. The limbic system is also easily aroused. Memory, reactions, and lower-order decision making is part of the responsibilities of the amygdala.

The amygdala is closely tied to the *hypothalamus*. The hypothalamus keeps all of our functions in balance through the autonomic nervous system. It does this by secreting hormones into the autonomic nervous system. The hypothalamus tells us when we are hungry, controls our bodily functions, and lets us know when we need to sleep. This is also an area where fear processing takes place; the "fight, flight, or freeze" responses originate here. Notice the extra word *freeze*. Immobilization (the freeze) is a defense mechanism. Like "fight or fright," it is an involuntary reaction. Our brain's sensory areas are aware of what is happening around us, processing information at very high levels. This is not perception, it is sensory awareness. Perception is cognition in the PFC; sensory awareness happens in the limbic systems.

When these "fight, flight, or freeze" situations arrive, the hypothalamus signals to our pituitary gland, which then sends signals to our adrenal glands. The adrenal glands are not part of our brain; they are located on top of the kidneys. The adrenal glands secrete adrenaline and cortisol when we are under pressure or stress. Most law enforcement trainers have heard the term *adrenaline dump* when training law enforcement officers. "Adrenaline dump" is when these chemicals released by the adrenal glands begin to overwhelm us. The brain starts redirecting blood from the PFC (the decision-making area of the brain) and moves the blood to our muscles and other organs and glands. Our breathing will increase along with our heartbeat, and our vision will narrow. If your officers have not trained for these situations, problems are going to arise, and poor decision making and other physical problems are going to manifest themselves. Further, with blood being redirected to other portions of the body, the brain's memory center, the hippocampus, will shrink. To further exacerbate the situation, large amounts of

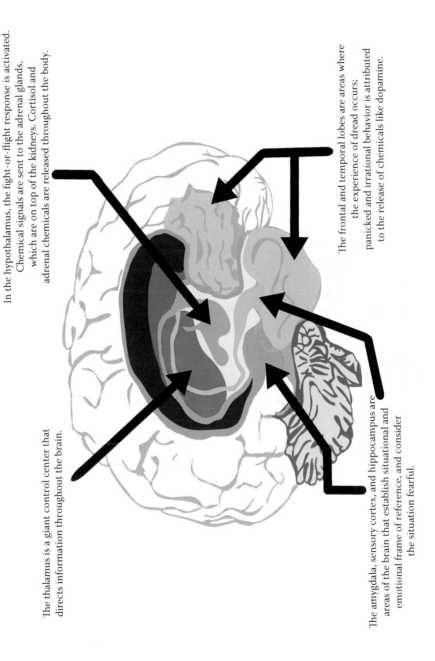

In the hypothalamus, the fight-or-flight response is activated. Chemical signals are sent to the adrenal glands, which are on top of the kidneys. Cortisol and adrenal chemicals are released throughout the body.

The frontal and temporal lobes are areas where the experience of dread occurs; panicked and irrational behavior is attributed to the release of chemicals like dopamine.

The thalamus is a giant control center that directs information throughout the brain.

The amygdala, sensory cortex, and hippocampus are areas of the brain that establish situational and emotional frame of reference, and consider the situation fearful.

Figure 2.3 Sensory areas of the brain.

cortisol will damage parts of the hippocampus. All this leads to a deterioration of memory and decision making (see Figure 2.3).

When officers have adrenaline and cortisol pumping at high levels in their system, along with blood being redirected to other portions of their body, other physiological factors will start to affect their performance. Their vision will narrow, sometimes referred to as "tunnel vision" or "perceptual narrowing." Objects will appear closer than they are, and close objects will not be seen at all. Sometimes, objects will be misrepresented, such as a wallet can be seen as a pistol or a long gun becomes a shovel. Dr. Alexis Artwohl and Loren Christensen (1997) in their excellent research on officer-involved shootings found that 21% of the officers "saw, heard, or experienced something during the event that was later found out had not really happened or happened very differently than how officers remembered it" (p. 67).

Many times, the officers under high-pressure situations suffer from "auditory exclusion," meaning they will temporarily lose their sense of hearing, but sometimes, it can have the opposite effect, their sense of hearing becomes more pronounced. Table 2.1 shows what can happen to an officer under pressure (stress being 175 heartbeats per minute [HPM] or higher).

When it comes to an officer's arousal and performance, you should be acquainted with the Upside-Down-U Theory of Arousal (sometimes referred to as Yerkes–Dodson law from their 1908 study). What the theory states is that as performance increases, along with mental and physiological arousal, performance reaches an optimal level. However, when the arousal increases too high, performance decreases. "The optimal level of arousal varies for different tasks, with complex tasks showing an earlier performance decrement

Table 2.1   Frequency of Perceptual Distortion under Pressure

85%	Diminished sound/auditory exclusion
80%	Tunnel vision
74%	Auto pilot
72%	Increased visual clarity
65%	Slow-motion time
51%	Memory loss for event
47%	Memory loss for action
40%	Dissociation
26%	Intrusive thoughts
22%	Memory distortion
16%	Fast-motion time
16%	Intensified sounds
7%	Temporary paralysis

Source: Adapted from Asken, M. J., Grossman, D., and Christensen, L. W.
               (2010). *Warrior Mindset.* Millstadt, IL: Human Research Group.

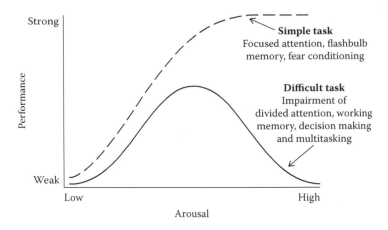

Figure 2.4 Upside-Down-U Theory of Arousal.

than simple tasks, for the same level of arousal. In other words, if we are performing a relatively simple task, then we can cope with a much larger range of arousal levels—the curve is flatter" (Hayes 2000, p. 45). However, the inverse is true, if we are performing a complex task, like a use of force situation, we cannot cope with a larger range of arousal levels—the performance curve goes down (see Figure 2.4).

Most of the research on stress and performance on officers has focused on HPM. Though HPM is a factor, most recent research has found HPM is not the single most important factor; the chemicals of adrenaline and cortisol pumping into an officer's mental functions also have an effect on how an officer performs in a high-stress situation.

Training for Stress and Pressure

Law enforcement training must include tactics for constructing mind maps that will assist officers in the evaluation of risk in a situation. Since it is well documented that stress can affect performance, how does your training prepare your officers for real-world performance? There are several ways to increase pressure during training:

- Reduced time to perform a task
- Increased number of tasks to be completed
- Increased expectancy of a possible threat
- Unwanted sounds or loud noise
- Unexpected turn of events
- Increased fatigue
- High consequences of error (FLETC 2011)

It is also important to understand that an officer's level of fitness performance under pressure can have little impact if the officer has not trained for the situation at hand. How many people have awakened in the middle of the night with their heart racing and beads of sweat coming off their body, and yet never moved a muscle? That is how the brain can ramp up functions in your body, and physical fitness has nothing to do with the situation. Your brain has control of the situation, not your body. Trainers need to get the body and the brain to work in sync with each other under times of pressure. This is not discounting physical fitness, which is very important. What is important is the brain and the body must be trained together.

Stress Inoculation Training

Stress inoculation training (SIT) is one of the best ways to prepare your officers for high performance under high-pressure situations. SIT is designed to intervene with officers at the psychosocial level, providing officers with the experience with pressure that fosters psychological preparedness and promotes resilience (Meichenbaum 2008). SIT helps an officer transition from a "fear" response to a high level of skill competency. SIT helps officers become aware of how their behaviors can be changed to help them cope with high-pressure situations. Through SIT, an officer can develop self-confidence in pressure situations. There is one caveat that must be discussed when talking about pressure training. Hancock and Szalma (2008) brought up two distinct issues. They noted the person's current state of mind when he or she encounters a high-pressure situation. Is he or she fatigued, tired from lack of sleep, or affected by some other variable (like work or family issues)? Second, what are the individual differences? Some people handle pressure better than others, and that can be based on a multitude of factors. Have they been involved in sports? Have they had previous military training? Though trainers try to train groups as homogenous individuals, it is still uncertain how any one individual will perform under pressure. Scenarios must be designed to heighten the level of pressure of officers being trained. Higher pressure can be dealt with an equally higher level of learning. The visual, auditory, and sensory stimuli place the brain into heightened states of alert. Let us look at this example. If you were to walk a plank 8 inches wide by 50 feet long placed on the ground, you would probably be able to perform the task in a low pressure level. However, if that plank was raised to 100 feet off the ground, your pressure level would be much higher, even though the psychomotor skills used to perform the task are exactly the same. Why? Because the threat of failure has a higher level of punishment, and therefore, a higher level of pressure.

Here is the difference between stress and pressure. You have choices when you are under stress. You can go for a walk, or take a yoga class.

However, when you are in a pressure situation, you do not have many options—it's a do-or-die situation. Dr. Hendrie Weisinger says in his book *Performing Under Pressure* (2015) that understanding the difference between *pressure* and *stress* is imperative to performing under pressure; failure to do so can make every small stressful situation feel like a pressure situation. Officers who believe that they are under stress the whole time can affect their performance when they are subjected to pressure. This is why managing stress is so important. So how do we as trainers prepare students to handle pressure and stressful situations? One way is to create the proper mindset.

The Law Enforcement Mindset

Let us make it clear at this juncture that not all stress or pressure is bad. Unmanaged stress is bad, but managed stress or pressure can create quality performance. Do you think Navy Seal training has high levels of stress embedded in it? Then how do you make it through Basic Underwater Demolition School? You build the proper mindset. Mindsets are beliefs that shape your reality, including physical reactions. Stress is a biological state designed to help you learn from experience. That means your stress response is extremely receptive to the effects of deliberate practice. Whatever actions you take during pressure situations, you teach your body and brain to do spontaneously. Every moment of stress is an opportunity to transform your stress instincts. Officers should have the mindset that stressful situations give them an opportunity to grow. Officers should view stress as a way to awaken their core human strength of courage, connection, and growth.

Mindfulness

Law enforcement is a profession with deep personal meaning. Trying to create a psychological shield to defend against stress can interfere with the ability to find purpose and satisfaction with the job. Law enforcement officers deal with the dark side of humanity, so officers should embrace the relationship between suffering and meaning, rather than reject it. There are a myriad of steps that can assist officers when dealing with, or coming out of, a stressful situation. One way is to create an inner resiliency to lessen the impact of a stressful situation. One method gaining traction in law enforcement circles is practicing mindfulness. A 2014 study conducted by Johnson et al. with US Marines going through Infantry Immersion Training (a 9-week course) found that Marines who were given Mindfulness Training had quicker recovery rates from extremely stressful/pressure situations.

Mindfulness is defined as the experience of paying close attention to the present in an open and accepting way (Rock 2009). It is an idea of living "in the present," of being aware of the experience as it occurs in real time, and accepting what you see. However, when we are distracted by past events, we activate that mind map. If you are thinking about that jerk boss you have, that mind map goes and retrieves that information. A picture of your boss will appear in your head, and memories of how he has mistreated you will surface. A narrative begins to play in your head. Then, all of a sudden, a routine traffic stop turns bad; now, your brain has to switch functions to adapt to what is happening now, different areas of the brain get activated, and in turn they try to activate other brain maps. The brain tries to find those training maps of use of force decision making, so hopefully your training will kick in, but because of the distractions, your reactions are slower. An officer needs to be completely focused on the moment to survive.

Listening to the perspective of others while also taking time to listen to the voice inside themselves can create an emotional balance within an officer. After a stress incident, officers can ask themselves these types of questions: (1) *What made the incident memorable?* (2) *What did I do that helped in the situation?* (3) *What did I learn about myself?* Writing these thoughts down can release some of the tension created by the incident. Speaking with fellow officers about the stress they are feeling also creates mindfulness. The sharing of experiences lets officers know they are not alone. Many agencies have created peer support programs composed of trained officers who are available to talk to officers who are under stress. Sometimes, just seeing a fellow officer creates a sense of brotherhood and sisterhood.

Psychologists have found the most important factor in how a person responds to pressure is how they think they can handle it (McGonigal 2015). When faced with any pressure situation, an officer needs to evaluate both the situation and the resources. An officer needs to think about how hard the situation is and assess whether he or she has the skills, strength, and courage to see the situation to completion. This assessment is critical to the performance of the officer. If the officer believes that the situation exceeds his resources, he will have a "fight or flight" response. However, if officers believe they have the resources to handle the situation, their performance will increase.

Another resilience training that has been widely discussed is the ability to keep the mind and the body in good physical condition. For people in good physical shape, their heart rates return to resting levels more quickly after a stressful event (Asken et al. 2010). Asken et al. (2010) found the following benefits of being physically fit:

- Reduced feeling of anxiety or depression
- Increased endurance, strength, and flexibility
- Increased physical resistance to stressors

- Increased pain tolerance
- Clear mental functioning under stress
- Increased stable positive mood
- Increased protection against injury

Keeping our body fit adds extra benefits by keeping our brain fit.

Other positive behaviors that can lead to increased resilience in officers are the benefits of meditation and yoga. Most officers shirk these practices as being too "out there" for them, but the research showing how these behaviors can increase the brain's ability to function before and after a stressful event is overwhelming. Yoga is not for stretching like most people think. Yoga grounds the person in the present moment and quiets the mind. If you are holding a yoga pose and you start thinking about that idiot boss you have, you will fall out of the pose. Yoga requires you to concentrate in the present moment and removes all of the chatter that can clog up our thinking. If the Green Bay Packers can do yoga (and they do), then law enforcement officers can do yoga as well. *Warrior Mindset* (2010) by Asken et al. is a very good book that delves into the many different aspects of creating a proper mindset and many different techniques that officers can use to make themselves more resilient.

The research on the benefits of meditation and stress reduction is staggering. Research conducted by Lisa Wimberger with law enforcement officers and meditation has shown how beneficial meditation can decrease stress reduction, including posttraumatic stress disorder. She has worked with a multitude of law enforcement agencies regarding her Neurosculpting method, a meditation technique.

Biofeedback is another way of assisting you in your meditation practice. Biofeedback has a mechanical device that hooks to your body and sends signals from your body back to the device, thus giving feedback regarding how relaxed you are. One organization that not only has a lot of information on meditation but also sells biofeedback devices is Heartmath (heartmath.org). Their devices can be added to a smartphone or a tablet to provide biofeedback during meditation.

Conclusion

You need to respect your body and how your body reacts under high-pressure or stressful situations. This goes back to more of the attributes of the sensory areas of the brain. By understanding how our sensory brain operates, we get a better understanding of the cues that our body is responding to. The bottom line is just a few moments each day of quietness with no distractions can have huge benefits to clearing the mind. These tools should be given to officers as soon as they start basic training. New officers should be taught these tools so that they can develop behaviors to assist them when dealing with stress and to become more resilient. This will assist officers to having a long successful career in law enforcement. We would be negligent to not provide officers with the tools to survive.

Life at the Academy

3

The More You Sweat in Training, the Less You Bleed in the Streets

Academy—An organization of people who work to provide training in special subjects or skills (*Webster's Dictionary*).

The training academy is where a new recruit is introduced to the profession of law enforcement. It is an introduction to a culture very few people (except those in the military) in our society understand. It is an indoctrination to a way of life that few have chosen. The academy should be the shining star of the profession. At the academy, perspectives are formed that may last a lifetime. It is also a place where those not fit for the profession are weeded out. Not everyone is cut out for the rigors of law enforcement. Many people think they would like to be in law enforcement based on their perspectives from television, movies, and so on, only to find out that the profession is not like what they thought it would be; the academy is where they need to come to this realization. Discipline is an integral part of being a law enforcement officer. If a new officer/agent does not come through the door with a sound understanding of discipline, where is he or she going to learn it? Do you want to put officers/agents in the field without a keen understanding of discipline? Someone falls asleep on a surveillance and misses a transfer, or someone runs up to the White House door, opens the door, and goes inside without ever getting apprehended before he gets there; these are examples of breakdown of discipline. Everyone does not get a trophy at the academy. Unfortunately, much of modern-day law enforcement training has been infected with the virus that everyone graduates and gets a trophy for "attending" training. This virus needs to be eliminated from law enforcement training. If you do not pass a standard, you do not graduate, and you do not get a trophy.

Effective training is not an isolated event in an organization. Training must be strategic in that it is designed to improve the knowledge, skills, and abilities of officers/agents to help them achieve the agency's strategic plan. Training warrants a long-term approach, multiyear investment, and strategic management. Therefore, effective training cannot be designed until we first understand the organization. This is done by conducting a Strength, Weaknesses, Opportunities, and Threats (SWOT) analysis to determine the strengths, weaknesses, opportunities, and threats to the organization, and therefore the academy. With this information and an understanding of the organization's vision, effective training creates a competitive advantage for the organization. After completing the SWOT analysis, a training needs assessment is conducted to identify the gaps between the officers' actual performance and desired performance. Careful analysis of performance gaps determines what training needs to be done or if there is a need for training at all. In some cases, the performance gaps are not related to training deficiencies and other interventions may be needed. Some experts suggest that you first consider outlining the external opportunities and threats before the strengths and weaknesses.

SWOT

Strengths

Strengths describe the positive attributes, tangible and intangible, internal to your academy. They are within your control. What do you do well? What resources do you have?

You may want to evaluate your strengths by area, such as resources and organizational structure. Strengths include the positive attributes of the people involved in training, including their knowledge, backgrounds, education, credentials, contacts, reputations, or the skills they bring. Strengths also include tangible assets such as available past performance, subject matter expertise, integrity, and work ethics. Strengths capture the positive aspects internal to your academy that add value. This is your opportunity to remind yourself of the value existing within your academy.

Weaknesses

Note the weaknesses within your academy. Weaknesses are factors that are within your control that detract from your ability to obtain or maintain a training edge. Which areas might you improve?

Weaknesses might include lack of expertise, limited resources, and lack of access to skills or technology. These are factors that are under your control but, for a variety of reasons, are in need of improvement to effectively accomplish your objectives.

Weaknesses capture the negative aspects internal to your organization that detract from the value of your training. These are areas you need to enhance in order to be the best at what you do. The more accurately you identify your weaknesses, the more valuable the SWOT will be for your assessment.

Opportunities

Opportunities assess the external attractive factors that represent the reason for your academy to exist. These are external to your business. What opportunities exist in your area, or in the environment, from which you hope to benefit?

These opportunities reflect the potential you can realize through implementing your organizational strategies. Opportunities may be the result of resolution of problems associated with current situations, positive perceptions about your academy, or the ability to offer greater value that will create a demand for your services. If it is relevant, place time frames around the opportunities. Does it represent an ongoing opportunity, or is it a window of opportunity? How critical is your timing?

Opportunities are external to your organization. If you have identified "opportunities" that are internal to the academy and within your control, you will want to classify them as strengths.

Threats

What factors are potential threats to your academy? Threats include factors beyond your control that could place your academy at risk. These are also external—you have no control over them, but you may benefit by having contingency plans to address them if they should occur.

A threat is a challenge created by an unfavorable trend or development that may lead to deteriorating funding. Other threats may include intolerable personnel turnover, governmental tide, devastating media or press coverage, a shift in agency behavior, or becoming stale in your training strategies. Get your worst fears on the table. Part of this list may be speculative in nature and still add value to your SWOT analysis.

It may be valuable to classify your threats according to their "seriousness" and "probability of occurrence."

The better you are at identifying potential threats, the more likely you can position yourself to proactively plan for and respond to them. You will be looking back at these threats when you consider your contingency plans.

The Implications

The internal strengths and weaknesses, compared to the external opportunities and threats, can offer additional insight. How can you use the strengths to better take advantage of the opportunities ahead and minimize the harm that threats may introduce if they become a reality? How can weaknesses be minimized or eliminated? The true value of the SWOT analysis is in bringing this information together, to assess the most promising opportunities and the most crucial issues.

An example
The Branch of Training is part of a medium-sized police department in the United States. Lately, it has suffered through steady budget reductions caused by an economic downturn. The following is the SWOT analysis included in its training plan.

Strengths
1. Knowledge. Your training personnel are top notch and enthusiastic about how they perform their job.
2. The branch's reputation for delivering top quality training is well established.
3. Your training equipment has been well kept and is in good working order.

Weaknesses
1. Some of the training equipment is in need of upgrading.
2. Additional expense of bringing officers in from the field for training.
3. An upcoming rise in retirement of high-quality instructors in the branch reduces training resources.

Opportunities
1. Explore new ways to utilize technology in training opportunities.
2. Do a needs assessment to see if there are any training gaps that need filling.
3. Do an internal audit to see whether there are better ways to leverage current human resources.
4. Promote the services your branch carries.

Threats
1. The budgetary cycle. Be prepared; there will be good times and bad times.
2. Changes in technology and keeping up with changes.
3. Generational changes and how to approach these changes.

Leveraging the insight the SWOT analysis can bring is time well invested.

Mission, Vision, Core Values, Outcomes, and Goals/Objectives Statements

Mission Statement

Every law enforcement academy needs to have a mission and vision statement. These statements provide a focus on what is expected from everyone that works at the academy. To illustrate this point, there is a story about a group of executives being given a tour of NASA's Cape Canaveral facility. One executive saw a person sweeping the floor and wandered over to speak to the person. The executive asked the person, "What do you do here?" The person sweeping the floor responded, "I assist in putting astronauts into space." Powerful! This highlights the point that mission and vision statements should not be created in a vacuum. Mission and vision statements should be a product of brainstorming sessions. Questions at these sessions should be as follows:

- What are the opportunities or needs that we must address?—This defines the purpose of the organization.
- How are we going to address those needs?—This defines the business activity.
- What principles or beliefs guide our work?—This defines the core values to guide decisions.

Look for patterns in people's statements in these sessions. Look at the passion behind their statements; these are clues on the direction of the academy. Through these sessions, a mission statement will begin to take form. Mission statements should not be too long and should not be too generic. You want a statement that speaks specifically to the academy. A mission statement must

- Be clear and understandable
- Be brief enough so everyone can remember it (the person sweeping the floor knew NASA's mission)
- Reflect the academy's distinctive competency
- Be broad enough to allow implementation flexibility, but be narrow enough to maintain a sense of focus
- Be a template by which personnel can make decisions
- Reflect the academy's values, beliefs, and philosophy

An example of a good academy mission statement is that of the New York City Police Department's Training Academy, which states:

The Police Academy Mission is to support the effectiveness of all NYPD members, in all of their daily activities.

Vision Statement

A vision statement refers to the category of intentions that are broad, all inclusive, and forward thinking. A vision statement should

- Provide aspirations for the future
- Provide a mental image of some desired future state
- Appeal to everyone's emotions and aspirations

When brainstorming for a vision statement, you need to ask your staff the following:

1. What do you like about being a part of this academy?
2. What do you like about the academy's mission?
3. When it's at its best, what do you like about the academy?
4. What legacy should we collectively leave behind?

Here is an example of an academy vision statement from the South Carolina Police Academy:

To foster a safer environment for the citizens of South Carolina through a prepared criminal justice population.

Core Values

Core values form the foundation on which the staff at the academy perform their work and conduct themselves. The values underlie how the staff interacts with one another and the officers, and the strategies the staff use to fulfill the academy's mission. Core values are essential and enduring, and cannot be compromised. The academy's mission and vision should align with the core values. An example of a core values statement comes from the Washington State Criminal Justice Training for the Basic Law Enforcement Academy:

- **PROFESSIONALISM:** We commit to service, while demonstrating a positive attitude and mastery of knowledge, skills, and abilities within our roles.
- **ACCOUNTABILITY:** We acknowledge that we are accountable to everyone we serve, and to each other for our actions and decisions. We welcome that responsibility.
- **INTEGRITY:** We value candor, honesty, and ethical behavior. We are committed to doing the right thing for the right reason.

Outcomes

Outcomes are the benefit that the academy seeks to achieve or influence. Outcomes control and affect the following:

- Identifying the impact the academy has as opposed to the activities in which it engages.
- Should be derived from many different stakeholders' perspective, expressed as expected results from the academy.
- Should encompass multiple stakeholder perspectives to ensure they are balanced.

Outcomes are not always under full control of the academy; there are a multitude of factors that can influence outcomes. Here is an example of outcomes regarding graduating officers from the Napa Valley Criminal Justice Training Center:

- Demonstrate oral and written communication skills.
- Confront and assess a problem and identify a solution using good judgment.
- Comprehend and retain factual and technical information related to the profession.
- Understand differences and work effectively with diverse populations.
- Demonstrate physical fitness, stamina, and fine motor skills related to the profession.
- Identify personal strengths and weaknesses.

Goals and Objectives

Goals and objectives are intentions that make the vision and mission actionable. Many times, goals/objectives are part of a larger strategic plan and therefore are sometimes referred to as "strategic goals." They typically encompass a shorter period than the vision statement. Goals should address all academy aspects, including mission, process, people, and resources. They should facilitate reasoned trade-offs and be achievable. Goals usually cut across functions and can counteract suboptimization.

To create goals or objectives, utilize previously developed material, such as outcomes and SWOT analyses. Make sure that your goals are attainable and within the academy's control. Try not to create too many goals; six to eight are generally enough. Here is an example of the goals of the Federal Law Enforcement Training Center:

1. Provide training that enables our partners to accomplish their missions.
2. Foster a high-performing workforce.
3. Provide mission-responsive infrastructure.
4. Optimize business practices.

Conclusion

A law enforcement academy's mission, vision, goals, objectives, and outcomes should be detailed for all stakeholders in the academy to focus on what they do. Inclusion of many stakeholders and staff at the academy needs to be part of the drafting of these statements; this creates buy-in and motivation. Having all of the facets of a mission, vision, goals, objectives, and outcomes ensures that everyone from the staff, to the personnel receiving training from the academy, and all stakeholders have a clear understanding of why the academy exists.

Law Enforcement
Ethics Training

4

Integrity is driven by an organization's culture.

National Institute of Justice
Enhancing Police Security, 2001

In the ancient Spartan community, self-discipline and high ethical standards were the goal of Spartan training. Sparta placed the values of liberty, equality, and fraternity at the center of their ethical system. The Spartans followed a strict laconic code of honor. No soldier was considered superior to another. Unethical recklessness, lack of team cohesiveness, and rage were prohibited in a Spartan army, as these behaviors endangered the phalanx. Recklessness and unethical behavior could lead to dishonor. Dishonored Spartans were labeled outcasts and were forced to wear different clothing for public humiliation.

Law enforcement is suffering from an ethics and integrity crisis. Law enforcement officers are finding themselves embroiled in an ethical and integrity situation almost every day. We have wandered from our core principle of conducting our business from a platform of ethics and integrity. The trust of the people in law enforcement professionals has eroded. Ethics and integrity are the guiding principles to any law enforcement agency. The foundation to any law enforcement training program or academy is the importance of ethics and integrity training. Many times, ethics training can be viewed as a "necessary evil" and can be glossed over up until the time an agency's name has hit the headlines on ethical scandals within a department. Many times, law enforcement leaders will make statements that these incidents involve just a few "bad apples." But is that really the case, or is it the case of a "rotten barrel"?

Dr. Neil Trautman, a leading expert in law enforcement integrity and ethics, states that officers need to be given sound ethics training using role-play situations that instruct officers on how to deal with ethical dilemmas. Further, annual ethics training needs to be fresh and relevant to current situations officers may confront. Generally, annual ethics training is in an e-learning format that rarely changes, which many officers try and click through the training as quickly as possible. An example on how this type of ethics training does not work can be seen in the Secret Service scandal that occurred in Cartagena, Colombia, where Secret Service officers who were on the president's forward security planning team were found to be soliciting and cohorting with local prostitutes. Here is the official testimony of Mark Sullivan, former director of the Secret Service, before Congress after the incident:

> "The Secret Service regularly provides ethics and standards of conduct training to our employees throughout their careers. Below is a list of training courses and programs where this information is covered.
>
> - Orientation for all new employees
> - Special Agent Recruit Training Course
> - Uniformed Division Officer Recruit Training Course
> - Seminar for First Line Supervisors
> - Emerging Leaders Seminar
> - Seminar for Mid-Level Managers
> - Emerging Executives Seminar
> - Ethics in Law Enforcement
> - Elicitation Briefing
>
> This training is reinforced yearly with each Secret Service employee certifying on a Secret Service form (SSF) 3218 ('Annual Employee Certification'), that they have read and reviewed agency policies, to include the Secret Service's 'Standards of Conduct.'" (Secret Service on the Line 2012)

Do you see a session for "Forward Security Planning in a Foreign Country" listed in Mr. Sullivan's statement? No. Remember ethics training should be fresh and relevant. Mr. Sullivan's statement meant the agents had already passed the Secret Service's mandated ethics training. However, was the training relevant to the ethical situations confronted by a forward security planning team? For training to be meaningful, it has to be relevant to situations performers may confront; otherwise, the training has no meaning. Lack of ethics in an organization destroys trust not only within the organization but also outside of the organization.

Frequency of ethics training relates to a positive ethical culture. Survey results done by the US Office of Government Ethics report found that frequency of ethics training is directly related to employees' positive perception of an ethical culture and ethical employee behavior in their agencies. Further, the report found in-person instructor-led training was rated the most effective type of training. Ethics training must be realistic; there are plenty of real ethical cases out there to develop real-world scenarios for ethics training. Ethics training should be embedded into your law enforcement training. Many training scenarios can have an ethical issue implanted into the scenario.

To address a more problematic cultural issue in law enforcement, Dr. Trautman states: "Top leaders must address their agency's ethical problems prior to ethics training being conducted. Administrators are viewed as hypocrites when 'the troops' are ordered to ethics training while glaring unethical situations within the department remain unaddressed"; the "rotten barrel" syndrome. Leaders must show ethical conduct if they expect their officers to do the same. Social learning theory clearly shows the power of mirroring behavior. If the chief misuses the government vehicle, do not expect the officers to behave differently. Social learning theory clearly shows the power of mirroring behavior and ethics, from supervisors to field training officers (FTOs) to new officers. This is why supervisors should be part of the discussions on ethics.

The "Business" of Law Enforcement Training

The use of contractors in law enforcement training is common. Many law enforcement agencies do not have a large array of subject-matter experts in their ranks, so they turn to contractors to fill the gaps. For instance, the Reid School of Interview and Interrogation is commonly used by law enforcement agencies to enhance their officers'/agents' interviewing skills. Before these contractors are allowed to teach in front of your officers, the subject matter they will be covering should be thoroughly reviewed. Be cognizant of people that are in the "business" of law enforcement training. There is a huge cottage industry of people parlaying law enforcement training; it is a multimillion-dollar industry. Though the certification of law enforcement training has recently been started by the International Association of Directors of Law Enforcement Standards and Training, there is no requirement that contractors be certified to teach law enforcement subject matters. What is the background of these people? Credentials and references should be verified. For example, a large law enforcement agency in the Midwest paid a private contractor to give some "cutting-edge" training on noncompliant subjects. This contractor alluded that he was previously KGB, but he could not "really talk about it." His noncompliant technique was called the "hook and slap technique," meaning if a person was noncompliant, the officer was to grab the subject by the ear (the hook) and then slap the subject across the face until the subject complied. Later, when this contractor's credentials were investigated, it was found that he had been banned from teaching in several states. One of the reasons for banning him was his failure to show up in court to testify on the validity of his "hook and slap" technique. Further, investigation found that he had been an automotive mechanic in Russia. What happens to the agency that has basically endorsed this technique on the public? They pay large sums of money in civil liability cases.

Be aware of contractors professing themselves to be a former FBI agent, CIA agent, and so on. Do a background check on contracted professionals to establish credibility. Even if they are former agents from those agencies, carefully scrutinize the material they will be instructing. Many times, these former officers/agents are teaching old or outdated material that has no present-day relevance. For instance, a former federal agent was teaching state and local officers that persons of a specific religious belief "do not have a First Amendment right to do anything." If your agency contracted this former agent and an incident in your local jurisdiction arose between one of your officers and a person of this specific religious belief, which resulted in a lawsuit, your agency could be found liable for using this contractor. The parameters of any written agreement should be detailed enough to protect your agency against any possible liability issues. Contractors provide a valuable service for agencies that do not have their own subject-matter experts, but agreements between the agency and contractor need to be thoroughly vetted and reviewed before they are allowed to train your officers.

Security Measures

Controlled substances, weapons, training records, explosives, equipment, and hazardous equipment need to have protocols to ensure that security measures are maintained. To many, this may appear somewhat obvious. But do you want your department or agency having to answer questions about several ounces of cocaine that came up missing at your training academy? Search the Internet and you will find this has happened on more than one occasion.

Controlled Substances

Several measures can be implemented regarding controlled substances. These measures should include the following:

1. Drug Custodian—The person who has overall responsibility for the safety and security of narcotics training and related equipment.
2. Access List—Persons who have authorized access to the drug locker.
3. Drug Supply Custodian—A person responsible for ensuring all drug supplies are maintained.
4. A secured room and a safe/vault where the controlled substances are kept.
5. Visitor Control Log—A logbook that is kept near the safe/vault and that shall be signed by all visitors not on the access list.
6. Controlled Substance Access Log—This logbook should be kept inside the safe/vault and should be signed every time the drug safe is opened. It should be signed by two *approved* individuals.

7. Controlled Substance Accountability Log—This log should be kept in the safe/vault and should contain both the signature list and a chronological record of the Substance Log.
8. Substance Log—This log is kept within the Controlled Substance Accountability Log and lists all narcotics present in the drug safe/vault. The log is used to record the weight of all narcotics before and after training. It should be signed by at least two instructors.
9. Transfer of Custody Log—This is used when drugs are transferred from one person to another, or transferred out of the safe/vault permanently.

Hazardous Materials

When storing hazardous material, the following protocols are suggested:

1. Follow the storage instructions on the label.
2. Be sure to store volatile materials in a well-ventilated area.
3. Ensure flammable products are kept at the recommended temperature range. You do not want to be called in the middle of the night regarding your training facility being on fire as a result of the improper storage of flammable material.
4. Use the original container to store hazardous material or an *approved* substitute.
5. Do not store too much hazardous material in one area. Purchase only what you need. There are a myriad of issues when it comes to proper disposal of unused material.
6. Periodically check the storage area for any possible issues, such as leaks or fumes. These can be early warning signs of possible problems.

A good source for further information on storage of hazardous materials can be found on OSHA or EPA websites.

Weapons and Explosives

Weapons, explosives, and other nonlethal training equipment (i.e., non-lethal weapons, Shockknives, etc.) should be closely accounted for. Weapons in particular should be held in a vault/locker with very limited access. Nothing could cause an agency/department more public scrutiny than a missing weapon.

Access to weapons should be limited to those persons authorized by command. A list of those designated persons should be posted on or near the vault/locker. Persons not authorized for those areas need to be accompanied by those who are authorized and a visitor log needs to be maintained. Keys/combinations/key cards should be kept under a stringent system of control and should be kept separate from other keys. Combinations should not be given to any people who have no authorized access. A weapons log needs to be maintained when weapons are checked in and out by authorized instructors.

Safety, Risks, and Hazardous Training

Every year, law enforcement training encounters a tragedy, and oftentimes, it is fatal. Many aspects of law enforcement training have safety concerns. At the same time, the best modality for training is for the situation simulation being as realistic as possible. How do trainers train for reality while maintaining a safe training environment at the same time? Chapter 11 will go into greater detail about high-risk training, but for now, the first thing to remember is that a safety officer, instructors, and officers are those involved in training. Safety is everyone's concern. Instructors cannot be the sole source for possible safety issues; officers can also see potential safety issues. The best answer is to try and mitigate any potential safety risk as much as possible. Checklists have proven to be a time-tested model that maintains high levels of integrity. A recognized best practice regarding training safely is the US Coast Guard's GAR (green, amber, red) sheets. These detailed checklists are a sound way for an instructor to try and mitigate training risks. These checklists do not prevent high-risk training but allow an instructor to think through the training evolution to see what steps he or she can take to lower the risks. Very high-risk training needs to be highly supervised and approved. Another good source for safety issues and law enforcement training is the Police Officers Safety Association (posai.org). Their website is a large resource on officer safety in and outside of the training venue (for a free downloadable safety template, go to humanperformance.vpweb.com).

What is Operational Risk Management? It is a continuous, systematic process of identifying and controlling risks in all activities according to a set of preconceived parameters by applying appropriate management policies and procedures.

1. **Supervision:** Supervision is the backbone of any training session. The simplest task may result in severe consequences without proper supervision. The higher the risk, the instructor should focus more on observing and verifying all steps in training. Questions to consider: How qualified is the instructor? How many instructors/backers are needed to safely monitor the session? Do the instructors know their responsibility? What will the instructor do if someone is injured?

2. **Planning:** Planning concerns how much information is available, how clear it is, and how much time is available to plan the evolution. Questions to consider: When is training scheduled? Where is the training located? Does the instructor understand what is required at the training location? Is the equipment updated and working properly? Is this a new training evolution?

3. **Selection:** Staff/Instructor/Role-player and student selection should be examined before engaging in training. Questions to consider: Do all persons know their roles in training evolution? Are they qualified to participate in their roles? How much experience do they have? If a person needs to be replaced, is there a qualified replacement? Will this decrease the quality of training?

4. **Fitness:** Team fitness should judge the person's/team's ability to safely conduct training. Persons should have at least 8 hours of rest before conducting training. Alcohol should not have been consumed a minimum of 8 hours before training. Instructors shall review all related incidents before training to ensure that officers who are injured or ill be exempt from physical training. Fatigue normally becomes a factor after 18 hours without sleep. Questions to consider: Does anyone feel they are not mentally or physically fit to conduct this training? Has anyone consumed alcohol 8 hours before training?

5. **Environment:** Instructors should consider all factors affecting personnel, teams, and resource performance including time of day, lighting, weather conditions, geographic and facility hazards, and other factors.

6. **Complexity:** Evolution complexity considers both the time and resources required to conduct a scenario. Generally, the longer the exposure to the hazard, the greater the risks involved. This is not always the case but should be considered. Instructors should be aware of hazards and monitor the length of time engaged near or with the hazard. Questions to consider: What will the effect be on the training or crew? Is this a safe evolution? Should we reevaluate the evolution?

7. **How do you calculate the risk?** Using the six elements, grade each with a score of 0–10, with 0 being no risk and 10 being maximum risk. Add all the scores for a total risk score. Use the GAR scale to determine risk: green, 0–23; amber, 24–44; and red, 45–60.

8. **What's next?** Identify your options. Change/redirect the training in your authority realm on how to conduct the training or reevaluate and consult with the training officer.

9. Remember that risk management is a continuous process and must be monitored.

What happens if training is determined to be at high risk (red)? The training plan should be reevaluated (possibly changed) and approved by a supervisor as "safe to train" (a sample of a risk assessment sheet can be downloaded from humanperformance.vpweb.com).

Training sites should have readily marked landline red phones (if available) for staff and officers to make emergency phone calls. Everyone needs to be made aware of where the phones are located. Emergency exits need to be clearly marked. At the beginning of a course/class, a safety briefing should be given to the officers. This briefing should include emergency phone numbers, foul weather procedures, and environmental concerns (hot humid weather for instance). First aid equipment should be readily available.

Policies and procedures need to be in place in case a hazardous situation arises (equipment failure, weather, and accidents). In case of an accident, training needs to be suspended until the situation is assessed. A training accident investigation needs to be conducted to see what caused the accident. If the training was video recorded, it will need to be taken and held for investigative purposes.

Maintaining Training Equipment

According to the academy's training throughput, a good majority of training equipment will have considerable use. The training equipment needs to be maintained according to the manufacturer's specifications. For instance, Intoximeters' Alco-Sensor for breath testing is commonly used to train law enforcement officers in alcohol intoxication. The manufacturer has strict guidelines to be followed, including a "Quality Assurance Plan." Follow their guidelines.

Besides just following manufacturer instructions, equipment should be maintained for health and safety reasons. Several years ago, many law enforcement training academies were hit with methicillin-resistant *Staphylococcus aureus* (MRSA) staph germs in their mat rooms; MRSA infections can be deadly. Now, most academies scrub down their mat rooms with alcohol after each class to reduce possible infections. Therefore, maintaining equipment reaches beyond the manufacturer's instructions.

Training Records

Many times, in civil liability suits, attorneys request for officer/agent training records to verify not only how the officer performed but also what the officer was actually taught. Paper training records (tests, student records, etc.)

should be kept in a locked, fireproof, file cabinet and maintained for around 40 years, the career of an officer/agent plus 10 years. Access needs to be limited strictly to persons authorized by command and a log needs to be maintained inside the file cabinet. Signatures, dates, and reasons for entry need to be maintained. Electronic training records need limited access, just like paper records, and need to be backed up in a separate hard drive that is kept in a secure fireproof area. These records need to include the following:

1. Syllabi and lesson plans
2. The course schedule and which instructors taught in each course
3. The class roster
4. Student exams and exam keys (this should include graded practical evaluations)
5. Documentation that a student successfully completed the training, or if a student did not complete the training, reasons for incompletion

Records also need to be kept when a request for training records is made.

Health

If there is physical activity involved in your training course, the officers need to undergo a thorough health screening by a qualified health professional. There are numerous incidents where officers have actually died from a health condition during training, which could have been prevented by a good health screening. Further, officers need to be completely honest when answering a health screening questionnaire. The health screening should closely align with the training being conducted.

Policies for Student Misconduct

The conduct of an officer in training defines his or her character as an officer, for both basic and advanced training. Everyone makes mistakes and officers are not immune to the fragile elements of being a human. However, the bar should be set very high regarding conduct in training. The agency should strongly consider how it will handle issues of misconduct in training. Consider this true story: an agency has a report of one officer cheating on an exam with the assistance of another officer, as witnessed by several instructors. The organization decides this is an isolated incident and decides to give the officers "a talking to." Do you have any idea what kinds of issues this has presented to the agency? First, the agency might as well do away with written tests, for trying to fire an officer after this incident will result in a claim of disparate treatment and open the agency up for civil liability. Second, the agency not only has just lowered the standard regarding acceptable conduct but also has a dim future in trying to raise the standard. There are also Giglio issues regarding the officer's testimony in court. Read more on this in the early section on ethics.

All issues regarding misconduct should be reported and investigated. The suspected student(s) should be notified of the allegation and be given an opportunity to respond to the allegation. The best plan of action is to have a review board go through all the facts collected regarding the allegation. This allows for different perspectives to be given to the circumstances and leads to a more balanced decision regarding how the misconduct should be handled. This also lifts the burden of decision making from the shoulders of just one person. There needs to be levels of discipline regarding misconduct including dismissal from the academy.

Most training staff understand that this is how misconduct is handled for basic training, but what about advanced or in-service training? There can be a little more flexibility regarding misconduct regarding in-service, but that does not mean anything goes regarding misconduct. Misconduct regarding in-service training needs to be treated on a case-by-case basis.

Orientation to Training

At the beginning of a training iteration, the officers need to be provided the following:

1. Course goals and objectives
2. The training schedule
3. Performance expectations
4. Practical evaluation and written examination requirements
5. Fire and emergency procedures
6. Safety rules and regulations
7. Code of conduct rules and requirements
8. Disciplinary procedures

Officers need to know what is expected of them. Get it out there on the first day. Some agencies also use written agreements regarding an officer's conduct and expectations while at training; this is a good practice (for a free sample of a downloadable written agreement, go to humanperformance .vpweb.com).

Legal Issues and Law Enforcement Instruction

Many times, law enforcement instructors do not think about the legal rami-fications of what they are teaching. Instructors have to realize that they are not immune from both criminal and civil liability. Tort laws in most states find that law enforcement instructors can be sued for negligence. This is very important when conducting high-risk training. The academy, the agency, and the training manager can all be sued. Harris et al. (2012) offer some sug-gestions regarding legal issues and law enforcement training:

- Is the subject matter appropriate for training?
- Are the instructors qualified/certified in the subject matter area?
- Is the subject matter instructed exhibiting the "best practices in law enforcement?" Everyone is searching for the best technique, piece of equipment, and so on for their officers, but be considerate of being too close to the edge of new training methods and equipment. Many of these new innovations are just passing fads.
- What are possible liability issues?
- Does the training material mirror existing law or the agency's policies?
- If you have a legal division, have them review the training material.
- Are all legal training topics being taught by a qualified legal instruc-tor? It is highly suggested that legal topics be taught by practicing lawyers, preferably prosecutors. Lawyers approach legal issues from a different perspective than officers do. Such a perspective can some-times keep you out of trouble.
- Have high-risk areas been identified and are safety officers in place?
- Do the testing methods ensure the officers' understanding of the material?
- Are evaluative processes in place to determine effectiveness of the training?
- Were the lesson plans followed?
- Are there proper documentation procedures in place regarding all of the elements of the training (who, what, where, when)?

Plagiarism and Copyright Laws

Plagiarism is a relatively easy concept to understand. Take someone else's work and claim it as your own without a proper citation; that is illegal. Copyright laws delve into a more gray area. A copyright gives the owner the ability to manage who can use his or her material derived from the original work. One thing to remember is that the US government cannot copyright itself; however, some state material may be copyrighted; it varies upon each individual situation.

The laws regarding copyright material are confusing. One of the rights accorded to the copyright owner is the right to reproduce or to authorize others to reproduce the work in copies. This right is subject to certain limitations found in sections 107 through 118 of the copyright law (Title 17, US Code). One of the more important limitations is the doctrine of "fair use." The doctrine of fair use has developed through a substantial number of court decisions over the years and has been codified in section 107 of the copyright law. Section 107 also sets out four factors to be considered in determining whether or not a particular use is fair:

1. The purpose and character of the use, including whether such use is of commercial nature or is for nonprofit educational purposes
2. The nature of the copyrighted work (is the work commendable to copyright protection?)
3. The amount and substantiality of the portion used in relation to the copyrighted work as a whole (how much of the material is going to be used, is it too much?)
4. The effect of the use upon the potential market for, or value of, the copyrighted work (has there been economic distress as a result of the use of the material?) (US Copyright Office 2012)

The first factor is the most important one for law enforcement training. There is no distinction on how many times the material can be used. The distinction between what is fair use and what is infringement in a particular case will not always be clear or easily defined. There is no specific number of words, lines, or notes that may be safely taken without permission. Acknowledging the source of the copyrighted material does not substitute for obtaining permission.

The 1961 *Report of the Register of Copyrights on the General Revision of the U.S. Copyright Law* cites examples of activities that courts have regarded as fair use: "quotation of excerpts in a review or criticism for purposes of illustration or comment; quotation of short passages in a scholarly or technical work, for illustration or clarification of the author's observations; use in a parody of some of the content of the work parodied; summary of an address or article, with brief quotations, in a news report; reproduction by a library of a portion of a work to replace part of a damaged copy; reproduction by a teacher or student of a small part of a work to illustrate a lesson; reproduction of a work in legislative or judicial proceedings or reports; incidental and fortuitous reproduction, in a newsreel or broadcast, of a work located in the scene of an event being reported" (p. 24).

Copyright protects the particular way authors have expressed themselves. It does not extend to any ideas, systems, or factual information conveyed in a work. The safest course is to get permission from the copyright owner before using copyrighted material.

When it is impracticable to obtain permission, you should consider avoiding the use of copyrighted material unless you are confident that the doctrine of fair use would apply to the situation. If there is any doubt, it is advisable to consult with your legal division.

Conclusion

Sound ethical conduct begins at the academy. From the officers going through training, the academy staff, to all persons who have interactions with the academy, ethics should be the gold standard on which the academy conducts its business. Further, the safety, security, and general well-being of everyone attending academy training, including the academy's staff, need to be of the highest priority.

Developing Training Staff

5

The backbone of any training academy/program is the quality of the staff. Be it support staff or instructors, these people are the frame that holds the academy together. Personnel selected to train at the academy need to be the best. The best example that exemplifies this is the Marine Corps Drill Instructors. They look sharp, they act sharp, and they mean business. The instructors are the face of the academy. Yet, many agencies use the academy as a dumping ground for those who could not cut it in the field. Does this make sense? Taking the people who could not cut it in the field and put them at the academy to instruct? Bad instruction will lead to bad performance. Also, personnel should not be sent to the academy unless they want to go to the academy. Forcing someone to do something they have no desire of doing is a losing proposition for all of those involved. Bad attitudes radiate like a virus through any organization; do not introduce the bad attitude virus to your academy by force transferring someone to the academy.

When new personnel arrive at the academy, they need to be properly introduced to the academy's vision, mission, core values, objectives, and outcomes. Many times, people work for an organization with no clue of what the mission and vision of the organization are. The new personnel need to be oriented to the goals and objectives of the respective courses they will be teaching. Further, the new personnel need to have an understanding of the structure of the academy and the academy's role in the overall organization. The code of conduct, prohibited acts, and discipline need to be thoroughly outlined.

One particular area that needs to be addressed regarding academy staff personnel and students is the instructor–student relationship. A very bright line needs to be drawn between instructors and students for a multitude of reasons. Many great instructors have seen their careers disappear because of fraternization with students. There should be near-zero tolerance on this issue. The only possible exception is graduation parties, but even those need to be closely watched especially if there is any alcohol involved. There should be a designated nondrinker instructor at class parties entrusted and endorsed to stop bad behavior. There are careers involved; let us not end them.

Instructing the Instructor

What is instruction and how does it work? Mayer (2008) states that instruction is preparing the officer by guiding the officer's learning by selecting applicable material, organizing the material into a logical representation, and assimilating the representation with other relevant knowledge. Mayer (2008) further suggests that good instruction should include

- Reducing *irrelevant* information that does not support the instructional goal
- Managing essential learning by allowing the officer to mentally characterize the incoming material
- Organizing the material by making sense of the incoming material, including organizing it and integrating it with prior knowledge

New instructors need to be closely monitored, mentored, and developed. Some law enforcement academies have developed steps in instructor development, starting from being an apprentice, to becoming a journeyman, a master instructor, and a senior instructor. Developing an instructor qualification program ensures the officers are given the best instruction possible. A list of instructor competencies needs to be developed for the qualification process. The International Board of Standards for Training Performance Instruction (Klein et al. 2004) suggests some of the following competencies.

Competency 1. Communicate Effectively

a. Vary pitch, tone, inflection, and rate of speech.
b. Use proper spelling, grammar, punctuation, and language appropriate for the officers' level of understanding.
c. Use hand gestures and body motions to enhance the teaching points.
d. Use eye contact appropriately and effectively.
e. Maintain a comfortable distance from officers.
f. Use pauses appropriately to allow for officer reflection and comprehension.

Development Strategy

Verbal Communication
- Understand that communication is a two-way process and involves verbal and nonverbal factors.
- Create a common ground when communicating. Use words and examples that officers are familiar with.

- Remain aware of variations in vocal pitch that can help you understand underlying concerns or issues officers may have.
- Pause after asking a question in order to give learners time to respond.
- Add a brief period of silence before introducing a point to focus officers' attention.
- Repeat information that is very important.

Nonverbal Communication
- Use active listening skills such as paraphrasing, leaning forward, and making eye contact.
- Ensure that your verbal communication (words) matches your nonverbal (facial expressions, gestures, and body movements) communication.
- Use eye contact to demonstrate your attention to officers. Avoid extended eye contact or staring.
- Use eye contact from officers to assess their understanding, interests, and willingness to be involved.
- Use gestures to support or replace your words, but remember that certain gestures may have a different meaning in different cultures.
- Use distance to support your message (proximity is generally less formal and more intimate).
- Scan the audience to identify nonverbal cues regarding officers' emotions and problems such as confused looks, staring into space, or blank stares.

Eye Contact
- Use eye contact to demonstrate one-on-one attention to officers and to draw officers into the training process. Try to avoid making eye contact with some officers and not others.
- Recognize that a lack of eye contact from officers may mean that they do not want to participate, they are bored, they are distracted, or they had a late night. This could also be a signal that it is break time.

Competency 2. Update and Improve One's Professional Knowledge and Skills

Development Strategy

Continuous Professional Development
Continuous Professional Development (CPD) refers to the process of tracking and documenting the skills, knowledge, and experience that you gain both formally and informally as you work, beyond any initial training. It is a record of what you experience, learn, and then

apply. The term is generally used to mean a physical folder or portfolio documenting your development as a professional. Some organizations use it to mean a training or development plan.

Training and Development

These terms are often used interchangeably, though there is a distinction. As a rule of thumb, training is formal and linear. It has to do with learning how to do something specific, relating to skill and competence. Training can be as simple as using a PC application and as complex as learning how to be a pilot. Development is often informal and has a wider application, giving you the tools to do a range of things and relating to capability and competency. It involves progression from basic know-how to more advanced, mature, or complex understanding.

The CPD Process

- Needs to be a documented process
- Should be self-directed: driven by you, not your agency
- Should focus on learning from experience, reflective learning, and review
- Should help you set development goals and objectives
- Needs to include both formal and informal learning

What It Does for You

- It provides an overview of your professional development to date.
- It reminds you of your achievements and how far you have progressed.
- It directs your career and helps you keep your eye on your goals.
- It uncovers gaps in your skills and capabilities.
- It opens up further development needs.
- It demonstrates your professional standing and credibility.
- It helps you with your career development or a possible career change.

Competency 3. Comply with Established Ethical and Legal Standards

    a. Respect officers' rights to confidentiality and anonymity in safeguarding personal information.
    b. Avoid conflicts of interest with the staff and officers.
    c. Respect and comply with intellectual property laws.

Development Strategy

Comply with Organizational and Professional Code of Ethics
- Little things have a way of becoming big things, so watch what you say and do.

Respect Intellectual Property Including Copyright (see Chapter 4 for information on copyright)
- Copyrighted material will need permission from the rightful owner before it can be used.
- Copyrighted material should be clearly identified with appropriate symbols.
- Information sources should be cited and annotated.

Respect Requirement of Confidentiality and Anonymity
- Instructors often have access to confidential officer information through class registration, tests, or organizational requirements. Instructors have an obligation to protect such information.

Competency 4. Establish and Maintain Professional Credibility

a. Conform to academy uniform attire (or appropriate civilian attire).
b. Demonstrate subject-matter expertise.
c. Recognize and acknowledge mistakes and provide opportunities to correct them.

Development Strategy

Visual Appearance
- Present a sharp appearance.
- Demonstrate good posture (relaxed and comfortable, try not to slouch).
- Carry yourself with smooth movements and exude confidence.
- Avoid inappropriate or distracting movements and gestures.

Demonstrate Subject-Matter Expertise
- Do not ever, ever start a class by saying you have never taught this subject before (even if it is true).
- Demonstrate content expertise to bolster credibility.
- Work toward professional certification.
- Convey subject-matter expertise by describing your work experience that relates to the training topic.
- Be very familiar with the training material.
- Prepare, prepare, and prepare for training delivery.
- Make sure you review your lesson plan.
- Answer questions accurately and thoroughly.
- Accept difference of opinion and experiences of officers.
- Never humiliate or become defensive with those who pose objections or difficult questions.

Model Professional Interpersonal Behavior
- Display respect for all officers and avoid bias and favoritism.

- Demonstrate consistency in your words and actions during training and outside of training.
- Use appropriate terminology and avoid jargon.
- Be cognizant of the overuse of acronyms. Make sure your audience knows the same acronyms as you do.

Build Trust
- Handle sensitive issues discreetly.
- Demonstrate openness to officers.
- Show respect for all officers by listening, being open to dissenting opinions, and treating all officers with respect and dignity.

Acceptable Manners and Behaviors
- Directly address unacceptable manners and behaviors.
- Provide all officers with equal amounts of attention and avoid favoritism.
- Avoid inappropriate humor.

Personality and Character
- Admit mistakes or lack of knowledge and avoid placing blame on others.
- Accept responsibility for correcting errors or getting the right answer for officers.
- Always follow up with officers and keep any promises.
- Be aware of your personal conduct and correct any inappropriate words or deeds.

Planning and Preparation

Competency 5. Plan Instructional Methods and Materials

a. Plan or modify instruction to accommodate for officers' experiences.
b. Personalize lesson plan to check for understanding.
c. Select (or adapt) instructional methods, strategies, and presentation techniques.
d. Adapt lesson plan to accommodate different instructional settings.
e. Create and publish course agenda for officers.
f. Sequence the lesson plan in a logical order.

Development Strategy

Making Adjustments before Training
- Arrive at your classroom a minimum of 30 minutes before class to see if all of the audiovisual equipment is working correctly, the officers have the necessary materials, there are markers (and

they have ink in them), the heat and cooling are working, and the classroom is arranged properly.

Strategies for Gathering Officer Information

- Recognize that the intended (who the training has been designed for) may not be the same as the actual audience. If possible, review the officers' profiles to determine the characteristics of the audience.
- Ask the officers questions at the beginning of training to learn more about them.
- Ask the officers what their expectations are from the training (to maximize training transfer, officers should recognize that newly learned material would improve their work performance).

Managing Group Dynamics

- Use a variety of methods to engage officers. All officers have different comfort levels and expectations from the training.
- Be proactive with perceived officer issues. Create guidelines and monitor groups to prevent potential problems from arising.
- Try to maintain a balance between officers' input with respect to their own experiences. Although having officers share their own experiences can be of great value to other officers, it can become distracting if the conversation goes off tangent or if one officer dominates.

Making Adjustments during Training

- Continuously monitor officer attention during training by asking questions and making quick adjustments if necessary (i.e., if a large percentage of the officers appear to be lost or confused, you may need to slow the pace of the training).
- Make sure you report (verbally or in writing) adjustments made during the training to the appropriate people. Include the rationale for the adjustments and the positive and negative results of the adjustments. The training may need to be readjusted to align with the officers.

Use Training Methods Appropriately

- Use a variety of training methodologies to stimulate interest, arouse curiosity, and promote understanding and retention.
- Provide an overview of activities with clear objectives and directions.
- Debrief activities to tie the results and key learning back to the objective-driven content.
- Ask for feedback from officers about the training methods that you are using, which you can use to identify what is working and what is not working. Obtain this feedback during the debrief.

Lecture

- Use the lecture to transmit cognitive information to the officers in a short period and with large audiences.

- Combine lecture with other training methodologies (i.e., case studies, group discussions) to stimulate interest and enhance the learning.

Role-Plays

- Use role-plays to provide officers the opportunity to practice new skills in a controlled environment.
- Combine role-plays with behavior modeling to create a stronger likelihood that the newly practiced skills will be beneficial to their jobs. Make sure you incorporate feedback into role-plays.

Individual Exercises

- Use assessment tools to promote individual reflection.
- Use reading assignments with a follow-up question/answer period.
- Use interactive simulations to teach analysis skills, problem solving, and priority setting.
- Use case studies individually or with groups. This training method can often demonstrate the complexities of interrelated variables.

Group Exercises

- Use games and other group activities to promote teamwork and to stimulate motivation and enthusiasm.
- Circulate through the groups to monitor progress without being intrusive. Inform officers in advance that you will be doing this. Tell them how and why so it is not distracting to officers.

Discussion

- Use discussions to engage officers and encourage participation.
- Start discussions by asking questions to stimulate thinking. Discussions are prone to tangents. Be sensitive to group dynamics, ensuring that the discussion remains focused.
- Arrange seating so that it is conducive to discussion and participation. Arranging seats in a U shape or in a circle generally works best.

Competency 6. Prepare for Instruction

a. Rehearse lesson plan timing with another qualified instructor.
b. Make available all necessary resources, supplies, and reference materials to officers.
c. Confirm logistical arrangements and equipment readiness before the class convenes.
d. Ensure that the environment is set up and conducive to learning.
e. Test equipment operation and functionality before the class convenes.
f. Eliminate (or minimize) internal and external distractions that prohibit learning and performance.
g. Provide a safe and clean learning environment.

Development Strategy

Logistical and Physical Arrangement
- Examine schedule, details, and room assignments. Check and double-check logistical arrangements to ensure everything is properly prepared.
- Visit the training site in advance to inspect. Create a checklist that includes the important logistical considerations.
- Match the physical venue of the facility to the training you are delivering.

Control the Physical Environment and Minimize Distractions
- Try to anticipate and plan for environmental distractions and other problems (i.e., bad weather, construction, etc.).
- Make a checklist of equipment and supplies needed for the training. Create a backup plan to handle broken equipment or lost supplies.
- Determine how to control the physical environment before training (temperature, lights, sound).

Instructional Methods and Strategies

Competency 7. Stimulate and Sustain Learner Motivation and Engagement

a. Match learning outcomes (expectations) to officer and course goals.
b. Plan (and deliberately use) feedback and positive reinforcement during delivery of instruction.
c. Use stories, analogies, and examples to gain and sustain officer attention.

Development Strategy

Increase Officer Motivation
- Emphasize the importance of the training results and the benefits to the organization and to the learners.
- Involve officers in setting their own training goals to increase their commitment and motivation in achieving them. Make learning goals specific, measurable, challenging, and realistic.
- Motivate officers by providing them with timely, specific feedback and recognition.
- Use positive as well as negative reinforcement (not the same as punishment) to encourage positive behavior.

Use a Variety of Motivational Strategies to Maintain Impact
- Use stories, anecdotes, icebreakers, and other introductory activities to capture learners' attention. Also, inform officers why they need to know this new information and how it will help them with their job.
- Provide officers with opportunities during training to successfully use the new skills to build their confidence. Emphasize how the new skills enhance their current skills and job performance.
- Monitor officers for signs of motivation (or lack of motivation) such as verbal activity, eye contact, level of participation, and a general sense of excitement and enthusiasm. Use these signs as indicators of when to employ more or different motivational strategies. Use activities when you detect officers getting sleepy, tired, or generally disinterested. These activities help you generate interest by moving to a new topic and encouraging participation.
- Incorporate frequent behavioral activities that promote relevant psychological processing of content presented (Clark 2015).

Competency 8. Demonstrate Effective Presentation/Facilitation Skills

a. Use a lesson plan to deliver instruction.
b. Present key ideas and concepts in a variety of ways.
c. Provide examples to clarify meanings or teaching points.
d. Involve officers in presentations for discussion, questions, and reflection.
e. Use examples, anecdotes, stories, analogies, and humor to reinforce teaching points.
f. Use props and teaching aids effectively and appropriately.

Development Strategy

Use Your Voice Effectively
- Vary your vocal tones to convey enthusiasm, sincerity, and seriousness.
- Use volume, rate, tempo, and inflection to ensure that everyone can hear, to stimulate interest, and to enhance your message.
- Identify distracting speech mannerisms ("ahh," "like," "you know") and attempt to correct them. This can be identified and corrected during videotaped practice sessions.
- Use a microphone for a large audience.

Competency 9. Demonstrate Effective Questioning Techniques

   a. Ask clear and relevant questions.
   b. Promptly follow up on officer questions and concerns.
   c. Use a variety of question types delivered at various levels.
   d. Direct and redirect questions effectively.
   e. Build responses to questions in current (or subsequent) learning environments.
   f. Repeat, rephrase, and restore questions from officers.
   g. Provide positive reinforcement to officer responses.
   h. Provide opportunity to involve all officers in discussions.

Development Strategy

Use Questions to Assess Officer Understanding, Identify Officers, Encourage Participation, Enable Reflection, and Capture and Hold Officer Attention

- Tell officers up front that you plan to ask questions and would like their participation.
- Ask questions that are challenging enough to hold officers' interest, but not too difficult that officers are unable to answer.
- Vary questions from officer to officer. Avoid forcing officers to answer questions so that you do not put them on the spot.

Levels of Questions

- Use different levels of questions to assess the depth of officers' understanding and their readiness or confidence to provide answers.
- Begin by asking easy questions and gradually move to more difficult questions. Embed several test questions in your questioning to determine the officers' current level of comprehension. (However, do not let the officers know you are using test questions.)

Strategies for Using Difficult Types of Questions

- Ask a variety of open, closed, and follow-up questions to elicit different responses depending on the level of participation you are seeking. For example, instead of asking, "Does anyone have more questions?" ask, "What questions do you have?" This technique encourages officers to respond with something other than a simple yes or no.
- Use closed questions to gauge participant reactions.
- Use open questions when you want to encourage more dialogue and participation.

- Use a direct question when you want to elicit responses or gain the attention of an individual officer.
- Use follow-up questions when you want to probe deeper into an officer's response.
- Use a reverse or reflective question to clarify an officer's question to the rest of the group.
- Subtly use a redirect question to the entire group to avoid informing learners that they have given an incorrect response.
- Redirect officer questions to the entire group to encourage everyone's participation and capitalize on the group's knowledge.

Once You Ask a Question
- Use silence to provide officers with time to reflect. If you begin talking too quickly after asking a question, officers assume they do not have to answer the question if they wait long enough. However, do not wait too long.
- Use active listening skills to demonstrate that you sincerely care about the response. Make eye contact with other nonverbal cues such as nodding or leaning forward. Repeat or paraphrase what you heard for clarity.

Competency 10. Provide Clarification and Feedback

a. Provide clear, timely, relevant, and specific feedback.
b. Provide opportunities for officers to request clarification to teaching points.
c. Assist officers in giving and receiving feedback.
d. Provide feedback targeted to the performance (and not to the officer).
e. Promote peer-to-peer feedback.

Development Strategy

Provide Officers with Feedback
- Watch for signs that officers need feedback such as incorrect responses to questions, confused looks, blank stares, avoidance of eye contact, or convoluted questions and comments.
- If feedback or clarification could be potentially embarrassing to the officer, delay the feedback for a later time. As the adage goes "Praise in public, correct in private."
- If the officer feedback calls for a lengthy response, delay the feedback until you can meet with the officer one on one.
- Provide feedback in a timely manner. The closer the feedback to the behavior, the greater the impact.

- Maintain a good balance between positive and corrective feedback. Too much positive feedback can come across as insincere, while too much corrective feedback can be overwhelming. Officers will typically only hear the corrective.
- Consider this formula when providing feedback:
    1. State the officer's name.
    2. Describe observable behavior that you are addressing.
    3. Specify the consequences or the result of the behavior in question.
- Never give feedback unless it is sincere. Insincere feedback undermines your credibility because it raises questions about your honesty and integrity.

Competency 11. Promote Retention and Transfer

a. Encourage officers to elaborate on concepts and ideas.
b. Provide opportunities to integrate new knowledge and practice new skills.
c. Provide opportunities for reflection, review, and self-guided learning.
d. Provide opportunities to practice in realistic settings.

Development Strategy

Encourage Officers to Elaborate on Concepts and Ideas
- Link the training content and activities to the course objectives.
- Have officers create metaphors, analogies, examples, pictures, applications, interpretations, paraphrases, and clarification related to the new knowledge or skill.
- Use examples and content that are tied to the organization and the officers' experience and work environment.
- Use transitions to bridge one topic to the next.

Link Learning Activities to Prior Knowledge
- Tap into officers' previous knowledge, skill, and experience during training. This helps reinforce understanding, which relates new information to what the officers already know.
- Recognize the life or career stage that may be different and the major goals or tasks they might have.
- Have officers generate questions, objectives, summaries, graphs, tables, main ideas, concept maps, diagrams, and outlines to establish relationships between new ideas and prior understanding.

Use Activities, Application, and Practice in Realistic Settings
- Design and conduct training in a job context to make abstract principles more concrete.

- Use case studies and simulations to assist officers to apply a learned skill.

Provide Opportunities for Reflection and Review
- Allow time for reflection by using tools such as journals and review.
- Provide officers with summaries at the end of training segments to help them synthesize important learning points.

Explore with Officers the Conditions That May Assist in Training Transfer
- Ask officers for real-life examples from their job or life experiences and tie them back to the training in a meaningful way.
- Provide opportunities for self-directed learning.

Assessment and Evaluation

Competency 12. Assess Learning and Performance

a. Communicate assessment criteria to officers.
b. Monitor individual and group performance during practice and assessment.
c. Provide officers with opportunities for self-assessment.
d. Assess officer performance outcomes.
e. Provide opportunities for remediation.

Development Strategy

Training Objectives
- When writing or reviewing objectives, they should be clear and measurable. Be certain that officers understand the behavior that is demonstrated, how the behaviors will be measured, and the conditions under which the officers must demonstrate the behavior.
- Remember that even though evaluation is usually conducted at the end of training, it is really a front-end responsibility. The instructor's responsibility is to be certain that the goals are in place and they match the officers' needs.

Officer Evaluation Guidelines
- Use multiple methods for evaluating officer performance such as written test, observations, interviews, and performance evaluations. Multiple methods will give you a 360-degree view of the officers' skill and abilities.
- Try observing officers at a distance to get a clear picture of performance.

- Create checklists of the behaviors that you are looking for; this minimizes subjectivity.

Management

Competency 13. Manage an Environment That Fosters Learning and Performance

a. Introduce oneself, co-instructors, and officers at the beginning of the course (if necessary).
b. Present clear expectations and ground rules for learning and interaction.
c. Address undesirable behavior effectively, appropriately, and timely.
d. Resolve officer conflicts appropriately and timely.
e. Manage group-paced and individual participation.
f. Manage instructional time effectively and avoid digressions.
g. Provide a positive learning environment for all officers.

Development Strategy

Managing Time
- Start on time. Welcome latecomers to the classroom without allowing them to disturb the class.
- Start class promptly after a break (use a countdown timer that the officers can see for themselves). This sends a message to the officers on how important the class is to you.

Communication
- Convey your expectation regarding the format and style of the class as well as expectations on the officers' conduct.
- Ask the officers what their expectations of the class are. Try and incorporate some of their expectation into the class whenever possible, and address those that will not be met during training.
- The orientation to the course should include the following:
  1. Course goals and objectives
  2. Training schedules
  3. Performance expectations
  4. Practical evaluation and written examination requirements
  5. Fire and emergency procedures
  6. Safety rules and regulations
  7. Code of conduct rules and requirements
  8. Disciplinary procedures

Competency 14. Manage the Instructional Process through the Appropriate Use of Technology

a. Use visual aids that support the objective(s) and teaching points.
b. Use visual aids that are simple and easy to read and understand.
c. Incorporate the use of job aids, handouts, or other printed materials in the learning environment.
d. Incorporate different media to appeal to all learning styles.
e. Establish a contingency plan in the event media fails during instruction.

Development Strategy

Turn Charts and Whiteboards
- Write clearly and legibly with no spelling errors using dark-colored markers. Avoid red and yellow because they can be difficult to read from a distance.
- When working on a whiteboard, *be certain* you are using an erasable marker.
- Use bullet points and capital letters.

Computer and Overhead Presentations
- Stand in the back of the training room to test the clarity of the presentation.
- When using video clips, adjust the lighting so that learners can see the video, but are not totally in the dark to enable them to take notes if necessary.

Computer-Aided Instruction and Computer-Based Training
- Keep in mind that many adults may not want to use computers during training.
- If using the Web, precheck before the class that the Internet connection is working. Plan for download time.

Contingency Plans and Other Things to Consider
- Practice using your media in advance to identify potential problems, breakdowns, or troubleshooting needs before training starts.
- Avoid replacing training with technology. While using technology can be exciting and can enhance your presentations, remember that officers learn from each other and many times want to interact with one another as well as the instructor.
- *Always* have a contingency plan when using technology. Have a backup plan in case of a power failure or some other unforeseen event.
- Whiteboards and turn charts are great backups, if the power goes down.

- Keep additional supplies close at hand such as masking tape, additional markers, light bulbs for projectors, and power packs for computers.

These competencies should help you develop an evaluation system for your instructors (for a free sample Instructor Competency Evaluation, go to humanperformance.vpweb.com).

A qualification process should have some of the following steps:

1. Proper schooling in the principles and methodologies of instruction.
2. Attendance of an Instructional Systems Design course.
3. Complete all of the requirements to meet the qualifications for the subject matter they will be required to instruct (i.e., physical fitness, etc.).
4. Have at least three successful officer presentations evaluated by qualified instructors.
5. Complete an oral board made up of qualified instructors.

Clicker Training

One of the most revolutionary learning techniques for classroom instruction is the use of clickers to engage officers. What is clicker training (and we are not talking about dog clicker training)? The basics of clicker use in the classroom are that each officer has a handheld clicker that connects wirelessly to the computer. An instructor can ask just one officer a question for them to answer via the clicker or they can ask the entire class a question. The officer's answers are then displayed on the computer screen. Clickers are generally used to enhance lectures and engage learners. Here is an example: A law enforcement instructor is giving a lecture on the Fourth Amendment. During the lecture, the instructor checks the comprehension of the material by asking questions and then having officers click on their answers. This gives both the instructor and the officers in the class a gauge on how well they comprehend the material. The instructor sees where there are learning gaps he or she needs to focus on, and the officers see areas where they need to spend more time learning. Mayer et al. (2009) found learners who answered questions in a lecture with a response clicker gained, on average, a one-third grade-point improvement compared with other learners who either answered questions on paper or were not asked questions.

Characteristics of a Motivating Instructor

Can instructors motivate adults? Yes, is the simple answer. But how? Wlodkowski (2008) outlines several characteristics of a motivating instructor:

1. They know something beneficial to the audience. Most officers are pragmatic learners. They want to know how to solve problems, build new skills, advance in their jobs, or decide if something is of value to them.
2. Instructors know their subject matter really well. An instructor gives several analogies to show depth of their knowledge of the subject matter. An instructor can demonstrate the skill properly. Instructors also know what they do not know.
3. Instructors are prepared to convey knowledge with officers through the instructional process. Quite simply, be prepared. Be organized. Readiness enhances confidence.
4. Instructors have a realistic understanding of the officers; goals, perspectives, and expectations for what is being learned. Be open and be flexible. Understand the officer's expectations.
5. Instructors adapt their instruction to the officers' level of experience and skill. Are you instructing a basic course or an advanced course? You change your instruction to the level of the officers you are teaching.
6. Instructors value what they teach. How do athletes approach their sport? How do musicians approach their art? How do you approach your subject matter?
7. Instructors create a safe, inclusive, and respectful learning environment. Officers will make mistakes in training; it is where you want mistakes made, not in the field. Mistakes are opportunities to enhance learning. Do not humiliate an officer for making a mistake in training; use it as a teaching opportunity.

Instructor Accountability

Instructors should be held to the highest level of competency; in other words, they must be able to know and do better than any of the officers they are teaching. For any subject matter they are teaching, they should be able to pass the exam given to officers by at least 90% (if not higher). They should also be evaluated as often as possible. Any instructor not maintaining competency should be pulled out and remediated until competency is achieved.

Instructors should be allowed to perform special functions related to field work not only to keep them in touch on how their instruction is being applied to field work but also to see what new issues may need to be addressed back at the academy. The academy runs the risk of becoming an ivory tower out of touch with the reality of field work if a link is not maintained with the field.

All of the instructor's professional development should be maintained in a database not only to have a record of his or her instructional competencies, but also to ensure that certifications are up to date. Instructors should be encouraged to seek outside professional development and advanced education. The academy should try to accommodate the instructors as they try and better themselves as best as the academy can.

The academy should develop specific criteria and document supervisor quality checks of instruction preparedness, class preparation, and performance. Further, the academy should develop a firm instructor qualification guidelines not only for full-time instructors but also for part-time and adjunct instructors.

Here are some steps to develop your instructors to being the best:

1. They should attend a qualified instructor development course.
2. They should be considered subject-matter experts in the area they are teaching.
3. They need to be physically fit.
4. They should be mentored and evaluated for courses they will be teaching. There should be some unannounced evaluations.
5. They should stand in front of an oral board of already qualified instructors.
6. There needs to be a decertification process, which addresses conduct, behavior, or competency of instructors.

The instructors are the face of the academy. Their conduct during training determines not only their credibility but also the credibility of the academy. Instructors have to maintain a high level of competency both before they are put in front of an officer and while in front of officers.

Approaches to Feedback

A primary skill set for a law enforcement instructor is providing feedback to officers. More and more research show how important feedback is to an officer's learning; sometimes, it improves learning by 15 to 50% (Shepherd and Godwin 2010). Yet, this is a tricky area: feedback can create a strong threat to officers in most situations. First, feedback causes anxiety. Thus, an instructor needs to realize that feedback needs to be constructive. Yet, officers need feedback to know how well they are progressing toward the proficiency of the objectives so that they can use that information to improve their performance. Without feedback, officers will not know what they are doing well and where they need to improve. The first question an instructor needs to ask before giving feedback is whether the feedback is needed.

Sometimes, officers themselves can provide their own feedback on how they are doing. Self-correcting feedback is valuable in effective learning. Schmidt and Wrisberg (2008) suggest two factors instructors need to consider before providing feedback: (1) complexity of the task and (2) experience of the officer. There are many types of instructional feedback outlined in Table 5.1.

Practice feedback reinforces capable performance and redirects progress toward the proficiency of the performance objective. Here are some guidelines instructors can use:

- Feedback should be immediate and precise. For instance, saying "Spread your feet further apart" is not precise. Instead, saying "Move your feet out 6 inches more" is more precise in feedback.
- Practice scenarios should be properly sequenced—from easy to more difficult.
- Allow officers to make errors and then provide immediate feedback and demonstrate the correct way.
- Reinforce good performance or effort.
- Ensure that the officers know exactly what is expected of them.

Table 5.1   Types of Instructional Feedback

Type	Function or Consideration	Example
Program	Assists officers in developing fundamental relative motion patterns More useful for beginners or inexperienced officers	"Power comes from the hips not the arms" to convey the importance of force of impact from a baton
Parameter	Assists officers in adjusting fundamental relative motion pattern More useful for experienced learners	"Unholster faster" to convey need to increase the quickness getting the pistol from the holster
Visual	Provides officers with visual depiction of their action More useful for experienced officers Beginners may need additional verbal cueing	Videotape replay of unholstering of a pistol to convey image of action from several different viewing perspectives
Descriptive	Directs officers' attention to a particular aspect of the action More useful for experienced officers	"Your feet need to be closer together by six inches" to convey observable characteristic or action
Prescriptive	Suggests specific alteration or correction for the action Most useful for beginners	"Sight alignment and sight picture" to convey adjustment that might correct an observed error

Source: Adapted from Schmidt, R. A. and Wrisberg, C. A. (2008). *Motor Learning and Performance: A Situation-Based Learning Approach* (4th ed.). Champaign, IL: Human Kinetics.

Feedback Strategies

It has been said that feedback is a "gift." In other words, a person's feedback to another is a form of either endorsement of one's behavior, or a way to improve one's behavior. Either way, it is important for both the officer and the instructor. There are four styles of feedback:

1. **Corrective:** Given to identify performance that is unsafe, ineffective, outside the policy, or inappropriate. It provides areas for improvement and expectations. This should be specific to give officers the ability to use the feedback in order to improve their performance or technique during future training.
2. **Supportive:** Given to identify performance that is safe, effective, within the policy, or appropriate. It provides areas in which officer performance met or exceeded training expectations. It reinforces positive performance.
3. **Elaborative:** Provides officer with additional information or guidance on how to improve performance that was unsatisfactory or specific guidance to improve satisfactory performance. Elaborative feedback can be used in conjunction with corrective and supportive feedback.
4. **Knowledge of Results:** Conveys to the officer whether the observed performance met acceptable standards. Officers need to be made aware of success or failure in order to determine the need for review, practice, or more instruction.

Feedback should be given as soon as practical after training, which must be given before continued training, and can last as long as necessary. The purpose of feedback is to

- Reinforce positive behavior (supportive/elaborative)
- Identify areas for improvement (corrective/elaborative)
- Provide results of objectives met or not met (knowledge of results)

Assessing Officer Performance

Another important skill set a law enforcement instructor needs is how to evaluate performance. *Performance* can be defined as the accomplishment of a task in accordance with a set standard of completeness and accuracy, for example, frisking a suspect. Skills can be divided into open skills and closed skills.

Open Skills versus Closed Skills

Skills differ in terms of the environment in which the skill is performed and the goal of the skill. Open skills demand that the officer be adaptable, flexible in response, able to read the situation, and able to anticipate what will happen next; for instance, interviewing a suspect can be considered an open skill. On the other hand, a closed skill allows the performance of a fixed, unchanging pattern of movement. Any variation in that one fixed pattern will destroy what you are trying to achieve; for instance, shooting a firearm is a closed skill. There are 10 techniques for evaluating open skills:

1. Know the learner (pre-brief, ask questions).
2. Be familiar with the scenario and tasks to be evaluated.
3. Observe carefully.
4. Take notes.
5. If using role players, ask for their feedback.
6. Ask the officers what they did, what they were thinking, and so on.
7. Consider new ways to meet the objective (don't limit options to your experience).
8. Coach appropriately.
9. Discuss with another evaluator.
10. Document.

A closed skill occurs in a stable and predictable environment, where the timing of the skill is self-paced, and to a large extent, the performer determines the place where the skill will be performed. These environments are more conducive to skill learning as the officer is not distracted by other factors, for example, shooting a firearm. The learning of closed skills tends to happen faster than the learning of open skills. If a skill is open by nature (e.g., kicking a training pad), it will be easier to learn if it is "closed down" (e.g., shooting a stationary target rather than a moving target). Most skills fit on a continuum between totally closed and totally open.

Pygmalion Effect

The Pygmalion effect is a well-researched phenomenon that states that the greater the expectation placed on officers, the better they perform.

The opposite of the Pygmalion effect is the *golem effect*, which states that the lower the expectation placed on officers is, the lower their performance is. Instructors need to be keenly aware of these effects. How they instruct, how they provide feedback, and the level of their expectation on officers are greater than they may realize. Positive feedback = positive performance; negative feedback = negative performance.

Interrater Agreement

Instructors need to be consistent when evaluating an officer's performance in training. Interrater agreement is the measure of reliability used to assess the degree to which different raters (instructors) agree in their assessment decisions. Agreement measures how frequently two or more evaluators assign the exact same rating: if both give a rating of "4," they are in agreement. Reliability measures the *relative* similarity between two or more sets of ratings, regardless of the *absolute* value of each evaluator's rating. Thus, even if two evaluators never assign the same numerical score, they could still have high interrater reliability if their ratings are in the same relative order (Tinsley and Weiss 2000). All officers want a fair and reliable assessment of their performance. If some instructors are "easy" on performance evaluations, and other instructors are "hard" on their performance evaluation, this is going to cause issues with officers involved in the training.

Why is interrater agreement important? Here's why:

- It ensures that officers are trained to the same standard.
- It ensures fairness in evaluations.
- It clarifies possible "gray" areas.

How can you enhance interrater agreement? When qualifying instructors run them through numerous laboratory exercises using videotape vignettes. On the basis of their qualitative analysis of evaluators, Nijveldt et al. (2009) recommend that instructors discuss all of the relevant judgment processes, including personal biases and the mental processes needed to adjudicate between ratings or standards, so that raters will be more attuned to the ways in which their ratings might stray from objectivity.

Another way to improve interrater agreement is to ensure that the evaluation rubrics are easily understood. If an instructor is having difficulty understanding what they are actually evaluating, then there are going to be issues of interrater agreement. Lumley (2002) found that when instructors are unsure on how to evaluate an issue based on the rubric, they choose to heavily weigh one aspect of the criteria or they resort to criteria that are not part of the rubric. This problem can be addressed not only through training but also by refining the rubric in a way that addresses assessor difficulties in applying it. Further, a yes/no or go/no-go checklist can produce higher rates of agreement than a Likert 1–5 scale.

How to Rate Performance

Instructors have to maintain reliability in their ratings of officers. What does this mean? If two instructors are evaluating how an officer performs on a certain practical exercise, they should come close in rating how the officer performs. It is not good when one instructor gives one rating and another instructor gives a completely different rating. Therefore, you have to train your instructors on how to rate performance to where they come close in their ratings. Frame of reference (FOR) training can help. FOR training is one of the latest attempts at increasing the accuracy of performance ratings. This method usually involves the following steps:

a. Participants are given descriptions of each measurement of compe-tence and are then instructed to discuss what they believe the quali-fications that are needed for each measurement.
b. Participants are given video vignettes that show performance (from unsatisfactory to average to outstanding) (FOR).
c. Participants use the vignettes to provide ratings on a behaviorally anchored rating scale; yes/no or go/no go is best.
d. The session trainer then provides feedback on what the "true" ratings should be along with an explanation for the rating.
e. The training session wraps up with an important discussion on the discrepancies between the participants' ratings and the "true" ratings.

To ensure that instructors maintain their FOR, FOR should be part of their own individual feedback and appraisal.

Conclusion

Instructors are the face of the academy. Instructors have to be at the top of their game every time they step in front of a class. Through a sound instructor qualification and monitoring process, you will ensure the instructors remain the star players on your team. Make sure your instructors stay current in their professional development and in their course material. If you take care of your instructors, they will ensure that the academy maintains a high level of expertise.

Curriculum Development

6

If instructors are the backbone of the academy, then curriculum is the foundation in which the academy and all of its courses are built. Most training curriculums are built on the industry standard ADDIE process (see Figure 6.1). ADDIE is defined as

A—Analysis
D—Design
D—Development
I—Implementation
E—Evaluation

Most of this chapter will be spent discussing each one of these processes.

Analysis

A thorough analysis is key to any training intervention. For one, analysis will answer whether training is even needed. Many times, it is mistaken that training will provide a solution to any identified problem. Yet, many times, problems can be easily solved with a job aid or lower form of intervention. This portion of the process is where many law enforcement training programs fail; a lack of analysis. Many programs are driven by opinion, guessing, subjective thought, or following what is currently in vogue with no thought given to analysis. This causes "training creep," meaning an ever-expanding training program with no evidence for the expansion. A good analysis will assist in understanding if training is needed, how the training should be completed, and when the training needs to be done. How do you know if your training is valid without an analysis? How do you know if your training is reliable without an analysis? How do you know if your training is relevant without an analysis? Gagne et al. (2005) suggest the following basic guidelines to an analysis (we will go into more detail on each one of these during this chapter):

1. Determine a need for which training is the solution.
2. Conduct an instructional analysis to determine the target cognitive, affective, and psychomotor goals for the course (Bloom's Taxonomy).

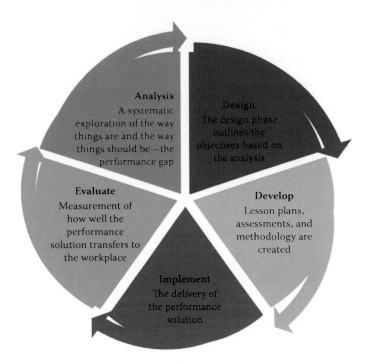

Figure 6.1 ADDIE model.

3. Determine what skills the officers are expected to have.
4. Analyze the time available and how much might be accomplished in that period.

There are mainly two types of analysis: a Front-End Analysis (FEA) and a Job Task Analysis (JTA).

FEA

Typically, an FEA is used to

- Define current and desired performance
- Identify the performance gap

The performance gap is the difference between where the organization or individual is and where they want to be. An FEA determines the influences on the gap by conducting a series of analyses—performance analysis (which includes organizational and environmental analyses) and cause analysis (which includes the organization's environmental support and the individual's behavioral repertory). Designing the appropriate intervention closes the gap. The intervention could be training, or it could be something else.

Joe Harless (1973), the father of FEA, has said that the purpose of front-end analysis is to

- Ask a series of Smart Questions in order to prevent spending money on unnecessary activities
- Come up with the most appropriate solution
- Produce the desired performance outcomes

These are Harless's Smart Questions for FEA:

These first five questions could be categorized as Performance Analysis:
1. Do we have a problem? (Based on what evidence can you say you have a problem?)
2. Do we have a performance problem (versus an attitudinal problem)?
3. How will we know when the problem is solved? (When indicators from the first question are the exception.)
4. What is the performance problem?
5. Should we allocate resources to solve it? (Do the benefits of solving the problem outweigh the costs?)

The next three questions could be categorized as Cause Analysis:
1. What are the possible causes of the problem? (Lack of data, tools, incentives, knowledge, capacity, motives?)
2. What evidence bears on each possibility?
3. What is the probable cause?

The final five questions fall under Intervention Selection, Design, and Development:
1. What general solution type is indicated?
2. What are the alternate subclasses of solution? (What else could you do to solve the problem?)
3. What are the costs, effects, and development times of each solution? (Research the costs of each solution.)
4. What are the constraints? (Research the constraints of each solution.)
5. What are the overall goals? (What goals would management like to adopt?)

FEA includes all the Smart Questions that a manager, specialist, trainer, and consultant should ask before deciding what specific solution to develop for a performance problem. Asking the Smart Questions helps agencies (1) spend money on performance problems that are worth solving, (2) thoroughly investigate the causes for the problems, and (3) determine the most cost-effective solutions.

JTA

Another type of analysis is a JTA. A JTA aims to answer questions such as the following:

1. Why does the job exist?
2. What physical and mental activities does the officer undertake?
3. When is the job to be performed?
4. Where is the job to be performed?
5. How does the officer do the job?
6. What qualifications are needed to perform the job?
7. What are the working conditions (such as levels of temperature, noise, equipment, light)?
8. What equipment is used in the job?
9. What constitutes successful performance?

There are a multitude of data points for collecting information for a JTA: agency policies and regulations, interviews with subject-matter experts (SMEs) and star performers (SPs), databases an agency may have regarding enforcement actions performed by officers (arrests, public contacts, etc.), and observations of officers doing their jobs. Just a brief note on the differences between SMEs and SPs. SMEs are recognized experts on specific subjects. The person heading up a firearms program is probably an SME on the type of firearms a department carries. An SP, on the hand, would be the person that uses the firearm best within the department. In other words, an SME may be a staff person, whereas an SP is the person who has a proven track record providing exemplary results in the field.

As data are being collected, it is important that the data are verified for their accuracy by vetting through persons identified as having technical exactness for the tasks. The content of your training should mirror how your SPs perform in their job. The content of your training should closely align with work practices (Elliott and Folsom 2013).

A task analysis should include the following:

- **Behavior**—The actual steps an officer takes in performing the tasks. Some of these steps are readily observable (disassembly of a firearm) or not observable (decision making).
- **Condition**—Under what elements are the tasks actually performed (such as wearing body armor, on horseback, or from a snowmobile).
- **Criteria**—What is the quality or quantity attached to the job? How clean is an officer's weapon supposed to be? What is the firearm qualification score for an officer?

- **Characteristics**—What tools are required to do the job (e.g., breathalyzer for making DUI arrests)? What are the safety concerns (take into consideration the speed, frequency, complexity, or consequences the job entails)?

Many agencies do not have the resources to do a full FEA or a JTA themselves and contract out to consulting companies to perform these functions. This is money well spent, for a JTA will provide all of the elements to build a curriculum.

Informal or Rapid Analysis

Since many agencies do not have the money to hire an outside consulting firm to do their JTAs or FEAs, there is a less costly way of doing the analysis from the inside, but first you have to do a quick needs assessment.

Instructional needs may be present when

- A problem surfaces in an area where there is no current instruction
- Technical or doctrinal changes make existing instruction obsolete
- A new weapon system is planned
- Instruction in a topic is mandated
- Educating for future assignment

One informal way of carrying out a pseudo-FEA is via the difficulty–importance–frequency (DIF) model. When determining if training is necessary, many agencies use the DIF model.

- **Difficulty**—The number of steps to perform a task, and the mental activity and psychomotor coordination required to perform the task.
- **Importance**—The prospect of danger to self or others, national security, or the community if the task is not done correctly.
- **Frequency**—The number of times the task is performed in a given period.

This model allows a simple process when deciding to conduct training. Quite simply, the model can be used as follows:

1. If a task is difficult, important, and infrequent, it is of high priority. Examples of such tasks are shooting and certain tactics. This type of task is something an officer must be able to act instantly on and perform automatically, but does not do it frequently.

2. If a task is not difficult, but important, and frequent, it is of medium priority. An example would be interviewing suspects or witnesses. For this type of task, an officer must be able to demonstrate proficiency in performing the task at a normal speed.
3. If a task is neither difficult nor important, it is of low priority. Much of this can be considered "nice to know" information, such as administrative updates. This task in reality does not require any formal training.

Generally, numbers are assigned to each section of the DIF on a Likert scale of 1–5 as seen in Table 6.1.

If the numbers are seven or above, then formal training is suggested (a DIF spreadsheet can be downloaded from humanperformance.vpweb.com).

Subject-Matter Experts

SMEs are essential to forming your training. However, you have to be careful that you do not allow SMEs to run your training program. You have to

Table 6.1   Explanation of How to Rate DIF for Tasks of *Average* Performers

Difficulty (or Complexity)	Importance (or Consequence of Error)	Frequency
1. **Very low**—Anyone can do it.	1. **Very low**—If task is not done correctly, no possibility of human loss or injury to self or others.	1. **Very low**—Infrequent/not predictable
2. **Low**—Usually less than 5 steps, not much judgment, application of rule with no exceptions, no hand–eye coordination.	2. **Low**—If task is not done correctly, very small possibility of human loss or injury to self or others.	2. **Low**—Semiannual
3. **Moderate**—Usually 5 to 10 steps, gross judgment, application of rule with few exceptions, or gross muscular movement.	3. **Moderate**—If task is not done correctly, would require some correction but would probably not cause human loss or injury.	3. **Moderate**—Monthly
4. **High**—Usually 10 to 15 steps, fine judgment, application of rules with many exceptions, precise hand–eye coordination.	4. **High**—If task is not done correctly, possible human loss or injury to self or others.	4. **High**—Weekly
5. **Very high**—Usually more than 15 steps, requires extensive skills, knowledge, or support.	5. **Very high**—If task is not done correctly, injury, loss of human life likely.	5. **Very high**—Daily or hourly

Table 6.2 Questions for Your SMEs

Ask	If	Then
Is the information critical to the officers performing their job?	Yes	**Need to know**
	No	Nice to know
Do the officers already have this information from prior experience or training?	Yes	Nice to know
	No	**Need to know**
Is the information available from another resource (e-learning, manuals, policies, etc.)?	Yes	Guide officers to that resource
	No	**Train**

love the passion your SMEs have for their subject matter, but you may have to build a comprehensive program using multiple SMEs. SMEs nearly always want more time and more information added to their course of instruction. Again, this adds to cognitive load to your officers along with more cost to your training. Table 6.2 is a good reference to assist you with developing your program and working with SMEs. There should be no nice-to-know information in your resident training program.

Design

A well-designed training is an effective and efficient tool for transferring the requisite skills, knowledge, and information to officers who are assigned a new role. The JTA or FEA will provide the foundation to design the course. Instructional objectives regarding knowledge, skills, and abilities will be fleshed out through a JTA or FEA. During the design phase, training objectives will be written. Instructional materials and activities will be added to provide task proficiency. The design phase provides a blueprint for the course.

Training design begins with the decisions made in the needs analysis process and ends with a model for the training program. Using learning objectives as a guide, trainers must determine what content to include in the curriculum, how detailed the content should be, and how it is to be presented. From these decisions, a lesson plan is created and training materials are developed.

As with any course development, the target audience must be known. This is a common problem throughout law enforcement training systems. Courses, material, and instructors are placed in a course for the wrong audience. There is little use if the course is valid and reliable if it is given to the wrong audience.

Merrill (2007) advocates for a Task-Centered Strategy that builds the curriculum from the tasks identified in the analysis. An illustration of the Task-Centered Strategy is shown in Figure 6.2.

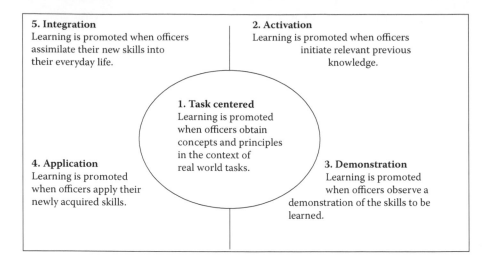

Figure 6.2 Task-centered strategies.

Identify the Real-World Task

A real-world task should come from your analysis—real-world tasks are not contrived, and many times they do not have one correct answer. There should be a standard for what acceptable performance is. Management of cognitive load is very important to recognize as tasks build upon one another.

Course Objectives

Clearly defined learning objectives are useful for instructors, instructional designers, and officers, for the following reasons:

- In order to select and design instructional content, materials, or methods and have a sound basis by which success can be measured.
- To give designers and instructors an objective method to determine how successful their material has been. By clearly stating the results we want the learners to accomplish, instructors can identify whether officers have gained the appropriate skills and knowledge.
- Because objectives should be stated before learners begin to use their instructional materials, they provide officers the means to organize their efforts toward accomplishing the desired behaviors.

Components of an Objective

Objectives clearly communicate what is measurable and what is observable. When writing learning objectives, avoid terms that cannot be clearly understood by the reader (there will be more on this later in this chapter). It is necessary to communicate an objective as clearly as possible to avoid misinterpretation.

A useful objective successfully describes an intended instructional result by describing the purpose of the instruction. The BEST statement is one that excludes the greatest number of possible meanings other than the one intended. In other words, it succeeds in communicating the intent of the instruction yet avoids misinterpretation.

Bloom's Taxonomy

Bloom's Taxonomy is a way of organizing according to some hierarchical order. Benjamin Bloom developed educational goals he published, called the *Taxonomy of Educational Objectives* (1956). Today, Bloom's Taxonomy is the most widely used method of creating learning objectives. Instructional designers use Bloom's Taxonomy levels to measure outcomes and compare everything from programs to methods of learning. While several modifications have been proposed, Bloom's description of learning domains and levels of complexity is still widely used. Bloom identified four principles that guided the development of the taxonomy:

- It should be based on behaviors.
- It should show logical relationships among the categories.
- It should reflect the best current understanding of psychological processes.
- It should describe rather than impose value judgments.

Next, he described three learning domains:

- Cognitive—knowledge-based domain
- Affective—attitude-based domain
- Psychomotor—physical skills–based domain

Cognitive Domain

The cognitive domain of Bloom's original taxonomy had six levels organized in a hierarchy. The base of the pyramid is the foundation of all cognition, knowledge. Each ascending level of the pyramid depends on the one below it. For example, officers must understand the elements of the Fourth Amendment (knowledge) before they can apply the definition of what a search is (comprehension). Knowledge and comprehension are often referred to as lower-order thinking skills. The skills above them are termed higher-order or critical thinking skills.

In the 1990s, a former student of Bloom, Lorin Anderson, revised Bloom's Taxonomy and published *Bloom's Revised Taxonomy* in 2001 (Anderson et al. 2001a). The key change is the use of verbs rather than nouns for each of the categories and a rearrangement of the sequence within the taxonomy. They are arranged below in increasing order, from low to high. There are some subtle differences from the original (see Figure 6.3).

The **remembering** level at the bottom of the hierarchy is defined as remembering or retrieving previously learned material. Learning objectives at this level often include defining key terms, listing steps in a process, or repeating something heard or seen. For example, let us take an objective for a new hire's orientation to his or her newly issued semiautomatic pistol. The new hire would be given an introduction to the nomenclature of the pistol. In this case, knowledge-level objectives are clearly critical, as they are foundational to understanding additional materials. However, designers tend to write too many knowledge-level objectives because they find it so easy to pick out definitions and details. How much detail does the new officer need to know about his or her new firearm? Do not provide information they do not need to know beyond the basics; doing so contributes to cognitive overload.

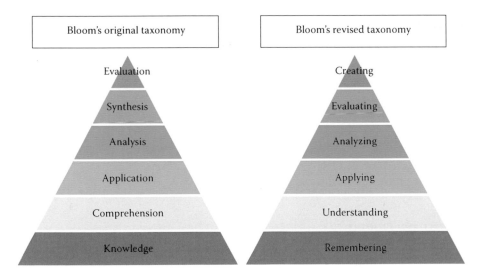

Figure 6.3 Bloom's Taxonomy: six levels of the cognitive domain (original and revised).

Understanding represents the largest category of cognitive skills and abilities. The key skill at this level is processing new information. For example, have the new hire explain the cycle of operation of a semiautomatic pistol.

At the *applying* level, the officer should be able to solve a new problem by applying information without having to be prompted. Objectives at this level might require learners to interpret information, demonstrate mastery of a concept, or apply a skill learned. For instance, have an officer demonstrate immediate action procedures to correct a sidearm malfunction.

Analyzing requires officers to recognize relationships among parts. Objectives at this level of the hierarchy often include verbs such as *differentiate, compare* and *contrast, criticize,* or *experiment*. In this case, the officer may be asked when to use a sidearm versus a long gun during force encounters.

Evaluating involves making judgments about value. Learning objectives at this level require officers to measure, value, estimate, choose, or revise something, or solve a problem. This time, officers would be given a practical exercise where their decision-making process is evaluated on when, where, and why they used different firearms during force encounters.

At the top of the pyramid, *creating*, officers have used all of the lower levels to design and produce something. To create a raid plan, for example, officers should have a clear understanding of the Fourth, Fifth, and Sixth Amendment rights, as well as techniques for searching, arresting, and documenting. In the end, they would have to create a raid plan, determine the suspect's location, and then fully implement their plan.

Instruction that stops too low on the taxonomy does not give officers the chance to think critically enough about what they are learning. When objectives focus solely on recall and comprehension, officers may understand what they have learned but fail to recognize when to apply their knowledge. Higher-order objectives require officers to use what they have learned and may provide practice for developing new approaches to problems, identifying critical variables, making needed judgments, and performing quickly and accurately. Both the original Bloom's Taxonomy and its later revisions can be used to develop much-needed critical thinking.

The cognitive levels range from lower-order thinking skills to higher-order thinking skills. Below each level is a list of suggested activities for that level (see Table 6.3). Below each sublevel is a list of verbs that might be used to create objectives targeted to that cognitive level. Officers are expected to move through the levels and master each step.

Psychomotor Domain

Psychomotor learning refers to learning a skill and task that involve mental ("psycho") as well as physical ("motor") aspects.

Table 6.3   Verbs Used in Bloom's Six Orders of Cognitive Thinking

Lower-Order Thinking → Higher-Order Thinking

Remember	Understand	Apply	Analyze	Evaluate	Create
Recognizing • Identifying Recalling • Retrieving	Interpreting • Clarifying • Paraphrasing • Representing • Translating Exemplifying • Illustrating Classifying • Categorizing • Subsuming Summarizing • Abstracting • Generalizing Inferring • Concluding • Extrapolating • Interpolating • Predicting Comparing • Contrasting • Mapping • Matching Explaining • Constructing models	Executing • Carrying out Implementing • Using	Differentiating • Discriminating • Distinguishing • Focusing • Selecting Organizing • Finding coherence • Integrating • Outlining • Parsing • Structuring Attributing • Deconstructing	Checking • Coordinating • Detecting • Monitoring • Testing Critiquing • Judging	Generating • Hypothesizing Planning • Designing Producing • Constructing

Motor skills can be divided into two categories:

1. Gross motor: Involving large muscle groups (running, jumping, punching).
2. Fine motor: Precise control of small muscle groups (shooting, manual dexterity). Fine motor skills generally demand more practice time than gross motor skills.

Psychomotor skills build upon cognitive thinking (Bloom's Cognitive Domain). They are symbiotic to one another. Think of psychomotor in terms of the proficiency an officer demonstrates when performing a movement. Skill proficiency implies that an officer is able to meet the performance objective with maximum certainty. The cognitive domain mainly emphasizes knowing what to do, while the psychomotor domain emphasizes doing it effectively. When an officer performs a purposeful movement, he or she is coordinating the cognitive, psychomotor, and affective domains. Internally, there is continuous movement, and externally, an officer's movement is modified by past learning, environmental surroundings, and the situation at hand. Therefore, we must be prepared to understand muscular, physiological, social, psychological, and neurological movement in order to recognize and efficiently utilize the components of movement in totality.

Anita Harrow's (1972) interpretation of the psychomotor domain is based on the development of physical fitness, dexterity and agility, and control of the physical "body," to a considerable level of expertise. There are six levels to the law enforcement psychomotor model: reflexive movements, imitation, basic fundamental manipulation, precise skilled movement, synchronistic movement, and automatic response (see Figure 6.4).

At the level of reflex, there are three movement forms: (1) inherited reflective forms, (2) exploratory forms, and (3) conditioned reflexive forms.

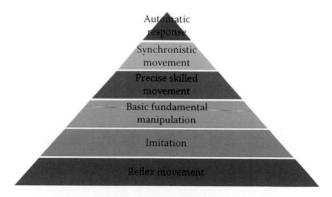

Figure 6.4 Law enforcement psychomotor domain.

A *reflexive movement* involves purely internal responses to external stimuli. For instance, a doctor taps on your knee and your lower leg kicks up; that is a reflexive movement. *Exploratory forms* are learned through trial and error; these movements are refined and develop into neural schemas, for instance, learning to throw a punch. *Conditioned reflexive forms* can be described as learned automatic motor responses to external stimuli. For instance, an officer's response to someone trying to take his weapon from his holster should be a conditioned reflexive form.

Imitation refers to movements learned by watching and imitating actions. They are often components for more complex actions. Practicing strong-arm takedowns after watching the instructor perform the movement would be imitation.

Basic fundamental manipulation should address skills related to kinesthetic (bodily movements), visual, auditory, tactile (touch), or coordination abilities as they are related to the ability to take in information from the environment and react. Performing a strong-arm takedown would be basic fundamental manipulation.

Precise skilled movement should be related to endurance, flexibility, agility, strength, reaction response time, or dexterity. Shooting a firearm at a target under timed conditions would be a precise skilled movement.

Synchronistic movement refers to skills and movements learned for games or sports. Several skills are performed together in a harmonious way. From the holster, firing a firearm at a moving subject and accurately hitting the subject would be a synchronistic movement.

Automatic response refers to a high level of performance achieved with actions becoming second nature. Being able to detect a threat and automatically responding correctly would be an automatic response.

Every psychomotor skill is a form of memory. When a championship martial artist skillfully defeats his or her opponent, he or she is using the structure of memory, telling his or her muscles what to do and when to do it. Anders Ericsson is a psychologist who has studied human performance for more than 40 years and has looked into how a great performance is achieved. According to him, every high performer in every field he studied (this included SWAT operators) found that around 10,000 hours of practice was needed to approach the *automatic response* level (Ericsson 2006). So what does this mean as trainers of law enforcement officers? It means that when training entry-level officers, you can expect these officers to only reach the *precise skilled movement* level. However, when training more advanced level officers, you strive to get them to attain the *synchronistic movement* and *automatic response* levels.

But there is more. There is a plateau effect on psychomotor domain levels as your cognitive domain level becomes higher. In other words, the more cognitive load there is, the less chance there is to move to higher psychomotor

Table 6.4 Description of the Six Levels of Psychomotor Movement

Level	Category	Description	Evidence of Measurement	Verbs Describing Activity
1	Reflex movement	Involuntary reaction	Respond physically instinctively	React, respond
2	Imitation	Basic simple movement	Alter position, move, perform a simple action	Copy, follow, repeat, replicate, reproduce
3	Basic fundamental manipulation	Basic response	Performs actions by memory	Implement, perform, execute, act
4	Precise skilled movement	Skilled action	Performance becomes exact	Control, master, show, calibrate
5	Synchronistic movements	Complex operations	Execute and adapt advance integrative movements	Combine, adapt, coordinate, create, integrate, modify
6	Automatic response	Actions become natural with little thought	Accurate active response in very little time	Automatic, very little thought, fluid

Table 6.5 Motor–Cognitive Interactive Skills

Motor Skills ◄──────────────────►		Cognitive Skills
Decision Making Minimized Motor Control Maximized	Some Decision Making Some Motor Control	Decision Making Maximized Motor Control Minimized
Running	Shooting	Writing a report
Takedowns	Handcuffing	Interviewing
Punching/kicking	Baton strikes	Writing a ticket

Source: Adapted from Schmidt, R. A. and Wrisberg, C. A. (2008). *Motor Learning and Performance: A Situation-Based Learning Approach* (4th ed.). Champaign, IL: Human Kinetics.

domain levels. Hence, the more an officer needs to know (i.e., law, policy, procedures), the less likely it is for the officer to advance to the *synchronistic movement* and *automatic response* levels. Table 6.4 breaks down the psychomotor domain into category, description, evidence of measurement, and verbs describing the activity.

Table 6.5 describes the interaction of motor skills and cognitive skills.

Situation-Based Approach to Psychomotor Performance

There are three elements that an instructor needs to be cognizant of about psychomotor performance: person, task, and environment (Figure 6.5).

Person Schmidt and Wrisberg (2008) state this is the most important element when it comes to teaching and evaluating psychomotor performance. They cite

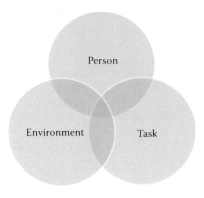

Figure 6.5 Three elements of psychomotor skills.

that individual background, such as emotional makeup, levels of motivation, sociocultural background, and previous experience, influences every person. If an officer has previous experience with the movement, has motivation, has high motivational emotions, and is in alignment with his or her sociocultural background, then he or she should be able to perform at a high level.

Task There are several components to consider when it comes to the task. Some tasks have sensory perceptual demands, such as detecting aggressive movements. Then, there are the cognitive decisions the officer must make about how to perform the task, such as active countermeasures. Last, there is the level of skill required to perform the task. There is a vast difference in skill level between accurately placing a round at center mass on a target at 15 yards and throwing a punch at arm's length.

Environment In what environment will the officer be required to perform the task? Will the officer have to step on the brakes on a wet surface? Will he perform crowd control? The optimal scenario is to have officers perform the task in the environment they will be performing the task in when they are in the field.

Three Levels in the Psychomotor Instructional Process

There are three basic levels or steps in the overall instructional process: imitation, practice, and habit.

1. **Imitation:** In this level, the instructor shares the knowledge content and demonstrates the skill. This level is where the instructor shares the essential information about the skill (such as facts, background information, safety considerations, etc.), breaks down the skill into small steps, demonstrates the skill, and allows the officer to reenact or copy the skill (sometimes referred to as "chunking").

2. **Practice:** In this level, the officer is allowed to practice alone or with the instructor to practice the skill over and over, with feedback from the instructor until the basic skill is learned. The officer is able to ask questions, receive feedback, and try in a friendly safe environment. Remember: "Practice does not make perfect; perfect practice makes perfect." Well-known professional football coach Pete Carroll states how we practice defines who we are. He further states, "Practice is something we want to be the best at for its own sake" (Carroll 2011, p. 90). Carroll emphasizes that it is the coaches that "establish an energy" and a "high level of intensity" to every practice session (Carroll 2011, p. 92). Instructors need to create an environment that will permit each officer to reach his or her maximum potential, and one way of doing so is to practice with great focus. An officer who is fully prepared in the training environment will feel ready to meet whatever comes his or her way when operating on the street; he or she will be more confident and able to minimize distractions such as fear or doubt.

3. **Habit:** The last level is where the officer develops such proficiency that he or she is able to perform the skill in half the time or at an expert level. Performance of the skill becomes second nature. When the officers reach this level, they are able to create their own versions of the skill and teach others.

Basic knowledge and skills start low and progressively increase to more sophisticated skills and to higher levels of ability, and learners develop a critical understanding of performance. There needs to be an awareness of *learning plateaus*, which occur often in psychomotor learning. There are several factors that contribute to learning plateaus: fatigue, need to practice, low motivation, and complexity of the skills trained. Many times, these plateaus occur as the officer moves to a higher level within the domain. Make your officers become aware of these plateaus so that they can adjust accordingly.

Hard Skills and Soft Skills

Hard, high-precision skills, such as shooting a firearm, are actions that are performed as consistently and correctly as possible, every time. Hard skills are about repeatable precision. Daniel Coyle (2012) in his book *The Little Book of Talent* states that to develop reliable hard skills, you need to connect the right wires in the officers' brain. It is advised to go slowly, making one skill move at a time, repeating and perfecting the officers' actions before moving on.

Soft, high-flexibility skills are those that have many paths to good results, not just one. These skills aren't about doing the same thing perfectly every time, but rather about being nimble and interactive, and about recognizing patterns as they unfold and making smart, timely choices, such as interviewing witnesses or suspects. Soft skills are developed in different portions of the brain and therefore are developed through different methods of practice. Soft skills are developed over time.

Affective Domain

Affective learning deals with emotions, attitudes, behaviors, and values (Rovai et al. 2009). There are five levels in the affective domain: receiving, responding, valuing, organizing, and internalizing by value set (Figure 6.6) (Krathwohl et al. 1964).

1. **Receiving:** The willingness to hear and be aware. It can be expressed through listening and attending to others with a good attitude and demeanor. Some verbs that can describe *receiving* are as follows:
   - Feel, sense, capture, experience, pursue, attend, and perceive
2. **Responding:** The experience of being actively involved in learning activities; this can be engaging with peers, instructors, and content. The officer has a willingness to respond and is motivated to have a satisfying learning experience. Some verbs that can describe *responding* are as follows:
   - Conform, allow, cooperate, contribute, enjoy, and satisfy
3. **Valuing:** The worth or value the officer attaches to a behavior. It can be reflected in an internalized set of values and beliefs. Some verbs that can describe *valuing* are as follows:
   - Believe, seek, justify, respect, search, and persuade
4. **Organizing:** The capacity to conceptualize the development of values as part of a professional identity. Some verbs that can describe *organizing* are as follows:
   - Examine, clarify, systematize, create, and integrate

Figure 6.6 Five levels of affective domain.

5. **Internalizing values:** The development of an internal guidance system of values that is consistent, predictable, pervasive, and characteristic of the learner. Some verbs that can describe *internalizing values* are as follows:
   - Internalize, review, conclude, resolve, and judge

Affective domain learning is firmly linked to the cognitive domain, similar to the psychomotor domain. It is easier to evaluate officers in the cognitive and psychomotor domains than in the affective domain. For the affective domain, one evaluates within the perspective of an officer's values orientation (in the case of law enforcement) rather than just looking at performance of a specific skill (Allen and Friedman 2010). When you engage in the learning process, you notice the process and analyze the processes in your mind. The job of law enforcement training is to use Bloom's Taxonomy and human performance technology to train the officer at every domain (Figure 6.7).

Writing Performance Objectives

Knowing what you now know about Bloom's Taxonomy, it is now time to start building performance objectives. Performance objectives must be accurately designed to accurately depict the performance, standards, and conditions of the task. Generally, there are two types of objectives: Terminal Performance Objectives (TPOs) and Enabling Performance Objectives (EPOs). TPOs describe the task the officer will be required to do upon completion of the instruction, hence the word *terminal*. EPOs describe the steps (thinking, acting) to reach the TPO. For instance, a TPO may be disassembling, cleaning, and reassembling a firearm. The EPOs would be (1) making the weapon safe by removing the magazine and safely clearing the chamber and (2) applying

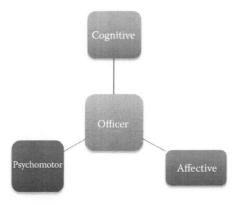

Figure 6.7 Bloom's learning domains.

the steps to disassemble the issued firearm. The goal of the TPO is to accurately describe the real-world expectation of the officer.

Dick and Carey (2011) provide several steps to follow when writing objectives:

1. Write objectives for each step in your instructional analysis.
2. Write an objective for each group of substeps, or for each individual substep.
3. Write objectives for all subordinate skills.
4. Write objectives for entry behaviors, if some officers are likely to not possess them.

According to Mager (1997), there are three main components of writing effective TPOs: **performance**, **conditions**, and **criterion**. From the human performance technology (HPT) perspective, add the component **performer**.

1. **Performer** (the officer): Identify who it is that will be doing the performance (not the instructor).
2. **Performance** (officer performance): What is the measurable behavior you want the officer to do as a result of your course? Make sure it is something that can be seen or heard.
3. **Conditions**: The conditions under which the officers must demonstrate their mastery of the objective: What will be allowed to use? What will not be allowed to use?
4. **Criterion**: At what level the behavior must be performed. Common degrees include speed, accuracy, and quality.

Performer
This is quite simply identifying who will perform the objectives. Is it basic students, advanced students, line officers, or supervisors?

Performance
The performance component is a description of the behavior that learners are expected to perform. It should be measurable and observable. It describes what the officer will be doing when demonstrating mastery of an objective. Mager (1997) distinguishes between two types of performances—visible and invisible. With a visible performance, the main intent is visible or audible. The following are examples:

- To be able to shoot a Sig Sauer P226
- To be able to handcuff a suspect
- To be able to write a report

Conditions

The conditions component of an objective is a description of the circumstances under which the performance will be carried out. It also includes a description of what will be available to officers when they perform the desired behavior. Specifying the conditions further helps prevent misunderstanding of your intent.

1. What will the officer be expected to use when performing (e.g., duty belts, forms, laptops, etc.)?
2. What will the officer not be allowed to use while performing (e.g., checklists, notes, or other study aids)?
3. What will be the real-world conditions under which the performance will be expected to occur (e.g., in an automobile, in elements of weather, in front of a large hostile crowd)?

Here are some examples of conditions:

- Using a Glock semiautomatic pistol…
- When driving at high speed…
- When confronting an intoxicated individual…

Criterion

The final component of an effective objective is the criterion. The criterion is a description of the standards for acceptance of a performance as sufficient, indicating *proficiency* of the objective. In other words, how well must it be done? Stating the criterion lets officers know how well they will have to perform to be considered competent. In addition, it provides a standard against which to test the success of the instruction and gives you a way of evaluating whether or not the officers can, in fact, do what you set out to teach them.

The criterion you specify should be what you consider to be the desired or appropriate level of performance, not necessarily the minimum level. In some cases (an officer's individual physical ability), a certain amount of error might be acceptable, while in other cases, no error is acceptable. In addition, you should only impose criteria that are important.

Mager (1997) describes three important criteria to consider when writing objectives:

1. They are related to intended outcomes, rather than to the process for achieving those outcomes.
2. They are specific and measurable, rather than broad and intangible.
3. They are concerned with officers, not instructors.

Here is an example of an objective with criteria:

Given a laptop computer, be able to write a report with minimal spelling and grammatical errors.

There are two main ways to define a criterion of acceptable performance: speed and accuracy.

1. *Speed*—providing a time limit within which a given performance must occur. If a time limit is important, it should be stated as part of the objective. If a time limit is not important, then do not impose a time limit. The following are some examples:
   - In under 15 seconds
   - Within 15 minutes
   - Before midnight
2. *Accuracy*—giving a range of acceptable performance. The following are some examples:
   - Within 2 inches of accuracy
   - Within 6 inches of a cone
   - With no more than two incorrect entries in a log

Here is an example of an objective containing all four components:

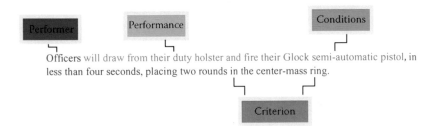

Outcomes versus Process

Teaching and lecturing are part of the process of instruction, but they are not the purpose of the instruction. The purpose is to facilitate learning. When writing objectives, make sure you are describing the intended results and not the process. The following are descriptions of the process, rather than of the intended results:

- To provide a lecture on the "Broken Windows" concept
- To be able to read in front of the class
- To provide practice and feedback
- To develop confidence

Specific versus General

If your objectives are not specific enough, then they are pretty much useless for their intended purpose. They need to be specific so that they will help you make sound instructional decisions later in the instructional design process. Here are some fuzzy statements:

- Understand motivation.
- Know the President.
- Be able to think clearly.

Here are some statements that are clearer:

- Put on a tourniquet.
- Assemble a weapon.
- Use your name when addressing suspects or witnesses.

With the specific statements, you would easily be able to determine if someone has met the objective.

Measurable versus Immeasurable

Measurable objectives describe tangible outcomes that can be observed. The statement that states "tie a shoe" is measurable because we can watch someone tie a shoe and determine if they have met the objective. The statement "understand motivation" is not measurable. How would we know if someone understood the concept of motivation? This would need to be broken down into much more specific, *observable* behaviors.

Officers versus Instructors

The last point is that instructional objectives should describe the officer's performance rather than the instructor's performance. Here are some that relate to the instructor's performance:

- Lecture on the Fourth Amendment.
- Teach the importance of keeping a weapon clean.
- Arrange instructional activities.

Here are some that relate to the officer's performance. These examples relate to specific, measurable officer outcomes:

- Shoot accurately.
- State the fundamental elements of the Fourth Amendment.
- Place a subject under arrest.

Now that we have discussed each of the three points, here is an example of an objective that violates all three of them:

- Officers will be taught about why people commit crimes.

One of the biggest problems with poorly written objectives is the choice of words used to indicate the type of performance expected. In the example above, "will be taught" is not a clear enough statement of what the learners will actually be doing. There are many slippery words that are open to a wide range of interpretation when writing objectives. It is important not to use broad or vague terms when trying to convey a *specific* instructional intent; otherwise, you leave yourself open to mis-interpretation. Table 6.6 lists some of the most common unclear words used in goals and objectives, as well as more specific, better alternatives.

When looking over your objectives, ask yourself if you could observe someone doing the behavior. It is hard to observe someone *knowing* or *understanding*. If any of your objectives contain these vague words, rewrite them to include verbs that actually describe the intended behavior. What you want to do is state how officers are going to *demonstrate* that they know or understand the skills. Try using words from the list on the right.

Table 6.6   Words for Writing Objectives

Common Ambiguous Words	"Better" Performance Words
• Know	• Choose (or select)
• Understand	• Solve
• *Really* understand	• Write
• Determine	• Identify
• Appreciate	• State
• *Fully* appreciate	• List
• Grasp the significance of	• Recite
• Enjoy	• Apply
• Become familiar with	• Sort
• Become aware of	• Assemble
• Believe	• Adjust
• Learn	• Build
• Have faith in	• Align
• Internalize	• Compare
• Be happy	• Contrast
• Value	• Disassemble
• Acquire	• Use
• Develop	• Perform
	• Execute
	• Classify
	• Draw
	• Construct

Table 6.7 Category of Learning Verbs

Category	Common Verbs
Verbal information	State, recite, tell, declare, name, list, define
Intellectual skills: concrete concepts	Identify, label
Intellectual skills: defined concepts	Classify instances, sort, categorize
Intellectual skills: rules	Solve, show, demonstrate, generate, develop, create, determine, calculate, predict
Intellectual skills: higher-order rules (problem solving)	Solve, show, demonstrate, generate, develop, create, determine, calculate, predict, defend, support
Motor skills	Execute, perform, swim, walk, run, climb, grab, pull, assemble, punch
Attitudes	Choose, decide, participate

To help you in writing your own objectives, Table 6.7 shows a chart listing the categories of learning along with some of the more common verbs used when writing objectives for that category.

The following represent some poorly written objectives taken from a number of commercially produced instructional materials.

- The officer will demonstrate knowledge of the principles of crime scene investigation.
- The officers will be able to recognize that the practical application of democratic ideals requires time, adjustment, and continuous effort.
- The officers will understand the use of commas.
- The officer will recognize a legal brief.
- Officers will demonstrate positive habits of a clean uniform.

Another common problem with objectives is the use of superfluous wording that often makes the actual performance fuzzy. For example, using "Officer will learn how to…" tends to emphasize the teaching rather than the learning (permanent change in behavior). Another common problem with poorly worded objectives is the description of instruction as part of the condition. These objectives might state "After viewing a PowerPoint…" or "Given a tactical worksheet…" and then indicate that officers will be given some type of instruction. Things like instructional procedures, descriptions of the target audience, or format requirements are not useful and should be left out of objectives. For example, look at the following statement:

- Following two lectures on search and seizure, …
  This statement does not serve a useful purpose and is limiting. An instructor might be able to accomplish the same thing in one lecture, or some officers may not need any lecture to achieve the goal. The

objective should only be concerned with officer outcomes. Here are some other poor examples, this time with improved versions:

Bad: The officer will demonstrate disassembly and reassembly of a Glock 19.

Better: Given a Glock 19, the officer will be able to disassemble and reassemble the weapon to be fully operational.

Bad: The instructor will learn about objectives.

Better: The instructor will construct well-written instructional objectives.

Bad: The officers will solve surveillance problems with 80% accuracy.

Better: The officer will correctly solve at least 8 out of 10 problems that can arise in a surveillance.

Development

At the development stage of ADDIE, materials are coalesced into a working product. This phase elaborates and builds on the learning objectives and learning steps that were produced in the design phase. It basically fleshes out all the previous content built in the prior two phases (Analysis and Design) into a complete learning platform. The end result is the instructional courseware—the media and its content (such as software, lesson plans, and video) that contains the instructional content and activities that will aid the officers in their quest for better performance. At this stage, test materials are developed, instructional activities are developed, and instructional materials (e.g., PowerPoint presentation) are produced. In this section, we will examine cognitive tests, remediation, practical exercises, instructional media, and officer materials.

Rosenberg (2012) said that the lesson should address expectations of the officers, such as the following:

1. What will I learn?
2. Why am I here?
3. Why is this important to me?
4. How will I use what I learn?
5. How will this benefit my job performance and my career?
6. Why is this important to the organization?
7. How will my job change based on what I have learned?
8. Does my supervisor support this training?
9. What do I need to be ready?
10. What is expected from me when I leave this training to go to my workplace?

After generating a list of objectives, you will be ready to proceed to subsequent stages of the instructional design process, including the creation of assessment items and the development of instructional activities. At this stage, you can now start drafting your lesson plan. It is important to begin with determining the objectives and then decide on the most effective activities, NOT the other way around. Too often, instructors decide that they have a really neat activity they want to do and have little idea of what objectives that activity will meet. It may be that the activity meets no relevant objectives, in which case the difficult decision may have to be made to eliminate the activity. This is not entirely bad, though, because it opens up the possibility of new, more relevant activities being created that do address the objectives.

There are basically eight steps to creating a lesson plan:

Step 1—Level of Simulation

    The main point of this step is to choose the highest level of simulation that matches the job task. The first level should be as high as the officer can handle without error.

Step 2—Select Instructional Methods

    How is the content of the subject going to be delivered? Most people think of this as a classroom. However, modern learning theory is slowly moving away from the butt-in-seat classroom. Many times, cognitive material can be delivered via other media such as online learning, guidebooks, videos, or a combination of all three. This allows the officer to show up in the practical exercise area ready to practice and perform the task, with the instructor serving more as a facilitator to learning.

Step 3—Design Instructional Strategy

    Methods of instructional strategy for delivering material include self-instruction, lecture, demonstration, practicals, and assessment.

Step 4—Design the Lesson Introduction

    Simply write out the introduction.

Step 5—Describe the Content

    Write out the content to be delivered.

Step 6—Select the Media

    This can be paper, video, audio, computer based, or other graphics.

Step 7—Determine Instructor/Officer Ratios

    The standard is generally 1 instructor to 10 officers; obviously, lectures can go higher. Conversely, practical exercises can go lower depending on risk and safety factors.

Step 8—Sequence Activities for the Lesson

    Robert Gagne published *Conditions of Learning: Training Applications*, which outlined the relation of learning objectives to appropriate instructional designs (Gagne and Medsker 1995). Gagne's 10 general steps of instruction for learning are as follows:

1. Gain attention.
   - For example, present a good problem, a new situation, advertisement, ask questions.
   - This helps ground the lesson and motivate people.
2. Describe the learning objective.
   - For example, state what officers will be able to accomplish and how they will be able to use the knowledge; give a demonstration if appropriate.
   - This allows officers to frame information.
3. Stimulate recall of prior knowledge.
   - For example, remind the officers of prior knowledge relevant to the current lesson (facts, rules, procedures, or skills). Show how knowledge is connected; provide the officers with a framework that helps learning and remembering. Quizzes can be included.
4. Present the material to be learned.
   - For example, text, graphics, simulations, figures, pictures, sound, and so on. Chunk information (avoid cognitive overload, recall information).
5. Provide guidance for learning.
   - For example, presentation of content is different from instructions on how to learn. Use of different channels (e.g., side boxes).
6. Elicit performance "practice."
7. Let the officer do something with the newly acquired behavior, practice skills, or apply knowledge.
8. Provide informative feedback.
   - Show correctness of the officer's response, analyze learner's behavior, or perhaps present a good (step-by-step) solution to the problem.
9. Assess performance test, if the lesson has been learned. Give general progress information as well.
10. Enhance retention and transfer.
    - For example, inform the officer about similar problematic situations and provide additional practice. Put the officer in a transfer situation. Let the officers review the lesson.

Table 6.8 shows some tips on how your lesson plan enhances the training experience and makes it more meaningful using adult learning theory.

Table 6.8   Tips for Using Adult Learning Theory

Adult Learning Issues from the Officer's Perspective	Questions to Be Answered by the Instructor/Designer	Where Questions Can Be Addressed in the Course Design and Delivery
1. Need to know—What will this course cover?	Where can the officers know about the training scope and why should it be learned to be addressed?	• Target audience analysis and description • Objectives • Course description • Course introduction and syllabus • Copy of lecture slides
2. Officer's self-concept—Can I agree with the process/approach for my learning?	Where in the course will we give officers an opportunity for self-direction?	• Course introduction and outline • Practice and case studies
3. Role of the officer's experience—What do I already know?	What do the officers know, and how should I use this information?	• Icebreaker • Reflection and discussion • Inclusion of life experience
4. Readiness to learn—What are my expectations in this area?	What are the officers' expectations, and can I satisfy them?	• Course background survey • Icebreaker
5. Orientation to learning—How do I approach this subject?	What methodology should I use to ensure understanding and application?	• Delivery method selection • Practice and group projects • Effective questioning
6. Motivators—How can I use this information myself?	What will the officers take away with them?	• Setting assumptions and expectations • Introduction • Transitions/breaks • Reflection and practice • Officer summary

Lesson Plan Development

Lesson plans (sometimes referred to as instructor guides) are basically the screenplay of the class, which means it will have everything necessary for the class and how the class will be taught. The following are the elements of a lesson plan:

- Lesson title (i.e., Search and Seizure)
- Length of the presentation (1 hour)

- Venue of the class (i.e., classroom, mat room)
- Method of presentation (lecture, demonstration, practical exercise)
- TPOs
- EPOs
- References (if necessary)
- Safety brief (if necessary)
- List of materials or props for the lesson (i.e., red gun, handcuffs)
- Date when the lesson plan was developed
- Names of the developers
- Gagne's ten general steps of instruction for learning, as mentioned above

Assessment Development

Assessments are used extensively to qualify officers. It is important to define the context of assessment in the training process. Each type of assessment used in the training process is detailed and outlined in Table 6.9.

Every objective developed during the design process needs to be evaluated either by written tests or by performance evaluation. Tests, in general, are used to assess an officer's progress in the learning process against predetermined criteria. Chapter 7 will go into greater detail on test development. Baldwin and Ford (1988) contended that cognitive ability has an influence on the training venue. However, transfer of training is not purely based on an officer's cognitive ability (Blume et al. 2010). Further, some cognitive skills that officers possess directly affect whether or not the officers will be able to comprehend and transfer the content to the work environment (Noe and Schmitt 1986). Tests should focus on outcomes to be measured, and processes to achieve that outcome, not the instructional process.

Collection of assessment strategies involves methods that instructors have traditionally used to judge classroom performance (e.g., essay and

Table 6.9 Types of Assessments

Assessment	Any systematic method of obtaining evidence by posing questions to draw inferences about the knowledge, skill, attitudes, and other characteristics of people for a specific purpose
Exam	A summative assessment used to measure an officer's knowledge or skills for the purpose of documenting their current level of knowledge or skill
Test	A diagnostic assessment to measure an officer's knowledge or skills for the purpose of informing the officers or their instructor of their current level of knowledge or skill
Quiz	A formative assessment used to measure an officer's knowledge or skills for the purpose of providing feedback to inform the officer of his or her current level of knowledge or skill

objective testing) as well as approaches that reflect more recent attention to assessment-driven training–learning processes. These include embedded assessment strategies in which departments identify specific classes in which to embed assessments that are endorsed and designed by the department as well as classroom assessment techniques.

Cognitive tests (e.g., multiple choice, fill in the blank) have advantages and disadvantages, as outlined below.

Advantages:
- It displays good psychometric properties.
- It facilitates rapid feedback through ease of scoring.
- It develops norms.
- It is inexpensive.
- It is comprehensive.
- It improves test validity through item analysis.
- It facilitates differential group scoring.

Disadvantages:
- It usually involves testing low-level knowledge.
- Constructing high-quality test questions is difficult.
- Question banks are often of poor quality.
- It can be compromised by officer test banks that may foster differential access.

Although constructing solid objective tests that tap into officers' deeper levels is not impossible, it is challenging. Instructors need to help officers understand how objective testing can be designed to go after different levels of knowledge. Some find that teaching officers Bloom's Taxonomy as an organizer that faculty might intuitively use to create more targeted challenges will help officers understand questions and view them as challenging.

Performance Tests

Here are some advantages and disadvantages of a performance test.

Advantages:
- It provides realistic testing circumstance.
- It engages and motivates officers.
- It promotes transfer of information and application.
- It taps complex skills.

Disadvantages:
- It is difficult to construct and measure.
- Locating designed instruments is challenging.

- It is prone to history/context/age cohort effects.
- Officers may rely on common sense under pressure rather than their knowledge from the course.

Performance tests are really strong indicators of an officer's knowledge on how to perform the task. Instructors need to properly demonstrate the performance that the officers will be evaluated on. The situation should correspond closely to the learning conditions to promote the best transfer of knowledge. Evaluating performance will be facilitated by clearly developed criteria. The quality of the rubric and the training of the evaluators will influence validity. If interrater agreement is not high, the results will be of limited value. Rubrics will sometimes not provide for unexpected, creative responses.

Schmidt and Wrisberg (2008) suggest that an instructor should ask the following questions before attempting to assess an officer's progress:

- What are the officer's goals?
- What am I going to learn from this performance assessment?
- What is the officer going to learn from this assessment?
- How am I going to use the information I obtain from this assessment to assist the officer in achieving his or her goals?

The officers need time to practice. Practices should be constructed and should be built on previous knowledge and skills for the officer to ultimately perform to the level of simulation, that is, as close as possible to the conditions expected from them on the job. Practice is designed to elevate a behavioral and psychological response that will build goal-relevant knowledge and skills (Clark 2015). Practice is intended to help officers bridge performance gaps.

Take shooting a sidearm for instance. Do the officers work in a cold climate where they may wear a parka or layers of clothing and then practice and qualify shoot in those clothes? Are the officers going to drive vehicles off-road or on slick roads? If such were the case, then the practice should be closely built to simulate those conditions. Will undercover agents be wearing street clothes, under low-light conditions, with a concealed weapon? The agents should then practice under those conditions.

Clark (2015, p. 210) offers some practice guidelines regarding how much time to spend on practice:

- Consequences of error: If serious, you need more rather than less practice.
- Acceptable error: If yes, then fewer practice exercises will suffice.
- Complexity of the work: If high, drill and practice might be needed to automate requisite subskills.

Chunking

Most instructors have heard of the "chunking" technique when teaching practical applications. Basically, the instructor breaks the task down into small steps and delivers these steps in small "chunks" to the officers. Then, the instructor lets the officers practice those steps, and the instructor adds more "chunks" and so on. The practice times should ensure that officers are competent and confident in the task expected of them and that they are ready for the performance test. Every performance objective should have at least one series of practice exercises before the officer is asked to be tested on the performance. The performance test should closely mirror the task conditions. The amount of practice necessary will depend on some on the following factors:

- Complexity of the task
- Previous experience or prerequisite skills the officer brings to this performance
- Various situations and stimuli that can provide the multiple scenarios that can initiate the task, or decisions that result in different outcomes of the task

Deciding when and how often to assess progress is a quandary for instructors. The goal is to evaluate officers under circumstances that allow the most valid assessment of skills. In many ways, this depends on the officer. Some officers may wish to have an initial assessment of their performance to determine which areas require particular attention. The best time for an initial assessment is right after the officer attains the basic capability of producing the final outcome of the performance (Schmidt and Wrisberg 2008).

How to Develop a Practical Exercise or Scenario

Scenario-based (some may use the terms *reality-based* or *evidence-based*) training has the merit of enhancing officers' confidence in solving real-life situations by rooting learning in a simulated work environment; it tests learning through authentic cases. It also consolidates knowledge and skills learnt through their application to a law enforcement scenario. Scenario-based training is probably one of the best forms of transfer of training. The cues in a scenario will accumulate in memory and can be retrieved later. In scenario-based learning, the officer is fed with all information and resources required to solve the problem according to predetermined learning outcomes. The key concept here is making the scenario as realistic as possible. Unfortunately, oftentimes, scenarios are cut short from being reality. Here is an example. The scenario is a two-officer situation in which one partner gets shot and goes down. Now, the other officer is taught to say he or she will call for EMS, and then the instructor ends the scenario when the officer says, "I will call EMS." But is that reality? When out in the street in a real shooting, is the officer going to say, "I will call EMS?" No. The officer is actually going to have to call for EMS. Also, what are the department rules regarding an officer involved in a shooting? What happens next? Have the officer follow what the policies are going to be in real life in such a scenario; do not create training scars. The message here is do not let your scenarios end too soon. What the officer actually has to do in the field should be a replica of what he or she is doing in a reality-based scenario.

A scenario is an outline or a synopsis of a play, a plot outline used by actors to act out a sequence of events of an account or synopsis of a projected course of action. A scenario has many things to consider, such as the people involved, the type of vehicle or subject, the location of the incident, the actions of the people, and so on. For instance, consider a setting for your scenario. Is it a vehicle, a mat room, a shoot house, or even just a house? There are many limitations that can be placed on a scenario, such as weather, lack of facilities, or role players.

A law enforcement scenario should have three distinct components:

- A reasonable beginning
- An uncertain challenge
- A complete finish (FLETC 2011)

Reasonable Beginning

Every scenario should have a reasonable beginning. It could be simple cues that prompt an officer to take some type of action, such as a traffic stop for speeding. After a prebrief for the scenario by the instructor, the scenario begins with the officer pulling over a motorist. The scenario should be allowed to play out in totality. This allows the instructors to observe the actions and decision making of the officer(s). The instructors assess the performance of the officer(s) as the scenario progresses.

Uncertain Challenge or Problem-Based Learning

As a scenario progresses, certain cues can be embedded for a role player to do certain things based on the officers' actions or the lack thereof. A routine traffic stop could turn into a verbal altercation and progress into a use of force encounter, or it could just be a low-level traffic stop with the scenario ending with the officers issuing a ticket. Uncertainty confronts officers to widen their situational awareness, behavioral cues, and decision making. The officers need to be aware of how fast situations can change. A motorist, during a routine traffic stop, suddenly jumps out of the car and runs away. All of a sudden, a Taser does not work, and the subject continues his active aggression. Once an officer becomes proficient in a task, variables can be added to a scenario to build upon the decision-making tree.

Problem-based learning is useful at this stage of the scenario. Problem-based learning scenarios can provide a wide array of problems that include the following:

- The officer needs to consider a myriad of facts and issues.
- The scenario is not easily solved. This can be enhanced by leaving out certain facts.
- More learning occurs during the scenario.
- Officers are encouraged to "think" their way through the scenario.
- Officers are encouraged to collaborate with other officers (if working in a team setting).
- The right setting to add an ethical dilemma, such as a person trying to bribe the officer.

Thorough Finish

From *Violent Encounters* (Federal Bureau of Investigation 2006) found that during a postincident control of subjects, victims, and witnesses, officers fail to notice critical elements, such as securing a scene, poor handcuffing, and poor searching techniques. Thus, officers should routinely be assessed on how well they act on visual cues and on their decision making postarrest. Built-in behavioral cues should be embedded into the scenario. If an officer catches a behavioral clue and responds appropriately, then the role player complies. If the officer does not pick up a behavioral cue, then the role player takes a different course of action.

Realism

Just like a play, a scenario has props, which can be guns, narcotics, vehicles, foam batons, and nonlethal weapons. Props provide an element of realism to a scenario. Safety is a prime concern in any practical exercise or scenario. The more realistic the practical exercise or scenario is, the more safety concerns should be addressed. The more the officer begins to feel the realism of the event, the more likely the officer will have realistic reactions to the event.

When developing a scenario or a practical exercise, here are some things to consider:

- Location
- Time allotted

- Number of instructors
- Props
- Purpose of the exercise
- Background information regarding the exercise
- Objectives of the exercise
- Instructor role
- Officer instruction
- Role player instruction (if applicable)
- Safety consideration

Role Players

If you are using role players, then a script will need to be written. In the script, role players need to know who they are, what they are doing, and why they are doing what they are doing. They also need to react to the officer's comments (e.g., are they going to be compliant or noncompliant?). Role players need to be properly coached on how to play their role, just like a dress rehearsal, and just like a play, the role player has to understand proper "cueing" to get the correct response from the officer. The role player has to have a keen understanding (emotional state, physical state, psychological state, etc.) of who they are role playing. If the role player will be noncompliant, he or she needs to be cautioned on how far his or her noncompliance will go. Taking their role too far has injured many role players. Role players have to have a keen understanding that officers can have an adrenaline dump and lose part of their senses. The more intense the scenario is, the more attention needs to be paid to the officer's reaction. Instructors need to be prepared to jump in and stop the scenario if the situation gets out of hand. Role players and officers need to understand code words such as "out of role" as an indication to stop what they are doing. But this is not the end-all. When experiencing an adrenaline dump, some officers may experience physio-psychological phenomena such as occlusion of the sense of hearing. Therefore, they may not hear the code words; hence, the instructor must be situationally aware during scenario training. A good resource for developing scenarios is Ken Murray's book, *Training at the Speed of Life, Volume 1.*

How Role-Playing Relates to Training

Role-playing is a powerful way to enhance learning, for both the officer and the role player. It is often suggested that trainers, as they go through their qualification process, spend some time as a role player. This gives the trainers a different and beneficial perspective of scenario-based training. As a role player, you often see things that the instructors do not. Further, in a scenario, participants share the experiences of the role play, discussing such things as the role players' expressions, feelings, attitudes, and reactions to others.

Once all the observations are made, participants can begin processing what took place. To help officers process the patterns of behaviors observed, instructors should stress that active role players should stop acting and be their usual selves. Research shows that this helps officers become more receptive to discussion, as any possible negative comments/observations are taken less personally since the participant is no longer emotionally involved in the role that is being critiqued or analyzed. Instructors could also use recordings of the role play in this phase, as it could help with officer recall and focus.

Once observations are processed, officers should begin the next phase, generalizing role-play experiences to real-world situations. Instructors can help officers develop generalizations by asking them to write declarative statements about outside experiences related to the role play or by asking them to come up with cause-and-effect hypotheses about observations that arise from the role-play experience.

Because role play often focuses on critical but rarely occurring events, the final phase, applying, becomes important. Most importantly, instructors should urge their officers to focus on two crucial questions: "So what?" and "Now what?" Instructors should encourage a discussion of these questions individually and in small and large groups. If necessary, the role play can be performed again, as it is vital that lessons be learned from the role play; after all, it may be a role play about a situation that cannot be trained for in any other way (e.g., use of force, active shooter, etc.) that bears life-or-death consequences.

Overall, role-playing is one of the most exciting active learning activities instructors can use. It is highly flexible in terms of how it can be set up and the length of time it can be used. It fits well for teaching important tasks that occur infrequently but are vital to be learned. When conducted skillfully, role plays have high credibility, which reduces any resistance to learning. Role-playing is also an inherent skill that people learned through childhood play; thus, it is unnecessary for officers to learn new skills to participate. Additionally, role-playing is often fun for participants, as it lets them "play" while learning, thus taking greater ownership of their class experience.

Performance Evaluations

Many times, cognitive tests are not necessarily the best measurement for evaluation. Shooting a firearm is the perfect example of this concept. Cognitive knowledge about a firearm does not equate to rounds at center mass. Performance tests measure skills. In these cases, the officer must demonstrate shooting a firearm, disarming a suspect, searching a vehicle, and so on, to an acceptable level. Performance testing is done to determine if officers can accomplish the objective before satisfactory course completion and presupposes the transfer of task proficiency to ensure they are ready to perform their job. Performance tests should focus on outcomes to be measured and processes to achieve that outcome—*not* the instructional process. All performance tests will evaluate the quality of the output (task performance), but many will also evaluate the execution of the task procedure. The outputs of this task are performance tests that validate officer performance proficiency for each and every performance objective and serve as the foundation for validity and reliability. They combine the TPOs developed during the design phase and the step-level data captured during analysis with the evaluation criteria selection from design.

The process for developing performance tests has been outlined in the following steps:

Step 1: Identify the performance in each objective.

Step 2: Draft a criterion-referenced test, specifying the performance required.

Step 3: Identify the conditions under which the performance should occur. (If they cannot be emulated, match them as closely as possible.)

Step 4: Add the standards and any other evaluation criteria to the test.

Step 5: Establish the steps for a successful evaluation of this task (process and product).

Step 6: Define the testing criteria and instructions for administering the performance tests.

Remediation

Remediation, or a lack of training transfer, is the instruction given to officers by an instructor to increase an officer's competency in performing a particular task. Remediation involves the specific directions/plans you set in place to assist the instructors when they have identified an apparent gap in training transfer. The need for remedial instruction will be most prevalent once the officers begin their performance tests and instructors identify problems during initial attempts. The feedback and guidance provided by the instructor when these performance deficiencies are identified are critical to the officer's future performance and continuation in the course. The frequency of remediation depends on the type of training and policies of the agency regarding it. Remediation time needs to be factored into the course times. When is remediation going to be done? After hours? How long before a remediation needs to be conducted should also be determined. Is it right after the failure, the evening after the failure, the next day, or 48 hours afterward? All remediation needs firm documentation.

Remediation can have many possible solutions, all of which will direct the officers to the right source for further guidance. For example, they may include the following:

- Redirection of the officer back to text already covered in order to receive supporting context needed to perform a particular exercise or learning activity
- Additional practice exercises
- Review of standards for a particular task to ensure that expectations for performance are clear

Instructional Media

Instructional media are the means used to present information to officers. Instructional media ensure that the content of the course is presented to the officers in an efficient and effective means. Select instructional media that are appropriate to the training situation and feasible under existing resources and logistical constraints. Here are some examples of instructional media:

- Turn chart
- Whiteboard (or chalkboard)
- Computer (PowerPoint)
- Audio tape
- Wall chart
- Model
- Print handouts

Technical Accuracy

It is important that all instructional materials be reviewed for accuracy, spelling, and grammar. Nothing can be more embarrassing than an officer finding a typo or some other inconsistency in the training materials. This alone can damage an instructor's (as well as a program's) credibility.

Let us try and put together an action plan that brings into view all the elements covered up to this point into a workable plan. Table 6.10 shows an example of steps you can take to develop a course. In this particular instance, it will be a workshop (therefore no assessments) on problem solving.

The obvious question that comes at this juncture is, "How long does all this take?" Unfortunately, the answer is, "It depends." If an FEA or JTA has to be done, it will take at a minimum 6 months to 1 year just to do the analysis portion. Kapp and Deflice (2009) did a study of design and development hours (no analysis) for the American Society of Training and Development and came up with the numbers shown in Table 6.11.

Table 6.10   Example of a Training Plan

Training Program Elements	Application to a Sample Course— A Problem-Solving Workshop
Target audience analysis and description	**Analysis:** The audience consists of all first-line law enforcement supervisors. There are 50 first-line supervisors in this group. Supervisors have between 4 and 25 years of supervisory experience. All have varying degrees of experience with problem solving. **Description:** The course is designed for first-line supervisors with an interest in problem solving. There are no prerequisites for this course.
Objectives	**Objectives:** • Discuss a basic model for problem solving • Apply the problem-solving model to work-related issues
Selection of delivery methods	**Methods of delivery:** **Lecture** is appropriate to familiarizing the officers with the problem-solving model. **Discussion** is appropriate to ensure that officers understand the model, can apply the model, and can relate the model to prior problem-solving experiences. **Case studies** are appropriate for practice, especially if cases can be selected based on officers' issues.
Course description	**Sample course description:** **Title:** Problem-solving 101 This course is for supervisors who ever needed to apply problem solving to a work-related issue. **Objectives:** By the end of this course, you will be able to • Discuss a basic model for problem solving • Apply the problem-solving model to a work-related issue **Prerequisites:** None **Length:** 8 hours **Method of delivery:** Lecture, discussion, and case study
Course introduction Lesson introductions usually include 1. A hook or motivator 2. Objectives 3. Tie into past learning (if applicable) 4. What's in it for me (officer) **Course introduction also includes** 1. Admin information 2. Setting expectations 3. Get-acquainted activity/ icebreaker	During the course introduction for the workshop 1. The instructor provides a welcome and explains the administrative support procedure (5 minutes). 2. Participants are paired up and asked to introduce each other. They present their partner's name, an example of a problem-solving issue their partner has experienced, and what their partner would like to get from the workshop (35 minutes). 3. The instructor explains the course objectives in his or her own words (5 minutes). 4. Course materials are distributed and the instructor explains the material and schedule. 5. The instructor shows a film clip (motivator) from the movie *Heat* depicting problem-solving skills (5 minutes).

(Continued)

Table 6.10 (Continued)   Example of a Training Plan

Training Program Elements	Application to a Sample Course—A Problem-Solving Workshop
	6. The instructor ends the introduction with What's In It For Me, stating, "We all have been in situations where poor problem-solving resulted in poor choices for ourselves and our agency. By participating in this workshop, you will gain new tools to improve your problem-solving abilities at work, and may even find it helpful for your non-work activities."
Course outline/syllabus The syllabus/course outline may contain the following: 1. Course objectives 2. Length of time 3. Officer assignments	**The problem-solving workshop outline:** 1. Welcome and get acquainted (30 minutes) 2. A basic model for problem solving (2 hours) 3. Common issues for supervisors to solve (2 hours) 4. A case study for practice (2 hours) 5. Wrap-up (1 hour) **Time:** Majority of the workshop will be spent on topics 2–4. The workshop will start at 8 AM and end at 4 PM, with 1 hour for lunch.
Practice Practice issues selection can be done before the workshop, based on issues from managers and from suggestions from the officers	The designer/instructor wants to provide the officer the ability to practice the problem-solving model and apply it to issues experienced by first-line supervisors. A background survey was not sent out before the course to identify topics of concern; thus, the designer/instructor should spend 10 minutes in small groups to generate topics for class activities. The group prioritizes their top three or four topics. The participants are divided into small groups, for their discussion and the application of the problem-solving model, to identify topic areas before sharing in a large group discussion.
Icebreaker An icebreaker is any activity to help the officer become more comfortable with other officers	The designer/instructor pairs up the officers. They are given a set/list of questions to discuss with their partner 1. Name 2. Sample problem 3. Expectations
Setting assumptions and expectations	The instructor/designer wants to ensure that the officers know what the workshop offers and wants to check assumptions about what the officers want from the learning activity. In this workshop, the instructor verifies assumptions and expectations with the icebreaker activity.
Reflection	There are several places the designer/instructor builds in time for officer reflection: • Expectations as part of the instruction • Issues from past experiences • Reflection as part of the practice • Officer summaries as part of the wrap-up

(Continued)

Table 6.10 (Continued)   Example of a Training Plan

Training Program Elements	Application to a Sample Course—A Problem-Solving Workshop
Discussion	**It is not enough to provide knowledge via lecture.** The designer/instructor must provide an opportunity for officers to demonstrate that they understand and can apply the concepts. Discussion allows the officers to raise points and ask questions about unclear concepts.
Effective questioning	**The designer/instructor wants to make sure that the material and course as delivered are relevant, that officers are engaged, and that appropriate feedback was provided.** The designer builds questions (closed, open, probing) into the lesson plan. A simple example for introductions: How many of you have had experience solving a problem at work? (show of hands to engage officers) Open example for content of lesson: What type of problems do you typically have to solve at work? (no set answer) Probing for wrap-up: Tell me more. What did you learn from this workshop? (check depth of understanding)
Transitions/breaks Officers need time to think about how they can use the information	The instructor plans for a break every hour, recaps information periodically, and provides a transition between learning activities during the workshop. Example: After the course introduction, the instructor asks the officers to think about how they apply problem solving to their work issues. After the break, the instructor transitions into the model by saying, "I used to jump right into every problem with the motto 'Solve it quick.' I had no model. I lost a lot of time. What are some models you use?"
Officer summary	**To encode what was learned, the instructor wants a dynamic conclusion for the workshop. Suggestions:** • Cover key points with a review game and review of objectives. • Complete an end-of-course program evaluation.

Table 6.11   Allocated Times to Develop Training

Type of Training (per 1 Hour of Finished Instruction)	Most Experienced Design and Developer (per 1 Hour of Instruction)	Minimum Experienced Design and Developer (per 1 Hour of Instruction)
Traditional Design and Development of Instruction		
Stand-up training	43 hours	70 hours
Self-instructional print	80 hours	125 hours

Source: Reprinted with permission from Kapp, K. M. and Defelice, R. A. (August 31, 2009). *Time to Develop One Hour of Training.* American Society for Training and Development.

Implementation

Pilot Testing

Now that everything has been developed, it is suggested that the material be piloted in front of a real audience. Moviemakers even use the tactic of pilot testing. Before a new television series is purchased by a network, they show a pilot to see if the audience is interested in the program before they invest large sums of money in purchasing the program; you should do the same for your course.

Before you roll out the entire course in its complete form, front to back, you should try out portions of the course to see how they are working; this is sometimes referred to as "beta testing." Once you have the bugs worked out of the portions of the course, then the course is ready for a completed rollout; this is the pilot test.

It is important to have everyone involved in the pilot course. Officer input during the pilot should be gathered and analyzed, not only regarding course content but also concerning instructor feedback, testing, and methods of delivery. Tracking of start and stop times for lessons, practical exercises, and testing need to be recorded. Everything gathered from the pilot will be analyzed and modifications will be put in place. It is now time to roll out the final project.

Course Assessment

Regardless of course type (i.e., a new course or an ongoing course), there should be periodic course assessment procedures in place to ensure continuous improvement and course integrity. Unscheduled regular observations should be made in classrooms and practical exercise areas to ensure quality control of the material being presented and how it is presented. Annually, a course should have a thorough review, including the following:

- Whether any new policies, laws, or regulations have been implemented.
- Test and practical assessment item review to see if there are any items being missed at a higher rate.
- Kirkpatrick Level 1 through 3 reviews (if used). An analysis should be conducted to search for any issues that may need addressing.
- SME interviews need to be conducted to see if there are any tactical or procedural issues that need to be addressed.
- Interviews with course instructors to see if there are any timing, media, material, or other concerns that need to be addressed.

From this, an annual course report will be written and sent to course managers and eventually to the academy director or branch chief to ensure all-around communication regarding the status of the course.

The course administration should continually work on the following key tasks:

- Quality production of course materials
- Maintaining instructor, training, and equipment records
- Scheduling and tracking course equipment, officer throughput, schedules, quotas, and so on
- Identifying health, safety, welfare, and environmental hazards
- Ensuring that the course focuses on officer learning

Evaluation

In many law enforcement academies, formative assessments mainly take the form of officer input and officer assessments (Kirkpatrick 1976), whereas summative assessments can be described as learning that is *transferred* for use at a certain time and place (Harlen and James 1997). Formative assessments consist of criterion-referenced tests or officer-referenced feedback. Criterion-referenced assessment is beneficial to an instructor in providing any indication of problems related to an officer's understanding of the material. An ipsative assessment can provide the instructor feedback on any issues regarding how the material is being analyzed by the trainee. Harlen and James (1997) expressed the importance of validity in formative assessments in that they are used to improve learning and not just a formality.

Summative assessments are linked to formative assessments as long as they are reviewed against the criteria of what the officer was expected to achieve (Harlen and James 1997). In many ways, this can be problematic. For example, does the person providing the feedback on the performance of the officer know what criterion-referenced material the officer was held to while in training? If not, feedback from a summative assessment is viewed as merely opinions with no real validity.

The Kirkpatrick model (Kirkpatrick 1976) has been widely adopted in the industry and government as the standard of training evaluation (Holton 1996; Kyllonen 2000). Kirkpatrick postulated that training evaluations could be divided into four levels: reaction, learning, behavior, and results.

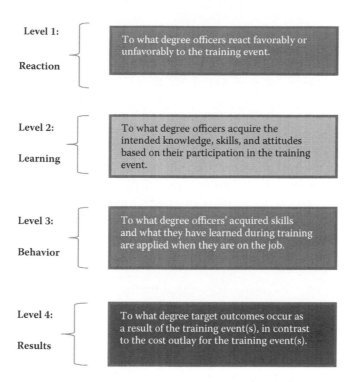

Level 1:

Reaction

To what degree officers react favorably or unfavorably to the training event.

Level 2:

Learning

To what degree officers acquire the intended knowledge, skills, and attitudes based on their participation in the training event.

Level 3:

Behavior

To what degree officers' acquired skills and what they have learned during training are applied when they are on the job.

Level 4:

Results

To what degree target outcomes occur as a result of the training event(s), in contrast to the cost outlay for the training event(s).

Level 1

Level 1 (reaction level) consists of handing out questionnaires to trainees at the end of a training intervention inquiring about their reactions to the materials, instruction, or other items to see if there are any glaring problems that need to be addressed (Kyllonen 2000). These are sometimes referred to as "smile sheets." Level 1 is mainly a formative evaluation (a sample Level 1 evaluation can be downloaded from humanperformance.vpweb.com).

What Are the Essential Questions for Level 1?

- Did they consider the training relevant to their own needs and the needs of the agency? This is more appropriate for advanced training versus basic training.
- How did officers perceive the practicability and potential for application of the learning?
- Did they consider it an effective use of their time?
- Were the styles, pace, content, delivery methods, and materials appropriate?
- Did the training act as a motivator toward further learning?

Is Evaluating at Level 1 Worthwhile?

It should be pointed out that while evaluations at this level are carried out widely, some evaluation experts have questioned the worth of evaluating participants' reaction. Sitzmann et al. (2008, p. 289) found "Reactions have a predictive relationship with cognitive learning outcomes, but the relationship is not strong enough to suggest reactions should be used as an indicator of learning." This is because they believe that getting feedback on, for example, whether the officers enjoyed the course will not result in any really useful data about whether the course was effective. Many times, a training course does not exist for the officers' enjoyment. While it is true that participant reaction evaluations cannot provide an objective measure of the effectiveness of the various elements of the course, this does not mean that they are not worthwhile. Capturing officers' views on the training can provide valuable information that can be used to:

- Identify popular courses (i.e., those that are likely to be attended well) and trainers
- Identify any unmet learning needs
- Provide clues as to how a training course may be improved
- Diagnose barriers to learning

The last two points are especially true when feedback from participant reaction evaluations is viewed alongside evaluation data from the other Kirkpatrick levels. For example, if a Level 2 (learning) evaluation shows that learning is not taking place and your Level 1 evaluation reveals that officers score all elements of the course highly except for the training materials, it would be a reasonable assumption that the training materials need to be improved.

Level 2

Level 2 is considered the learning level. This level aims to determine whether trainees actually acquired the knowledge and skills the training was designed for (Kirkpatrick 1998). Typically, these are written tests with multiple-choice or performance evaluations where an officer's performance level is evaluated by an instructor (Wexley and Latham 2002). Many times, these tests are analyzed to see if officers are having problems in any certain area that may need to be addressed in the curriculum (Kyllonen 2000). Level 2 would still be considered in the formative evaluation stage.

Level 3

Level 3 is considered the behavioral level, that is, where change in the behavior of the officer happens (Kirkpatrick 1998). The main purpose of this level is to determine whether officers are transferring their newly acquired knowledge and skills on the job. This is probably the most important and, yet, most problematic of the first three levels. This level is where you can see if the training you provided is actually transferred to the field. Typically, a questionnaire is sent to both the officer and the officer's supervisor after a certain period to assess the level of skills gained from the training (Kyllonen 2000). This level is considered a summative evaluation and falls into the training transfer area. Salas and Cannon-Bowers (2001) suggested a more rigorous method for collecting Level 3 data than what is currently practiced by many organizations, and this needs to be implemented; this will be discussed later in this chapter.

As stated, this level is also problematic. Why? Most agencies complain about the very low return rate of the questionnaires at Level 3. Unfortunately, a low return rate provides little validity to the training you provided even if the training was outstanding. As a general rule of thumb, without getting into in-depth statistical issues that come with external validity, approximately 30% is considered a good response rate. Yet, many agencies fail to even come close to 30%, which begs the question, should Level 3s even be done? The only answer to that question is another question: how can response rate be increased? The following are suggestions for increasing your response rate to surveys:

1. Tailor the survey to the intended audience.
2. Make the survey easy and user-friendly.
3. Do not make the survey very long. It should have no more than 20 questions.
4. Focus on essential questions.
5. Ensure confidentiality.
6. Personalize communication. If the respondents feel that the questionnaire is directed specifically to them, they are more likely to respond.
7. Hold managers accountable for tracking the performance of officers.
8. Send a presurvey message to let officers know that a survey is on the way. (Smith and Bost 2007)

What Are the Essential Questions for Level 3?

- To what extent were knowledge and skills acquired through the training course used in the workplace?
- Were there noticeable and measurable changes in the activity and performance of the officers who went back to their workplace?
- Was the change in performance and new level of knowledge or skills sustained?

- Were there any particular barriers to or promoters of training transfer to the workplace?
- What influence did factors such as the workplace environment, the support of managers and supervisors, target setting, and the availability of on-the-job support have on the application of learning?

Choosing Your Evaluation Questions
- Which particular job behaviors and competencies are expected to change as a result of the training course?
  - Focus on observable behavior, not thoughts or motives.
  - Limit each statement to a single description of behavior.
  - Write statements, not questions (Phillips 2012).
- Are data on these job behaviors and competencies currently collected (e.g., through performance appraisals)? If not, then, where possible, the initial data should be collected before the course begins.
- When, and over what time scale, will changes to the job behaviors and competencies be measured? You will need to bear in mind that, in most cases, it takes a minimum of 3 months before the impact of learning on workplace performance becomes evident.
- What factors other than the training course might influence changes to each job behavior and competency? For example, have managers and supervisors supported officers in applying their new skills, have there been changes to agency structures, have performance incentive schemes been introduced, or have there been other external environmental influences?

Level 4

Level 4 of the Kirkpatrick evaluation model has recently gone through some changes. Originally, this level is called the "results" level, which Kirkpatrick defined plainly "as the results that occurred because the participants attended the program" (Kirkpatrick 1998, p. 23). This summative evaluation step was conducted only after the results of all the steps turned out to be positive (Kyllonen 2000). This level aims to evaluate how the training was a return on investment (ROI) to the organization. Cannon-Bowers et al. (1995) stated that ROI entails an uncompromisingly high level of readiness at the lowest possible cost and in the shortest period. Oddly enough, most organizations do not collect Level 4 data (Salas et al. 2009). This is surprising since oftentimes the organization itself is the reason why training is requested.

Recently, Kirkpatrick and Kirkpatrick (2010) have changed Level 4 from ROI to return on expectations (ROE). Kirkpatrick now defines this level as "taking the data collected at each of the four Kirkpatrick levels, putting it into a logical Chain of Evidence, and presenting it to your jury in a compelling manner" (Kirkpatrick and Kirkpatrick 2010, p. 44). They defend the change in that ROI was "too narrow in its application, too financial for the training situation" (p. 71).

Analysis of Evaluations

The data collected via Kirkpatrick's level of evaluations need not just be collected—it needs to be analyzed. Though the value of Level 1s may be of little consequence, they need to be examined to see if there are any trends in the data. A good rule of thumb is to eliminate the evaluations that say this is the greatest training ever along with the evaluations that say this is the worst training ever (and yes you will see this for the very same block of instruction) and look for what is in the middle. For instance, there can be personality clashes between an instructor and an officer, which may be reflected in a bad Level 1 evaluation. However, if more than 50% of the class has noted a problem with this instructor, there is an identified problem that will need to be addressed.

For Kirkpatrick Level 2, there needs to be an analysis to determine if there is a certain question that appears to be incorrectly answered by a large number of officers. This could point to a poorly worded question. However, if this question is missed by a large number of officers in just one course, it is possible that the instructor failed to cover the objective correctly. Either way, analysis points to issues in testing. Level 2 does not measure learning transfer; it measures short-term memory comprehension. This is not to conclude that short-term memory cannot transfer to long-term performance.

Level 3 is the most important level because of its ability to validate transfer of training. However, the Kirkpatrick model does not specify the mechanisms of capturing and analyzing the data obtained. Further, the supervisor filling out a survey on the officer may not know exactly what the officer was trained in; it may have been more than 10 years since the supervisor had attended the same training. The Kirkpatrick model further ignores the other dependencies at the level of evaluation.

This discussion on Kirkpatrick levels of evaluation segues into the criticisms of the Kirkpatrick model. Originally, Kirkpatrick (1976) said that the levels of evaluation have to be done in a sequential order. Alliger and Janak (1989) questioned whether strict sequencing is necessary. For example, learning might occur at Level 2 and job performance might improve (Level 3) even if the officers thought the training was a waste of time (Level 1). Tannenbaum and Yukl (1992) specifically addressed that if an officer likes the training, it does not imply learning or the transfer of training. Holton (1996) argued that the Kirkpatrick model shows no causal linkages and is not well researched. Alliger et al. (1997) agreed with Holton stating that the Kirkpatrick model is vague and the model has shortcomings. They state that Level 1 reaction is more like unthinking responses.

Bates (2004) stated that the Kirkpatrick model is an oversimplified view of training effectiveness. His criticism continued on, saying that the model lacks contextual variables, which masks the complexities of the training process and does not measure training transfer. Bates (2004) continued and said that the Kirkpatrick model will result in a woefully uninformed training program about the important aspects of training effectiveness and could lead to erroneous conclusions. Bates ended his criticism by stating, "This results in evaluations that provide relatively little valid data about training effects or which may grossly miscalculate and inflate the influence and value of training" (p. 345).

Probably the largest criticism of the Kirkpatrick model is Level 4. First, Kirkpatrick gives no blueprint on how this level should be conducted. Further, is the ROE to be done by the training division, the budget division, or the human resources division? In theory, Level 4 is a good concept, but in reality, there could be better models to assess the ROI than the Kirkpatrick model.

For a human performance perspective, performance is better than reactions. For Level 1, it would be better to examine motivation than reaction. Motivation gets to the core of human learning. Training motivation is the intensity, persistence, and direction of learning-directed behavior in training venues (Colquitt et al. 2000). Bransford et al. (2000) stated that motivation affects the amount of time that people are willing to devote to learning.

Learning Transfer System Inventory

There is a more comprehensive training evaluation available called the Learning Transfer System Inventory (LTSI). When assessing training transfer, there is only one valid and reliable instrument that can diagnose factors affecting transfer of training described in the literature, which is the LTSI developed by Holton et al. (2000). Holton et al. (2000) based the LTSI on three parts: (a) a diagnostic instrument, (b) a set of constructs that influence transfer, and (c) a change process model.

The LTSI has gone through several revisions, but the latest version measures 16 transfer factors using 68 items. There are four domains in the LTSI: motivation, environment, secondary influences, and ability elements. There are 10 constructs: supervisor support, opportunity to use, peer support, personal outcomes positive, supervisor sanctions, personal outcomes negative, transfer design, resistance to change, motivation to transfer, and content validity. Then, there are six additional constructs: performance coaching, performance self-efficacy, transfer effort, learner readiness, opportunity to use, and personal capacity. Eleven constructs are training specific, and five constructs pertain to the generality of transfer.

There are 68 questions on the instrument. Subjects rate each of the questions from a 1 (strongly disagree) to 5 (strongly agree) Likert-type scale. Holton et al. (2000) advised practitioners to use the LTSI in a variety of ways:

1. To assess potential transfer factor problems before conducting major learning interventions
2. As part of follow-up evaluations of existing training programs
3. As a diagnostic tool for investigating known transfer training problems
4. To target interventions designed to enhance transfer
5. To incorporate evaluation of transfer learning systems as part of regular employee assessments
6. To conduct needs assessment for training programs to provide skills to supervisors and trainers that will aid in transfer (p. 357)

Many of the factors of the LTSI are linked to specific research in training transfer. The macro-structure of the LTSI assesses three functions, ability, motivation, and environmental influences, with three outcome levels, organizational performance, individual performance, and learning (Holton et al. 2000). Below is a listing of the elements and factors with definitions provided by Holton et al. (2000).

Ability Elements
There are four ability elements:

1. *Perceived content validity.* Definition: "Extent to which trainees judge training content to accurately reflect job requirement" (p. 45).
2. *Transfer design.* Definition: "Degree to which (1) training has been designed and delivered to give trainees the ability to transfer learning to the job, and (2) training instructions match job requirement" (p. 45).
3. *Personal capacity for transfer.* Definition: "Extent to which individuals have the time, energy and mental space in their work lives to make changes required to transfer learning to the job" (p. 44).
4. *Opportunity to use knowledge.* Definition: "Extent to which trainees are provided with or obtain resources and tasks on the job enabling them to use training on the job" (p. 45).

Motivation Elements

There are four motivation elements:

1. *Performance coaching (feedback).* Definition: "Formal and informal indicators from an organization about an individual's job performance" (p. 46).
2. *Personal outcomes—positive.* Definition: "The degree to which applying training on the job leads to outcomes that are positive for the individual" (p. 44).
3. *Personal outcomes—negative.* Definition: "The extent to which individuals believe that not applying skills and knowledge learned in training will lead to outcomes that are negative" (p. 44).
4. *Peer support.* Definition: "Extent to which peers reinforce and support use of learning to the job" (p. 44).

Environmental Elements

There are three environmental elements:

1. *Supervisory support.* Definition: "Extent to which peers reinforce and support use of learning to the job" (p. 45).
2. *Supervisor sanctions.* Definition: "Extent to which individuals perceive negative responses from supervisor/managers when applying skills learned in training" (p. 45).
3. *Resistance—openness to change.* Definition: "Extent to which prevailing group norms are perceived by trainees to resist or discourage the use of skills and knowledge acquired in training" (p. 46).

Secondary Influences

There are five secondary influences:

1. *Performance self-efficacy.* Definition: "An individual's general belief that he is able to change his performance when they want to" (p. 46).
2. *Transfer effort–performance expectations.* Definition: "Expectation that effort devoted to transferring learning will lead to changes in job performance" (p. 45).
3. *Learner readiness.* Definition: "The extent to which individuals are prepared to enter and participate in training" (p. 44).
4. *Motivation to transfer.* Definition: "The direction, intensity, and persistence of effort toward utilizing in a work setting skills and knowledge learned" (p. 44).
5. *Performance outcomes expectations.* Definition: "The expectations that changes in job performance will lead to changes in job performance" (p. 45).

Though validation studies are oftentimes ongoing, the LTSI has several studies validating the instrument (Holton et al. 2007). The LTSI has been used on numerous organizational settings (Holton et al. 2003), in training programs (Kirwan and Birchall 2006), and as a predictor of performance and motivation (Seyler et al. 1998).

The Bottom Line

In 2009, the American Society of Training and Development released a comprehensive report on training evaluation. From that report, they offered the following recommended actions:

- Collect data that are meaningful to leaders. Otherwise, they will never see the value of evaluations.
- Where possible, standardize evaluation data across different functions within the organization to make it easier to use the data effectively.
- Spend more time and money evaluating behaviors and results and less on participant reactions. At the very least, do not rely on reactions so completely.
- *Give supervisors more responsibility when it comes to evaluation training. They should give employees opportunities to use their training, and they should help track performance both before and after the training* [emphasis added].
- When evaluating changes in behavior, use strategies such as follow-up sessions, focus groups, and participant surveys. Used with action planning and performance monitoring, these strategies are the most highly correlated with evaluation success.
- When evaluating the impact that training has had on results, find some ways to help filter out factors other than training that may have an influence, but also keep in mind that organizations are not laboratories where all the factors can be controlled. The learning function should not be held to a higher standard than others.
- When evaluating results, focus on metrics such as proficiency and competency levels, and employee perceptions of training impact (pp. 36 and 37).

Spiral or Rapid Development

The ADDIE process can be a slow and tedious process, and many times, organizations do not have the time to complete the entire ADDIE process.

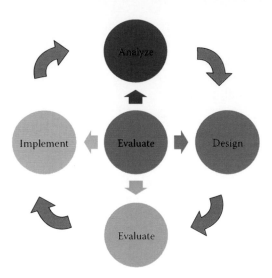

Figure 6.8 Spiral/rapid development.

Situations can change rapidly in the field, and officers may need to be trained hurriedly. The field can be a dynamic changing environment; thus, your training process should be dynamic and changing. Spiral development suggests two things. First, the work in the later stages can influence reconsideration of the work completed at the early stages. Second, the "spiral" shows that instructors/designers move dynamically back and forth during the process. The spiral process shows the work done during implementation and evaluation is fed back into the analysis phase (Figure 6.8). Therefore, the change is made and the evaluation of the change is folded back into the analysis at a later time.

Conclusion

The ADDIE process for a course to be developed can appear a little overwhelming, but the time and effort put in will show large returns. This process will ensure that you are delivering the best training to your officers. Further, the process adheres to the industry standard of sound course development and evaluation. It is imperative that if you have separate instructional systems designers, they should work closely with your instructors. When this happens, each person understands the role of the other, instructors will have a better understanding of the instructional design process, and instructional designers will have a better understanding of the perspective of the instructors.

Test Development 7

First off at this juncture, it should be stated that written tests are grossly overused in law enforcement training. As stated in Chapter 1, a good portion of a law enforcement officer's job is performance related, and a good test taker does not equate to a good job performer. Further, a lot more goes into planning a test than just writing a few questions. That is why this whole chapter is devoted to test development and analysis. Reliability and validity of test questions and performance criteria should be established right from the start. An assessment's results are considered reliable if they are dependable, repeatable, and consistent. The assessment is deemed to be valid if it measures the specific knowledge and skills that it is meant to measure.

Validity: A test is valid if it actually measures or assesses what it claims to measure or assess. A test is valid when
- Its individual items are consistent with the objectives the test claims to assess
- The items for each objective are representative of the range of items possible to develop that objective
- Objectives upon which the test is based have been adequately sampled

Reliability: A test or a performance evaluation is reliable if it consistently measures what it claims to measure and has confidence in the scores it produces.

You have to make your testing defensible. Therefore, you have to make sure that your test development processes have been clearly defined and documented. Can your test or performance evaluation be defended against a challenge? You will need to have specifications for your test, such as

- The conditions of which the test is administered
- The process for scoring
- The process for evaluating test performance
- The process for conveying scores to the test takers

Test Content Outline

A test content outline (TCO), sometimes referred to as a test blueprint, drives the test item development process. Test items developed this way can be easily mapped back to the objectives of the course or lesson. This ensures that your test is testing what it is supposed to test. The TCO describes the content areas to be covered in the assessment. Here are some suggestions for items to be contained in your TCO:

1. An introduction—A general description and schedule of the test
2. Required resources—What you need to complete the test (computers, pencil, and staff)
3. The objectives to be tested

There are several TCO templates to assist you that can be downloaded from the Internet. The process generally starts with examination of the Job Task Analysis (JTA). You need to understand *what* tasks a person in the position in question performs or supervises, *how often* the person does the task, *how important* the task is to the person's job, and *how hard* it is to perform the task. The results of the JTA are typically used to develop a competency model (all of this is covered in Chapter 6) (Figure 7.1).

The next step is to determine how many items should be written for each content area. There are several factors that must be taken into account when performing this step:

- **Criticality of the content**—Is this content "must know" or "nice to know"? Required knowledge necessitates more thorough testing, which means more items.
- **Size of the content area**—A larger content area requires more test items than a smaller content area.
- **Homogeneity**—Does everything in the content area require the same knowledge, skills, or abilities? If so, fewer questions are needed.
- **Consequences**—What happens if the officer does not grasp the concepts in the content area? Does he or she have to undergo more

Figure 7.1 Ensuring valid content.

training? Does the person lose his or her job? As the stakes go higher, you need more items to ensure that the officer's true knowledge is being assessed.

- **Available resources during testing**—If the test is going to be open book or open notes, you will need more (and more difficult) items to truly assess the officer's knowledge versus his or her ability to quickly look things up.

Having determined how many items you need to write for each content area covered by your assessment, there are a few more things to consider before you start writing items. You must balance the number of items you have determined that you need with any time limits imposed on the actual taking of the written test. Take a look at Table 7.1 showing the average amount of time a participant spends on different question types.

You will notice that true/false is not included in Table 7.1. The reason being is that you should stay away from true/false questions. Why? Because an officer has a 50% chance of getting the question right by just guessing; that is pretty good odds. You want your officers to know the material, not to take chances at guessing correctly. Other factors that can affect the length of the test include the following:

- How serious are decisions based on the results of the test (i.e., Use of Force issues)?
- What resources are available for testing?
- How significant is the overall objective being assessed?
- How interrelated are the objectives being tested?

The average written test question length based on difficultly is listed in Table 7.2.

Sharon Shrock and William Coscarelli's book, *Criterion-Referenced Test Development* (2007), provides some good advice on effective test writing:

✓ Always strive for clarity and readability. Remember, you only want to test for one thing, so make sure that you are not testing the officer's reading ability or comprehension ability as well as the specific piece of knowledge for which you are testing. Avoid "window dressing" or

Table 7.1 Test Item Time Response

Item Type	Time Estimate per Item
Multiple choice	1–1.5 minutes
Matching	30 seconds/response
Short answer	2 minutes
Fill in the blank	1 minute

Table 7.2   Test Item Difficulty Time Response

Test Difficulty	Easy	Moderately Easy	Moderate	Moderately Difficult	Difficult
Time per test item	42 seconds	54 seconds	66 seconds	78 seconds	90 seconds
50-item test time	0.58 hours (35 minutes)	0.75 hours (45 minutes)	0.92 hours (55 minutes)	1.08 hours (1 hour 5 minutes)	1.25 hours (1 hour 15 minutes)
100-item test time	1.16 hours (1 hour 10 minutes)	1.50 hours (1 hour 30 minutes)	1.83 hours (1 hour 50 minutes)	2.17 hours (2 hours 10 minutes)	2.50 hours (2 hours 30 minutes)

superfluous information that is not necessary to ask the question and get a response. Make sure that you are truly asking a single question. You don't want to ask something like, "What color is a stop sign and how many sides does it have?" or "Which of the following HotShot Show booths are the most popular?" You also want to make sure to avoid negative phrasing, such as "Which of the following is not an acceptable way to ..." because this increases the cognitive load and introduces confusion without increasing the value of the question.

✓ Use a style guide for consistency. You do not want anything to distract the officer, so make sure you use the same font size and family, including consistent bolding and italics, and so on. Test takers are nervous enough as they are; you do not want to unfairly add to their cognitive load by making them wonder why you used "item-writing" in one place and "item writing" in another. Was it on purpose? Is there a hidden meaning that they need to pick up on? Does the hyphenated one have a different meaning? A nervous officer may obsess over meaningless things like this—wasting time and preventing the person from showing you what he or she truly knows.

✓ If you are writing items that use distracters (e.g., multiple-choice questions), make sure the distracters are plausible. An obviously wrong distracter is a wasted distracter that only helps the officer guess correctly, making it look like the person knows something he or she doesn't. At the same time, make sure that you have only one truly correct choice and that you are not tricking the officer. Also, be careful about using keywords in the choice that are also used in the main body of the question, as this can clue in the officer to the correct answer or unfairly trick the officer into selecting the wrong answer.

✓ Also, keep in mind that the verb you use can raise or lower the cognitive level of the question. A simple recall question would use verbs such as *define*, *list*, or *identify* (from Bloom's Taxonomy). You could take that item to the next level by using "interpretation" verbs such as *differentiate, contrast, categorize,* and *distinguish.* An even higher cognitive level can be achieved by using "problem-solving" verbs such as *formulate, value, rate, revise,* and *evaluate.*

Avoiding Bias and Stereotypes

As you write and evaluate your assessment items, it is critical to avoid bias and stereotyping, as they can inhibit the impartiality, and therefore the fairness, of your assessment. *Bias* refers to giving a preference to one group over another. There are a number of ways that bias can creep into your item writing. For example, if you use language that is familiar to a group in a specific geographical location, it would give participants from that group an unfair advantage over participants from other parts of the globe. For example, some areas of the country use the term *tow truck* while others say *wrecker.* You can avoid bias by doing the following:

- Use neutral terms—for example, *police officer* instead of *policeman.*
- Strive for a balanced representation of various groups in diverse roles.
- Use standard, formal English. Avoid slang, idioms, and colloquialisms. Also, avoid obscure language or ambiguous acronyms unless they are standard, recognized terms with regard to the subject matter of the assessment.
- Be wary of using a condescending tone. For example, this could be a tone that implies that a person with differing abilities is incapable of caring for himself or herself, or that a person of lower socioeconomic status is not as intelligent as someone from a higher status.
- Avoid references to race, ethnicity, gender, age, and so on unless they specifically apply to the question. For example, it would be appropriate to mention age in a question about an emergency medical situation when age is pertinent to the emergency personnel who arrive on the scene, but it is not appropriate to mention age when age has nothing to do with the knowledge or skill being assessed.

Stereotyping is when you make generalizations or assumptions about a person on the basis of his or her membership in a group. There are several ways to avoid stereotyping:

- Include positive depictions of individuals in nontraditional roles. For example, do not assume that all nurses are female and all doctors are male.
- Make sure your items are reviewed by a diverse group of subject-matter experts (SMEs).

- Present people with disabilities in active, capable, and independent positions.
- Avoid common racial/ethnic stereotyping.
- Do not portray either sex as submissive or having an inferior status.
- Do not demean the elderly by portraying them as feeble, lonely, or dependent.

By avoiding bias and stereotypes, you help ensure that your assessment is testing only what it should be testing and that nothing is interfering with or distracting from participants' ability to demonstrate their true knowledge levels.

The test question itself is referred to as the *stem*. The portion of the question where the officer answers is called the *response*. The incorrect answers are called *distracters*. A distracter (1) is an answer that seems correct, (2) is an answer the test taker might be tempted to select, (3) is an answer that cannot be ruled out immediately, (4) can be a plausible answer.

There are two styles of stem formats, the *declarative format* and the *interrogative format*. The declarative format asks for only one portion of information, such as a fill-in-the-blank question. The blank should be at the end of the sentence. It is important to use a set number of spaces for the blank for the entire test, so you do not give away the answer.

Example:
   On a semiautomatic handgun, rounds are loaded into the _____.

For an interrogative format, there is only one question and the question begins with an interrogative word, such as who, what, which, how, and why.

Example:
   What do you load rounds into for a semiautomatic handgun?

The stem has to be written to where its meaning is immediately clear before reading the responses.

Example:
   The procedure to ensure handcuffs do not tighten after being placed on a subject is called _____.

Make sure you leave out irrelevant information in the question.

Poor example:
   Loyal Police Department's policy on pursuit driving is that lights and siren must be on. However, you may pursue without lights and siren when _____.

Better example:
> You may pursue a subject's vehicle without lights or siren when _____.

Include information in the stem, which sets limits for the correct response (e.g., first, maximum, least, minimum).

Poor example:
> The Sig Sauer P229 will hold _____rounds.

Better example:
> The Sig Sauer P229 will hold a MAXIMUM of _____rounds.

Place qualifying information in the first part of the stem phrase, dependent clause, or a separate sentence. Eliminate qualifying information and modifiers that are vague or ambiguous.

Poor example:
> What should you do FIRST after you remove a potentially dangerous subject from a crowded building?

Better example:
> After you remove a potentially dangerous subject from a crowded building, what should you do FIRST?

Write positive test items, unless the negative form is more appropriate for safety, critical decision, or exception items.

Poor example:
> Which function is not a function of lube oil?

Better example:
> The four MAIN functions of lube oil are to lubricate, clean, seal, and _____.

Do not omit words needed to complete comparisons.

Poor example:
> One advantage of hinge cuffs is that they can _____.

Better example:
> One advantage of hinge cuffs over chain cuffs is that hinge cuffs can _____.

Answer choices should be roughly the same length and kept as short as possible.

Poor example:
    a. In the chest
    b. In the kidney
    c. In the cranium
    d. In the groin

Better example:
    a. In the chest
    b. In the kidney
    c. In the head
    d. In the groin

Capitalize the first letter of each response to a stem that asks a question.

Example: *After arriving at the scene of a crash, what should you do FIRST?*
    a. Check the injuries
    b. Determine your position
    c. Set up a temporary shelter
    d. Operate the emergency radio

Other helpful hints for multiple-choice tests are as follows:

- Provide at least three answer choices and a maximum of five. Four is considered best.
- One answer should be completely correct.
- Another answer is mostly correct, but not completely. This will differentiate between those who really know the subject matter and those who have a more low understanding.
- You should have one correct answer and three distracters.
- Do **not** use "all of the above" or "none of the above" as an answer.
- Avoid using the words *always* or *never*.
- Avoid conjoining answers like "A and B" or "A, B, and C."

Test Complexity

There are three levels of test complexity: low, moderate, and high. A low test question generally requires one single fact of information, not multiple facts (i.e., knowing a name of a piece of equipment).

Example:
At Loyal Police Department, officers are issued what caliber sidearm?
    a. .22
    b. .40
    c. .357
    d. .45

    A moderate test question will require the test taker to know multiple facts or that two or more parts of information are combined to produce a new fact. The answer is dependent on factual knowledge that is definitive and complete.

Example:
Your sidearm misfires. You should _____.
    a. Raise your hand
    b. Tap and rack
    c. Strip out the magazine
    d. Reholster the weapon

    A highly complex test question requires the test taker to analyze multiple facts to solve a problem and make a decision. The correct answer may not be recognized until it is compared to an incorrect response. The test taker will have to select the best answer under conditions described in the stem. These types of questions are generally derived from real job situations.

Example:
You are drafting a search warrant affidavit and have used a confidential informant to gather evidence for your warrant. What is required to be included on your warrant?

1. All of the following are required:
   - Name of the informant
   - "Veracity" of the informant
   - "Basis of Knowledge" of the informant
   - Current information
2. All of the following are required:
   - Standards of probable cause
   - Current information
   - Address of the place to be searched
   - "Veracity" of the informant
3. All of the following are required:
   - Agency identifier of the confidential informant
   - Standards of probable cause
   - "Basis of Knowledge" of the informant
   - Address of the place to be searched

4. All of the following are required:
   - Items that may be searched and seized
   - Address of the place to be searched
   - Name of the confidential informant
   - Standards of probable cause

You can see that the highly complex questions require a higher level of cognitive load and recall to key out the right answer.

Test Question Analysis

When analyzing your test questions, you need to look at answer trends. For instance, if a high percentage of answers are wrong, there could be several variables affecting the outcomes, such as the following:

- The question may be poorly written.
- The wrong answer may be listed as correct.
- There may be a problem with what was taught in the class or the course materials.

Once you are confident that you have a complete set of well-written items that tie directly to your terminal performance objective, it is time to start putting the assessment together. In addition to determining which questions from your item bank you want to include, you must also develop test directions for the participant. These directions should include the following:

- Purpose of the assessment
- Amount of time allowed
- Procedures for asking questions
- Procedures for completing the test
- Procedures for returning test materials

As part of your officer's directions, you may want to consider including sample items, especially if the format is unusual or unfamiliar to the officers. Sample items also help reduce test anxiety. Remember, you want to assess the officers' true knowledge, which means you do not want a "stress barrier" getting in the way.

In addition to the officers' instructions, you also want to put together instructions for the assessment administrator—the instructor or test administrator who will be handing out the test and watching over the room while the participants take the assessment. Having a set of written instructions will help ensure consistency when different administrators in different locations give the assessment. The instructions should include the following:

- The participants' instructions, which should be read aloud
- How to handle and document irregularities
- The administrator's monitoring responsibilities and methods (e.g., no cell phones should be allowed in the classroom, walk around the room every 10 minutes, etc.)
- Hardware and software requirements and instructions, if applicable
- Contact information for technical help

Cut Scores

To be legally defensible in the United States and meet the Standards for Educational and Psychological Testing, a cut score cannot be arbitrarily determined; it must be empirically justified. For example, the organization cannot merely decide that the cut score will be 70% correct. Instead, a study is conducted to determine what score best differentiates the classifications of examinees, such as competent versus incompetent based on professional judgments. The minimal acceptable competence level is the level of performance on a test indicative of minimal competence (this is NOT the best or most qualified).

Therefore, what is a cut score? A cut score is based on the minimal acceptable competence level, which represents the threshold between officers who can do the job and those who cannot. The cut score must be defensible, as the most reasonable person on the job would accept.

The Angoff method is a widely used standard-setting approach in test development. In plain English, it is a kind of study that test developers use to determine the passing percentage (cut score) for a test. The passing grade of a test cannot be decided arbitrarily; it must be justified with empirical data. The Angoff method relies on SMEs who examine the content of each test question (item) and then predict how many minimally qualified candidates would answer the item correctly. The average of the judges' predictions for a test question becomes its *predicted difficulty*. The sum of the predicted difficulty values for each item averaged across the judges and items on a test is the recommended Angoff cut score. Here is a real-world example that illustrates the process:

Let us say a test developer needed to determine the passing grade for a written exam that tested an officer's knowledge of the Fourth Amendment. Using the Angoff method, the developer would employ a number of SMEs (in this case, Fourth Amendment experts) and ensure that they were properly trained on how to use the Angoff method, as well as informed on the test's purpose.

The Fourth Amendment–Angoff Panel would then rate each test item on the basis of whether a minimally qualified candidate would answer the item correctly or incorrectly. Once the first round of ratings had been conducted, everyone on the panel would be given access to the ratings of the other SMEs so that they could compare what they determined about a particular item. Then, the SMEs would be asked to rate the items again for a second round. The second round of rating would give the SMEs the opportunity to review their initial rating of an item and decide whether or not they might like to change their decision based on the expert judgments of the other panelists. This second round of ratings would be averaged across the SMEs to determine the final cut score for the test.

Jim Parry, test development manager for the US Coast Guard, explains the use of the Angoff this way: The probability estimate can never be less than 0.25 (25%) if there are four choices for a multiple choice question. Probability estimates are 0.25 through 0.95 for four-response multiple-choice questions. Therefore, 0.40 (40%) of minimally competent test takers should respond correctly. You need to agree upon an "allowable" percentage (from 0 to 1.00), but you should have nothing below 0.25 and nothing above 0.95.

Examine each stem (question), each correct response, and all distracters. Decide how many distracters a minimally competent performer would surely eliminate. This provides a "floor" to the rating of the item. Therefore, if a distracter on a four-choice item will be eliminated, the lowest possible rating for the item would be 0.33. If the choices between the remaining distracters are truly random, estimate the Angoff weight as the chance probability between the remaining options. For example, if there are two choices from four distracters, then the chance probability would be 0.50 (50%). Your SMEs estimate the difficulty of each item at the minimally competent test-taker level, NOT the SME's level as a judge. Do NOT estimate the level of typical test taker thinks of the minimally competent officer just entering the job would answer. This sets the standard that a minimally competent performer should be able to answer.

Your SMEs should not discuss their rating of each item; they are to work independently of each other. They should record their ratings between 0.25 and 0.95 for each item next to the item (this should be transferred to a spreadsheet). If there are any variation among the SMEs by a standard deviation of 10 after all items are rated and recorded, that item will need to be discussed. In the end, you will have your final cut score. Figure 7.2 shows what your spreadsheet can look like (to download a workable Angoff Excel spreadsheet, go to humanperformance.vpweb.com).

Be prepared that your passing test score may be something like 78.5%. In the end, using the Angoff method ensures that the passing grade of a test is

Test Item OID	Difficulty Metatag	Percentage Correct (Angoff Rating)	Expert 1 Name	Expert 2 Name	Expert 3 Name	Expert 4 Name	Expert 5 Name	Expert 6 Name	Expert 7 Name	Expert 8 Name	Standard Deviation
5.3.1.1/1	Moderate	67.50	55	55	70	75	75	75			9.87
5.3.1.1/2	Moderate	69.17	75	55	60	75	70	80			9.70
5.3.1.1/3	Easy	77.50	75	65	75	85	75	90			8.80
5.3.1.2/1	Easy	75.00	85	65	60	85	75	80			10.49
5.3.1.2/2	Easy	85.00	85	85	70	95	80	95			9.49
5.3.1.2/3	Moderate	68.33	75	55	60	65	80	75			9.83
5.3.1.2/4	Moderate	69.17	75	65	60	65	75	75			6.65
5.3.1.2/5	Easy	75.83	75	80	65	85	70	80			7.36
5.3.1.2/6	Moderate	69.17	75	65	50	75	75	75			10.21
5.3.1.2/7	Moderate	72.50	85	75	60	75	65	75			8.80
5.3.1.3/1	Moderate	69.17	75	65	60	65	75	75			6.65
5.3.1.3/2	Moderate	70.83	75	70	60	65	80	75			7.36
5.3.1.3/3	Moderate	73.33	75	75	60	75	80	75			6.83
5.3.1.3/4	Moderate	70.83	75	65	60	75	75	75			6.65
5.3.1.4/1	Moderate	69.17	75	75	60	65	70	70			5.85
5.3.1.4/2	Easy	76.67	85	75	70	75	70	85			6.83
5.3.1.4/3	Moderate	70.83	85	75	55	65	70	75			10.21
5.3.1.4/4	Moderate	68.33	65	75	50	75	75	70			9.83
5.3.1.4/5	Easy	80.00	85	80	80	75	75	85			4.47

Difficulty Rating

25 - 49.99	Hard
50 - 74.99	Moderate
75 - 95	Easy

Standard Deviation

A standard deviation of more than 10 will trigger an alert. Discuss the outliers with the judges who set them to determine why. Change as necessary.

6	Easy	In the section	24%
19	Moderate	In the section	76%
0	Hard	In the section	0%
25	TOTAL		100%

Figure 7.2 Sample of an Angoff cut score data sheet. (Courtesy of Jim Parry, US Coast Guard.)

determined empirically, which is necessary for a test to be legally defensible and meets the Standards for Educational and Psychological Testing.

Practicality

Many times, cognitive tests are not necessarily the best tool for evaluation. Shooting a firearm is a perfect example of this concept. Cognitive knowledge about a firearm does not equate to rounds at center mass. Performance tests measure skills. In these cases, the officer must demonstrate, to an acceptable level, how to shoot a firearm, how to disarm a suspect, how to search a vehicle, and so on.

Performance Test or Evaluations

Performance evaluations are a little different from written tests, and yet they are the same. The Terminal Performance Objectives should be criterion reference the same way they are in written exams. From there, you list the steps; many times, these are the enabling performance objectives, required for the successful performance of the task. From there, follow these steps:

1. Write the steps so that each point on your checklist is worded such that the performance standard results in a GO or YES being checked.
2. Word the actions such that the instructor observes the officer during the performance of the task, specifying the standards on how the performance will be measured.
3. Use words such as *who*, *what*, *when*, *where*, *why*, and *how* in the performance evaluation.
4. List the evaluation criteria, such as whether the performance was done safely.

Let us look at an example of a performance checklist to see how a performance evaluation actually looks. We will be using Use of Force Levels 1–5 as an example.

Terminal Performance Objective

Given the proper law enforcement equipment, training area, role player(s), an instructor, a vehicle stop scenario, and you acting as an officer working by yourself, combine Level 1–5 Use of Force techniques in accordance with the department policy.

Task		Yes	No
1.	The officer will **IDENTIFY** which levels of force are appropriate and **DETERMINE** the effectiveness of the level of force used. ☐ Uses the appropriate levels of force ☐ Articulates his or her actions ☐ Engages subject ☐ Maintains control of subject(s)		
	Level 1	Yes	No
2.	The officer will **DEMONSTRATE** officer presence. ☐ Communicates effectively ☐ Demonstrates the use of stances		
	Level 2	Yes	No
3.	The officer will **DEMONSTRATE** verbal commands (task direction with consequences).		
	Level 3	Yes	No
4.	The officer will **DEMONSTRATE** control techniques.		
	Level 4	Yes	No
5.	The officer will **DEMONSTRATE** aggressive response techniques.		
	Level 5	Yes	No
6.	The officer will **DEMONSTRATE** intermediate weapons.		
Evaluation criteria: To receive a pass, **all applicable tasks** must receive a Yes. (Circle one)		Pass	Fail

Conclusion

This is a substantial amount of information on test development. But to defend your testing the effort you put into test development will pay off in the end. Your tests have to be reliable and valid to be defendable.

Focus on Officer Performance

8

Officers are the consumers of your training. If you have poor training, you will have low performance. If your training is of high quality, you will have high performance; research data firmly support this statement. In his study of academy graduates from a midwestern police academy, Hundersmarck (2009) found that academy graduates found scenarios conducted in the academy to be powerful during field training. Recruits did not consider lecture classes as important as hands-on training. This supports Malcolm Knowles, in his adult learning theory, which said that adults learn by doing.

Armstrong (2012, p. 1) claimed, "...traditional education ignores or suppresses learner responsibility." He advocates that when officers take responsibility for their learning, they enhance their learning. The following provides a few examples of why officer-centered learning should be integrated into the curriculum:

- It strengthens officer motivation.
- It promotes peer communication.
- It reduces disruptive behavior.
- It builds officer–instructor relationships.
- It promotes discovery/active learning.
- It encourages responsibility for one's own learning.

Motivation—The Key to Learning

If you have noticed by now, the word *motivation* is used substantially in this book. Why? Motivation is key to learning. No matter how great your training is, without an officer's motivation, learning will be minimal. Officers who believe they are competent are more likely to remain motivated. Most of the theories on motivation are linked to Vroom's early research on motivation and work (Vroom 1964). Vroom's expectancy theory begins with the concept that people prefer certain goals over others, thus experiencing satisfaction when the goal is met (Miner 2005). In the context of training, the expectancy theory suggests that officers consider the usefulness of the training in reaching desired outcomes. The expectancy theory clarifies motivation as the relationship between one's efforts and one's rewards (Moorhead and Griffin 1992). The expectancy theory would enhance an officer's motivation through the transfer of trained tasks (Holton 1996).

Valence is an officer's beliefs regarding the outcomes received from training and is related to training success (Colquitt et al. 2000). By linking these elements together into one cohesive understanding, officers will have the greatest motivation, that is, believing that the new training material (expectancy) and the knowledge learned from this new material (instrumentality) are important to their careers (valence) (Knowles et al. 2005).

Intrinsic versus Extrinsic Motivation

Extrinsic and intrinsic motivations are components of motivation to transfer, which are closely linked to training outcomes (Burke and Hutchins 2007). Intrinsic motivation could be defined as behaviors that are not driven by physiological derivatives and not based solely on the reward itself, but based more on the internal satisfaction associated with pursuing the reward (Vanteenkiste et al. 2006). Thus, intrinsic motivation involves engagement in the activity based solely on that activity. Extrinsic motivation is based more on the reward and is not significantly related to the activity (Burke and Hutchins 2007). If an officer studies hard to get a good grade because there is a reward for doing so (i.e., recognition, competitive advantage) and not purely to obtain knowledge, that is extrinsic motivation (Shia 2005).

Relative to an extrinsic goal, a training activity helps in the attainment of goals, which should increase the perceived value of the training. The value is greater for the intrinsic goal than for the extrinsic goal, and with the same expectancy value for both goals, motivation should be greater for the intrinsic goal than for the extrinsic goal since motivation would be the product of expectancy × value.

Putting these theories to practice, to enhance an officer's motivation for training and learning, it is useful for instructors to point out the importance of the training material, especially when officers have a low interest. Simply urging officers to do their best is not enough because there is no external reference. Instead, instructors should set highly articulate goals, which reduces ambiguity and increases intrinsic motivation. Officers who are not certain of the significance of their training will lack motivation to transfer newly acquired skills (Grossman and Salas 2011).

Motivation plays a significant role in learning. Keller (1987) developed a general model integrating the various sources of motivation for learning. He

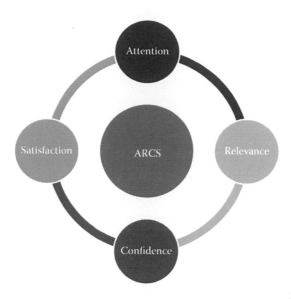

Figure 8.1 Keller's ARCS model.

calls it the ARCS model (Figure 8.1), an acronym for the four sets of conditions that should be met to have a motivated learner:

A for attention.

   Attention involves grabbing the learner's interest at the beginning of instruction and maintaining that interest throughout the lesson and course. There are two broad ways to garner attention: perceptual arousal and inquiry arousal. Perceptual arousal involves using a surprising event to grab the audience's attention. Inquiry arousal connects the officers to the instructor and material through asking good introspective questions or problems.

R for relevance.

   Relevance is the personal significance and value to the learner of mastering the learning objectives. Keller (1987) suggests six ways to connect relevance:

1. *Experience*: Just do not throw new knowledge at the officers; build on what they may already know.
2. *Present worth*: What is in it for them? Why are they there?
3. *Future usefulness*: The officers need to know how the current training will make a difference in their jobs in the future.
4. *Needs matching*: Drive home the advantage your training will provide in achievement, risk taking, and affiliation.

5. *Modeling*: The best instructor is always the best example. Never instruct anyone else unless you can do it better than those you are instructing.
6. *Choice*: Give the officers choices. Just do not tell, let them do.

C for confidence.

Confidence relates to the officer's expectancy of success. Officers have to feel they can accomplish what they have been taught. Feedback from instructors is crucial to an officer's success in training.

S for satisfaction.

Satisfaction comes from achieving performance goals. In many cases, satisfaction is derived from just completing the training. When officers feel they have not just learned something, but earned something as well, that is the root of satisfaction. Real learning comes from the inside out.

The following are some reasons for low motivation:

1. The officer perceives the knowledge component to be unimportant.
2. The officer believes that he or she does not have the necessary ability, power, or resources to learn or increase his or her competence relative to the knowledge component.
3. The officer has a negative emotional response to the knowledge component (Marzano and Kendall 2007, p. 59).

Adult Learning

Part of being an effective instructor involves understanding how adults learn best (Lieb 1991). Andragogy (adult learning) is a theory that holds a set of assumptions about how adults learn. Andragogy emphasizes the value of the process of learning. It uses approaches to learning that are *problem based and collaborative* rather than didactic, and also emphasizes more *equality between the instructor and the officer.*

Educators have understood pedagogy, the process of helping children learn, for a long time. Andragogy, as a study of adult learning, originated in Europe in the 1950s and was then pioneered as a theory and model of adult learning from the 1970s by Malcolm Knowles, an American practitioner and theorist of adult education, who defined andragogy as "the art and science of helping adults learn" (Fidishun 2000, p. 4; Zmeyov 1998). Adults bring specific characteristics to the learning environment. They have life experiences that they want incorporated into their learning. They are motivated to learn when they have a problem to solve. Therefore, they are more interested in the specifics of a topic than in its generalities. For adults, being a learner is often not their primary role; it is secondary to their other life obligations. Combine these adult learner characteristics, add a sprinkling of learning theories, and the result is a complicated mix that trainers must consider for the training to be well received and meet the needs of the adult audience.

Knowles et al. (2005) identified the six principles of adult learning outlined below.

- Adults are internally motivated and self-directed.
- Adults bring life experiences and knowledge to learning experiences.
- Adults are goal oriented.
- Adults are relevancy oriented.
- Adults are practical.
- Adult learners like to be respected.

Adults Are Internally Motivated and Self-Directed

Adult learners resist learning when they feel others are imposing information, ideas, or actions on them (Fidishun 2000). Your role is to facilitate an officer's movement toward more self-directed and responsible learning as well as to foster the officer's internal motivation to learn.

As an instructor, you can

- Set up a **graded learning program** that moves from more to less structure, from less to more responsibility and from more to less direct supervision, at an appropriate pace that is challenging yet not overloading for the officer.
- **Develop rapport** with the officer to optimize your approachability and encourage asking of questions and exploration of concepts.
- **Show interest** in the officer's thoughts and opinions. Actively and carefully listen to any questions asked.
- **Lead the officer toward inquiry** before supplying them with too many facts (the cognitive load factor).
- Provide **regular constructive and specific feedback** (both positive and negative).
- **Review goals** *and* **acknowledge goal completion**.
- **Encourage use of resources** such as field training officers, professional journals, supervisors, Internet, social media, and other department resources.
- **Set projects or tasks** for the officer that **reflect their interests** and which they must complete and "tick off" over the course of the placement.

Adults Bring Life Experiences and Knowledge to Learning Experiences

Adults like to be given the opportunity to use their existing foundation of knowledge and experiences gained from life experience, and apply it to their new learning experiences.

- *Find out about your officers*—their interests and past experiences (personal, work, and study related).
- *Assist them to draw on those experiences* when solving problems, reflecting, and applying field reasoning processes.
- *Facilitate reflective learning opportunities*, which Fidishun (2000) suggests can also assist the officer to examine existing biases or habits based on life experiences and "move them toward a new understanding of information presented" (p. 4).

Adults Are Goal Oriented

Officers become ready to learn when "they experience a need to learn it in order to cope more satisfyingly with real-life tasks or problems" (Knowles 1980, p. 44, as cited in Fidishun 2000). Your role is to facilitate an officer's readiness for problem-based learning and increase the officer's awareness of the need for the knowledge or skill presented. As an instructor, you can

- *Provide meaningful learning experiences* that are *clearly linked* to personal and fieldwork goals
- *Provide real case studies* based on real cases
- *Ask questions* that motivate reflection, inquiry, and further research

Adults Are Relevancy Oriented

Adult learners want to know the relevance of what they are learning to what they want to achieve. One way to help officers see the value of their observations and practical experiences is to

- *Ask the officer to do some reflection* on, for example, what they expect to learn before the experience, on what they learned after the experience, and how they might apply what they learned in the future, or how it will help them meet their learning goals
- *Provide some choice* of fieldwork project by providing two or more options, so that learning is more likely to reflect the officer's interests

Adults Are Practical

Through practical fieldwork experiences, interacting with real people and their real-life situations, officers transition from classroom and textbook mode to hands-on problem solving where they can recognize firsthand how what they are learning applies to life and the work context. As an instructor, you can

- *Clearly explain your reasoning* when making enforcement choices.
- *Be explicit* about how what the officer is learning is useful and applicable to the job.
- *Promote active participation* by allowing officers to try things rather than observe. Provide plenty of practice opportunity in order to promote development of skill, confidence, and competence.

Adult Learners Like to Be Respected

Respect can be demonstrated to your officer by

- Taking interest
- *Acknowledging the wealth of experiences* that the officer brings to the placement
- *Regarding them as a colleague* who is equal in life experience
- *Encouraging expression* of ideas, reasoning, and feedback at every opportunity

It is important to keep in mind that officers are still developing their law enforcement skills. However, with the theory and principles of adult learning in mind, you can facilitate the learning approach of the officer to progress from being novice to becoming more sophisticated. This facilitates greater integration of knowledge, information, and experience; the officer learns to distinguish what is important when assessing law enforcement situations and how to prioritize goals and caseloads.

Knowing the many roles of the instructor apply to the learning experiences instructors create, and build relationships that promote a safe and positive environment in which officers are responsible, self-motivated, and self-evaluating.

- **Relationships:** Build collaborative and respectful relationships with officers and colleagues. Consistently encourage, support, and appropriately challenge officers to ensure officer success. Facilitate development of relationships among officers to promote mutual respect and support in your classroom.

- **Procedures and Routines:** Structure the classroom to create an orderly learning environment, communicate expectations that support positive officer behavior to facilitate high levels of officer engagement, and build a shared community of learners.
- **Arrangement of Classroom:** Organize the classroom for a variety of learning opportunities that encourage both whole group and small group instructor-directed activities and independent and cooperative learning experiences (more on this later in this chapter).
- **Displays:** Support learning by using instructional resources (such as whiteboards, models, and turn charts) that are clearly accessible. Make officer work a focal point in the classroom. Post classroom and community expectations.
- **Tools:** Make appropriate materials that support learning and make them accessible for all officers.

Experiential Learning

The ultimate aim of reviewing exercises is to make reviewing a habit, thus stimulating and developing people's ability to learn from experience.

Creative Reviewing, 1989, p. v

Current research supports experiential learning as a solid means to facilitate learning in an officer-centered environment. Experiential learning has foundational elements from John Dewey, Kurt Lewin, Jean Piaget, and David Kolb. Experiential activities are among the most powerful teaching and learning tools available for law enforcement instructors. Experiential learning can exist without an instructor and relates solely to the meaning-making process of the officer's direct experience. It is described by Quinsland and Van Ginkel (1984) as "an activity that is used to encourage individuals to reflect, describe, analyze and communicate what they recently experienced" (p. 9). Though the gaining of knowledge is an inherent process that occurs naturally, for a genuine learning experience to occur, there must exist certain elements. According to David A. Kolb (1984), knowledge is continuously gained through both personal and environmental experiences. He states in order to gain genuine knowledge from an experience, certain abilities are required:

- The officer must be willing to be actively involved in the experience.
- The officer must be able to reflect on the experience.

- The officer must possess and use analytical skills to conceptualize the experience.
- The officer must possess decision-making and problem-solving skills in order to use the new ideas gained from the experience.

Figure 8.2 shows the three main experiential learning models.

1. Kolb's Experiential Learning Model

    David A. Kolb believes that "learning is the process whereby knowledge is created through the transformation of experience" (1984, p. 38). The four stages in his model are as follows:
    a. Concrete experience (or "Do")
    b. Reflective observation (or "Observe")
    c. Abstract conceptualization (or "Think")
    d. Active experimentation (or "Plan")

    Concrete experience is where officers actively experience an activity like a scenario. The second stage, reflective observation, is when the officers consciously reflect on their experience from the scenario. Abstract conceptualization is when the officer attempts to conceptualize an idea of what is observed. Finally, the fourth stage, active experimentation, is when the officer is trying to plan for the next experience.

2. Roger Greenaway's Experiential Learning Model

    Roger Greenaway (1992) believes that people ask themselves four questions:
    a. Facts (What happened?)
    b. Feelings (What did I just experience?)
    c. Findings (Why did it happen?)
    d. Future (What will I do?)

    The first stage is *Facts*. This stage is to relive what just happened. This stage is a reminder of the event and how the experience unfolded. If the event went well, then there could be an internal celebration. If there were problems, then the event is reviewed.

    The second stage is *Feelings*. At this stage, emotions of the scenario begin to surface. This stage focuses on the quality of the scenario, such as "What was it like?" or "How did it feel?"

    The third stage is *Findings*. The scenario is analyzed and reviewed. The officer begins to go through all of the portions of the scenario reviewing what went right and what went wrong, and how to correct the wrongs.

    The final stage is *Future*. At this stage, the officer begins to prepare and plan for the next scenario. The officer raises his or her awareness to a higher level. Officers may be careful in the next scenario or take bigger risks based on how they analyzed the previous scenario.

3. Argyris and Schön's Experiential Learning Model

Argyris and Schön's Experiential Learning Model is a highly theoretical model of learning incorporating many different theories. They proposed that all humans subconsciously operate through many different levels to explain their experience. Argyris and Schön (1978) state that when we go through an experience, we learn as *single-loop learning*, where the officers see their behavior and assess the consequences of their behavior. They then revise their actions to see if the outcomes are a success or a failure. If they fail, they again revise their actions, called *double-loop learning*. If they succeed, they implement their revised theory of what worked.

Let us take a look at an example of how an experiential learning model can be used in training officers. Most officers have gone through some type of oleoresin capsicum (OC) training requiring them to be sprayed in the face with OC spray. Therefore, when an officer gets sprayed in the face, this is the *experience*. They then *reflect* on experience, concluding, "This really sucks, and I don't like it." In the next stage, they figure out how they *reacted* to the spray, such as tearing of the eyes, inflammation of mucous membranes, and burning sensation in the face. Finally, they understand and *formulate* a plan regarding the effects of OC spray not only on themselves and other officers but also on suspects.

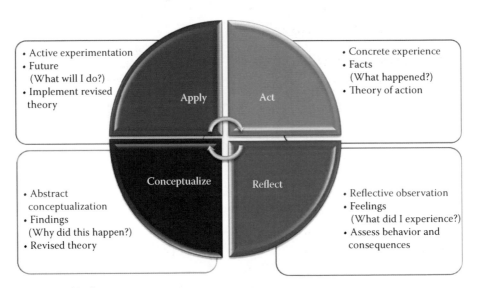

- Active experimentation
- Future
  (What will I do?)
- Implement revised theory

Apply		**Act**

- Concrete experience
- Facts
  (What happened?)
- Theory of action

Conceptualize		**Reflect**

- Abstract conceptualization
- Findings
  (Why did this happen?)
- Revised theory

- Reflective observation
- Feelings
  (What did I experience?)
- Assess behavior and consequences

1. David Kolb
2. Roger Greenaway
3. Chris Argyris and Donald Schön

Figure 8.2 Experiential learning cycles.

Learning Styles

Many trainers, instructional designers, and others involved with training officers have been taught officers learn through a certain learning style. A learning style can be described as the way an officer concentrates on, processes, and retains new information. Many trainers have been taught these styles:

- *Auditory*—A person learns primarily through hearing material presented to him or her.
- *Visual*—A person learns primarily through visual means presented to him or her.
- *Kinesthetic*—A person learns primarily through feeling and sensing things presented to him or her.

However, the literature is not very clear-cut on learning styles. In fact, the literature is not very definitive at all on learning styles. So much so that the name itself is not agreed upon; some researchers call them *cognitive styles*, some call them *learning preferences*, and others call them *learning strategy*. Clark (2015, p. 5) states that learning styles "represent one of the most wasteful and misleading pervasive myths of the past 25 years." There are some researchers, quite a few of them in fact, that state there is no such thing as a learning style. Pashler et al. (2008) embarked on an extensive study of learning styles. They specifically analyzed the theory of learning styles to determine what evidence would be needed to validate andragogical choices on assessment of student learning styles. At the end of their study, they found "...virtually *no evidence* for the interaction pattern mentioned above [a preference for a learning style], which was judged to be a precondition for validating the educational applications of learning styles" (p. 105) (emphasis added). They further added:

> The contrast between the enormous popularity of the learning-styles approach within education and the lack of credible evidence for its utility is, in our opinion, striking and disturbing. If classification of students' learning styles has practical utility, it remains to be demonstrated. (p. 117)

Many educational psychologists use many different learning style assessments to determine which styles to use with students. However, in the training world, who has time to assess each officer to see what style they use? Many times, trainers have to train the officers provided to them, and therefore, they do not have the time to assess each individual learning style. With so much controversy surrounding the debate on learning styles, most trainers should maintain focus on providing the best material (i.e., designed and developed correctly and presented in the best format available) and let learning styles (if they exist) work their way into the learning process.

Training Generational Differences

There is a very strong possibility in today's workforce that you may be training officers from at least three distinctly different generational backgrounds, and because of these different generational backgrounds, this makes training difficult to design; each background has different expectations about training. The more we understand these generations, the better we are in developing and delivering effective training programs. Be forewarned though these characteristics represent a broad generalization and may not apply across all members of a generational group; this definitely applies to people born at the very beginning or at the tail end of a generation. Here are some general tips to keep in mind when designing and developing training courses for different generational groups:

1. When you are trying to make a point, always keep the audience in mind. Tailor your communication to speak strongly to your target demographic.
2. Forget about "one-size-fits-all" thinking. Different things motivate different generations.
3. If possible, allow officers to choose their own training methods. Boomers like resident live classes, whereas Millennials may prefer a Webinar instead.

Let us quickly cover the different generations and then provide tips on how to address training these different generations.

Boomers: Born between 1943 and 1960 (some say 1964), they are the children of the WWII generation. Many Boomers are nearing retirement or have already retired. Many Boomers lived during affluent and nurturing times. It was during their time when there were advances in science and technology, a sexual revolution emerged among women, and the Vietnam War happened. The Civil Rights movement and the assassinations of John F. Kennedy, Robert Kennedy, and Martin Luther King all happened during the early years of Boomers. Boomers tend to be optimistic and individualistic, and place great value on instant gratification (Sandeen 2008). Boomers are known to work long hours, have little leisure time, and have common stress ailments as a result of the long hours.

Boomers place a high value on education and have seen how educational attainment can advance their careers. Thus, Boomers tend to be highly career focused and to have high expectations regarding salary, titles, and perks. Boomers can also be highly competitive and value recognition and visibility.

When designing and developing a training program, consider Boomers prefer classroom-based programs and welcome high-interaction formats. They will prefer instructor-led training over technology-based learning formats. They prefer critical reflection and value feedback, but prefer the feedback to be positive.

Generation X: Born between 1961 (some say 1964) and 1981, this generation is quite different from the Boomers. This generation experienced severe economic downturns during their early life. Many saw their fathers being laid off or downsized by big-name corporations. They saw that dedication gets you nowhere in an organization. This generation saw high levels of divorce in families. This made this generation more cynical, more suspicious, and more pessimistic than Boomers. They also saw music, art, and gym class removed from schools. However, the women's movement boomed as more and more women entered the workforce. This created more "latch key" kids (Sandeen 2008). Generally, Generation X kids scored lower in academic skills and fewer went to college. Compared to any generation in recent history, this generation saw fewer marriages and got married later in life. Also, they have seen that fathers have a more significant role in their life as more moms entered the workforce.

Generation X'ers look to build "mobile" careers. They perceive that loyalty gets you nowhere. However, they are very family oriented and, therefore, reject the Boomer 80-hour workweek. They see jobs as a way to pay for their creature comforts, hobbies, and leisure time.

Regarding training Generation X'ers, they like options and prefer shorter and more flexible training formats. They are comfortable with technology because it provides flexibility. They like instant messaging and short, highly-focused training. They like multimedia learning opportunities (Webinars, short-training clips, etc.). They place little value on feedback and have short attention spans.

Generation Y (sometimes referred to as Millennials): Born between 1982 and 2003, Millennials are projected to be 50% of the workforce by 2020. Millennials have seen a shift back to child-centered context similar to the Boomers. The terms *helicopter moms* and *soccer moms* were coined during their lifetime. Many Millennial kids' "resumes" began to be filled out as early as preschool. Millennials have been raised in a highly structured life; many have had their days scheduled from waking up to bedtime. This unfortunately has led them to be thrown out of balance when the structure is taken away. This generation, unlike any other, trusts authority and their parents (Sandeen 2008). They are very team oriented, optimistic, and confident.

Millennials love technology and have been around it their entire lifetime. Many children of this generation had cell phones by the time they were in third grade. They are prone to believe that Google has all the answers. These are the people who are quick to pull out their smartphone and Google for the answer to something. Thus, when Google fails to provide an answer, they are stuck. This has made the generation prone to poor problem-solving skills— no Internet access means no answers to problems. Like Boomers, they are very career oriented and expect rapid advancement. They like feedback and evaluation since they have been evaluated their entire life.

Millennials are multitaskers, networked, and technologically connected. They walk around with their tablet or smartphone in their hands. They prefer distance learning over classroom learning; they can get their information from their "wireless" tablet or smartphone. This means that they expect 24/7 access to the training branch and instructors. They like collaborative learning via Skype, GoToMeeting, and Blackboard. They like training via Webinars, Instant Messaging, Blogs, Podcasts, Avatars, and YouTube. They expect a "trophy" at the end of their training.

As you can see, developing and designing training for these generations are not easy. That is why the training branch has to be nimble and flexible in their approach to training.

Metacognition and Officer Learning

Great instructors and instructional designers understand the reason for knowing how their officers learn. The term *metacognition* can be traced back to Flavell (1979) who said that metacognition was "thinking about thinking" (p. 906). Metacognition refers to an individual's self-awareness about what they know and understand, along with ways of processing their own cognition through self-control and self-manipulation (Osman and Hannafin 1992). Many aspects of training transfer, especially in the officer characteristics, have a metacognitive element tied to it. Metacognition is a cognitive function, which includes understanding of relationships between learning tasks and individual capabilities (Ford and Weissbein 1997). A metacognitive skill is the ability to monitor and direct the process of cognitive skills to attain the best possible success (Geiwitz 1994).

Several training transfer factors are linked to metacognition. Motivation is linked to metacognitive strategies and enhances officers' performance (Pintrich and De Groot 1990). Metacognition lead to higher tests and practical evaluation scores for officers attending a resident 5-week training program basic law enforcement course and a 2-week basic law enforcement blended training course (Giovengo 2014).

There are two main fundamental components to metacognition: knowing about cognition and checking of cognition (Schraw and Moshman 1995). Schmitt and Newby (1986) described these components as metacognitive knowledge and metacognitive regulation.

Metacognitive Knowledge

Flavell (1979) defined metacognitive knowledge as stored knowledge that has to do with people as "cognitive creatures" (p. 906). Metacognition is a culmination of an officer's awareness of cognitive functions in relation to their tasks, goals, actions, and experiences (Schmitt and Newby 1986). Metacognitive knowledge is how officers learn and process information and knowledge of oneself in the learning process (Livingston 1997). An example of metacognitive knowledge is when officers know that *when* they take notes, they enhance their ability to recall material.

Metacognition can be divided into three kinds of "awareness" or domains of knowledge: declarative, procedural, and conditional (Schmitt and Newby 1986; Schraw and Moshman 1995, p. 352). Declarative knowledge is an officer's knowledge of his or her skills and abilities as a learner (Anderson et al. 2001b). Declarative knowledge is one's knowledge of self-weaknesses and strengths, as well as personal strategies. Declarative knowledge is what an officer intellectually knows (Pierce 2003); declarative knowledge is "knowing what" about a task. For instance, knowing how a Sig Sauer P229 operates is declarative knowledge. Schraw and Dennison (1994) used an example question of declarative knowledge: "I know what kind of information is important to me" or "I learn more when I am interested in the topic" (p. 473).

Procedural knowledge quite simply is *how* to use strategies (Anderson et al. 2001b; Murphy 2008). It involves the steps in the process of knowing how to do something (Pierce 2003). Using the same example as above, knowing how to shoot a Sig Sauer P229 is procedural knowledge. Procedural knowledge is set to context and can be difficult to transfer. Procedural knowledge is common to law enforcement training programs. A procedural knowledge indicator question would be "I have a specific purpose for each strategy I use" or "I am aware of what strategies I use when I study."

Haskell (2001) stated that when he classified types of learning transfer, he tied specific procedural knowledge and declarative knowledge together, which means that transfer is enabled for an officer to acquire supplementary abstract knowledge about a subject when the officer has practical experience in that subject. For example, a field training officer conducting a vehicle search may help the new officer in learning theoretical constitutional law.

Conditional knowledge is defined as *why* and *when* to use a strategy, such as why something works and when something does not work (Murphy 2008; Pierce 2003). Examples of questions regarding conditional knowledge would be "I learn best when I know something about the topic" or "I can motivate myself to learn when I need to" (pp. 473–474). An example of putting these domains into context would be that when an officer is given learning material, he or she also needs to be given direction on what is necessary for recall (declarative knowledge). The officer needs to be aware of how this material is used in a process (procedural knowledge). Finally, the officer needs to be given many circumstances where he or she can apply these processes (conditional knowledge).

Metacognitive Regulation

Metacognitive strategies are sequential processes an officer uses to control cognitive activities, which see that a cognitive goal is met (Coutinho and Neuman 2008). Metacognitive strategies involve *planning, monitoring,* and *evaluating* processes (Schraw and Moshman 1995). A definition of planning is "Selecting, predicting, planning, scheduling, goal setting, allocating resources and ordering coordinating and action or strategy necessary to accomplishment of an action or goal *prior* to learning" (Murphy 2008, p. 16). A *planning* indicator question is "I ask myself questions about the material before I begin" (Schraw and Dennison 1994, p. 473). An example of a planning type of statement would be something like "Before I did that [learn] I read through the Study Guide because that gives you an idea of what the chapter was about" (de la Harpe et al. 1997, p. 336).

A definition of monitoring (or regulation) is "Setting up, assessing, testing, monitoring, redirecting, modifying, maintaining, revising, re-scheduling and supervising plans and strategies, desired goals and the overall cognitive task *during* learning" (Murphy 2008, p. 16). A *monitoring* indicator question is: "I ask myself periodically if I am meeting my goals" (Schraw and Dennison 1994, p. 472). An example of a planning type of statement would be something like "I used the notes as well as my summaries, and that is a way of testing yourself" (de la Harpe et al. 1997, p. 336).

Finally, the third process is *evaluation* (Murphy 2008; Schraw and Moshman 1995). A definition of evaluation (revising or adapting) is "Assessment, appraisal, evaluation, analysis, or verification of one's knowledge, understanding, skills, performances, and strategy efficiency and effectiveness *after* learning" (Murphy 2008, p. 16). An *evaluation* indicator question is "I ask myself if there was an easier way to do things after I finish a task" (Schraw and Dennison 1994, p. 473). An example of an adapting type of statement would be something like "…and then when I did the test, if there were questions asked and I thought I have no idea, I went back and reread it" (de la Harpe et al. 1997, p. 336) (Figure 8.3).

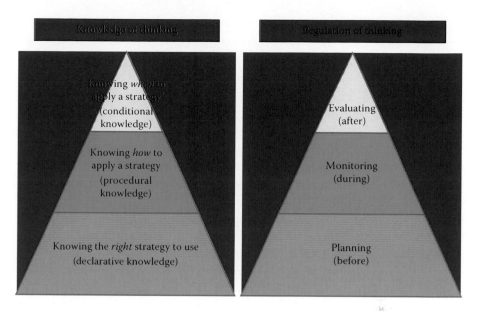

Figure 8.3 Knowledge of thinking/regulation of thinking.

Levels of Processing

There are two levels of processing officers utilize when confronted with learning material: *deep-level* and *surface-level* processing (Marton and Säljö 1976). Surface-level processing is when an officer rote-learns material that will be assessed later on a test. In deep-level processing, the officer directs his or her learning toward comprehending more of what the material is about. Spelling the words *fight* and *right* and hearing the word *sight* on the surface level can explain an example of the difference of the two; a student would be able to spell the word. However, if the word *height* were added, a negative transfer would result owing to the deep structures that would have to be known. Marton and Säljö's model has relevance with the understanding that officers may not have the time to "deeply" learn every aspect of training. Instructors need to be aware that training interventions have time limitations and parameters that can limit "deep" learning (Figure 8.4).

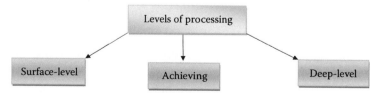

Figure 8.4 Levels of processing.

Instructional Strategies and Methods

The literature is robust regarding instructional strategies and methods. Over the last century, a myriad of books and research have been written about instructional design, strategies, and methods. Baldwin and Ford (1988) examined numerous training principles such as practice, reliability, sequencing, and Thorndike and Woodward's (1901) identical elements theory. Stemming from a task analysis, Merrill (2007) suggested using a task-centered instructional strategy. His idea is that engaging officers with realistic real-world problems will enhance their ability to form appropriate mental models and schemas. His principles are divided into a cycle of instructional phases composed of "activation, demonstration, application, and integration in the context of real-world problems or tasks" (p. 6).

Goal setting is an instructional strategy, both during and after training (Holton 1996). A goal is anything an officer is consciously trying to achieve (Wexley and Latham 2002). Goal-setting theory is important to training transfer (Kontoghiorghes 2001; Lim and Johnson 2002; Lim and Morris 2006; Yamnill and McLean 2002). Bandura (1997) has advocated for officers setting both proximal and distal goals.

Proximal goals are short-term goals that are influential in accomplishing distal goals (long-term goals). Bandura (1997) suggested that proximal plus distal goals produce better performance than just distal goals. Weldon (1998) supported Bandura's theory by stating that (a) proximal goals create a sense of urgency, which reduces procrastination; (b) proximal goals create a clear line of progress, which increases the feeling of accomplishment; (c) proximal goal attainment increases self-efficacy; and (d) proximal goal attainment leads to an officer's sense of mastery, which increases intrinsic interest. Bandura's theory is further substantiated by Brown and Warren's (2009) study of public sector midcareer employees where they found that trainees who had proximal and distal goals performed higher than those who just set distal goals, which increased self-efficacy.

There are three important inferences goal setting does in motivating trainees:

a. At the onset of the program, learning objectives should be articulated to the officers and should be reinforced throughout the training program.
b. Training goals should be difficult enough so that trainees are adequately challenged and thus derive satisfaction from achieving objectives.
c. Sprinkled throughout the program should be subgoals such as practice sessions and quizzes (Wexley and Latham 2002).

In her study of 4097 training professionals who were members of the American Society of Training and Development (now called the Association for Talent Development), Kontoghiorghes (2004) found that the development of training goals and objectives was significantly inter-related with transfer. This finding indicates officers are likely to transfer when they have a clear understanding of the goals and objectives of a training program.

There are many types of instructional methods, each with its strengths and weaknesses. Here are the different teaching methodologies:

Lecture—The type of method we are most familiar with. An instructor in front of a class teaching material. This typically takes place in a classroom.

Demonstration—Typically involves an instructor showing officers a process or modeling a behavior.

Games—A game can be computer based or a tangible event that leads to learning or review of material.

Case Studies—Officers are given a scenario (generally real-world) that requires officer analysis. Case studies can be done step by step; twists and turns can be added.

Student Teach Back—This requires the student to take charge of a class and deliver training material to the rest of the class.

Group Work—The class is broken down into smaller groups to discuss and analyze a situation.

Role Play—This requires the officers to assume a scripted role to be acted out with another classmate. The other officer may not know what is going to happen next.

Independent Practice—This may involve a series of questions that an officer has to independently answer on his own.

Reflection—This requires a large amount of time as officers try to self-analyze and understand their personal attitudes.

Simulations—This involves a scenario that resembles the real work environment that an officer may face.

Guided Learning—The instructor guides the officers through a situation where the officers have to provide input. The instructor ensures that the officers reach a sound conclusion.

Table 8.1 outlines some of these methods and their advantages and disadvantages.

Table 8.1   Learning Methodologies: Advantages and Disadvantages

Method	Advantages	Disadvantages	Tips
Lecture	• Presents large amount of information • Good for large groups • Quickest method • Saves time • Introduces material • Summarizes material	• One-way communication • Can be boring • Not student centered • Passive	• Requires good speaking skills • Must have clear-cut objectives • Should not be longer than 45 minutes in duration • Use realistic examples • Requires deep understanding of material
Demonstration	• Shows the concept • Replicates the task • Easier for officers • Applies to all officers • Easy to perform • Good for small groups	• Requires resources • Can be passive • Requires more time • Can be difficult for some students to see	• Position students and training aids for unobstructed view • Show/explain each step • Do not hurry • Observe safety rules • Check for student comprehension
Games	• Good for icebreaker or review • Makes students forget they are learning something • Relaxes students • Can create a positive learning environment • Good for large to medium groups	• Not always appropriate (know your audience) • May be seen as childish or a waste of time (choose your game wisely) • Can lead to overcompetition	• Make sure the game is appropriate to the audience • Emphasize the goal of the game • Have a prize for the winners
Case studies	• Perfect for examining specific situations • Encourages students to determine appropriate response • Teaches students to apply learned knowledge • Good for medium groups	• Time consuming • Instructor intervention may be necessary • Must be instructor led and controlled	• Give case studies as assignments or supplemental reading • Include a list of questions • Set up group rules for discussion and debriefing

(Continued)

Table 8.1 (Continued)   Learning Methodologies: Advantages and Disadvantages

Method	Advantages	Disadvantages	Tips
Student teach back	• Best for a student to learn a subject • Students learn the value of preparing for unexpected questions • Good for small to medium groups	• Time consuming • Not well suited for short training sessions	• Provide adequate time for preparation and presentations • Must cover all appropriate material • Ensure students realize they are responsible for all of the material covered (not just the topic they present)
Group work	• Officers exchange different ideas • Enhances team building • Encourages officer participation • Promotes problem-solving skills • Good for large to medium groups	• Officer may get off topic • Intensive instructor monitoring of groups • Large groups can lead to passive student involvement	• Instructor is to guide, direct, and monitor officers' performance • Clearly define the purpose of the activity • Set specific time limits and stick to those limits
Role play	• Prepares officers to respond to situations • Every officer takes part in the lesson • Provides vivid experiences • Officers assume active roles • Large to medium groups	• Must be instructor controlled • Should be well scripted • Time consuming • Officers must be willing to play	• Establish ground rules • Maintain safe environment • Debrief
Independent practice	• Identifies each officer's strong and weak areas • Provides for student practice • Good for any size group	• May have to switch to group work if too difficult • Instructor resource intensive	• Present information first, then practice • Instructor should have strong evaluation skills
Reflection	• Assists in transferring skills from the classroom to the real world	• May not always have enough time during the course of this activity	• Use officer information to adjust course (if necessary) to learning objectives

(Continued)

Table 8.1 (Continued)   Learning Methodologies: Advantages and Disadvantages

Method	Advantages	Disadvantages	Tips
Simulation	• Prepares officers to deal with various situations • Enhances problem-solving skills • Reproduces real-life scenarios • Medium to small groups	• Resource intensive	• Be very safety conscious • Make sure equipment is in good working order
Guided learning	• Officers actively involved • Officers internalize and remember the experience better • Medium to small groups	• Instructor resource intensive • Time consuming • Cannot rush officers through the process	• Instructor must master effective questioning skills • Use a variety of instructional media (i.e., handouts, whiteboards, props, etc.)

Death by PowerPoint (and How to Prevent It)

Thousands of PowerPoint presentations are given every day, and many are misused. Those in the business call it "death by PowerPoint." When Microsoft first introduced PowerPoint back in the early 1990s, everyone was amazed at the usefulness of the product. No more slide projector shows. However, more than 20 years later, PowerPoint has become a crutch for instructors. This crutch is attributed to the lack of (1) significance, (2) structure, (3) simplicity, and (4) rehearsal.

What is wrong with PowerPoint? First, it is text based, with six hierarchical levels of chapters and subheads, all words. Humans are visual-based species; we depend a lot on our visual cues (i.e., pictures). Brain researcher John Medina states, "We learn and remember best through pictures, not through written or spoken words" (Medina 2008, p. 240). Multimedia learning is learning from both pictures and words (Mayer 2008). Words can be spoken or in text. Pictures can take the form of a photo, a diagram, a chart, a map, or a video. Mayer (2008) says people learn through multimedia presentations by way of the following elements:

a. **Dual paths**—the notion that humans possess separate paths for processing verbal and visual material.
b. **Limited capacity**—the view that each path can process only a small amount of material at a time.

c. **Active processing**—the notion that deep learning depends on the learner's cognitive processing during learning. As noted in Figure 8.5, you can see how a multimedia presentation is processed in the brain.

This is not to suggest that you should just add pictures to a PowerPoint slide; the pictures have to have relevance to what is being taught. A "decorative visual" added to a slide does nothing to promote learning. Clark (2015) suggests simple visual graphics are often more effective than complex visual graphics. Try not to add any words to a visual that is self-explanatory.

Significance

To find significance to your PowerPoint presentation, you have to ask yourself these questions:

1. What is the purpose of your presentation?
   a. To pass on information?
   b. Your supervisor told you to do it?
   c. The regular instructor is out?
   d. To make *meaning*?
2. What is the subject and why does it *matter* to you?

A presentation is significant if it creates passion. Passion, in turn, attracts attention. Attention leads to action. Then, you must ask yourself: "Am I passionate about the subject matter of my presentation?" If you cannot find *meaning*, then do not present.

Structure

Just like building a house, structure is how you place the framework of your story. What structure to use then? It should be

1. Convincing
2. Memorable
3. Scalable

Here are some PowerPoint structure suggestions:

1. Problem → Pathway → Solution
2. Problem → Solution → Reasoning

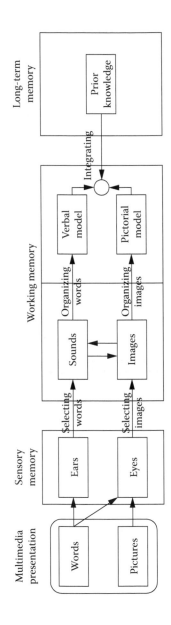

Figure 8.5 Brain processing multimedia. (From Mayer, R. E. et al., *Journal of Educational Psychology*, 93(1), 190, 2001. With permission.)

Try to give just three to four reasons to support your point. Here is an example:

Memorable opening

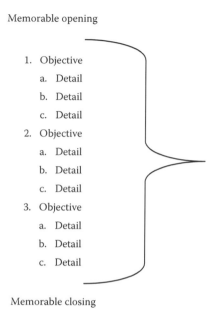

1. Objective
   a. Detail
   b. Detail
   c. Detail
2. Objective
   a. Detail
   b. Detail
   c. Detail
3. Objective
   a. Detail
   b. Detail
   c. Detail

Memorable closing

Simplicity

PowerPoint assists in (1) visualizing ideas, (2) creating key points, and (3) emphasizing a point. It is not a substitute for sound instruction. Here are a few slide design rules:

1. One point per slide
2. Few matching colors
3. Very few fonts
4. Photos, not clipart

In other words, less text and more imagery. Remember your slide presentation is to augment your instruction; it is not your instruction. Some great instructors black out the slide after they have presented it. This helps the officer to focus more on the instructor and not on the slide behind the instructor. Always put yourself in the officers' shoes.

Rehearsal

Perform a dry run of your presentation to fellow instructors and ask for their feedback. Practice, practice, rehearse, practice, revise, practice, edit, practice, rehearse, present.

Marzano's (1998) Nine Instructional Strategies for Effective Teaching and Learning

Researchers at Mid-continent Research for Education and Learning have identified nine instructional strategies that will most likely improve officer learning:

1. Identifying Similarities and Differences

    The ability to break a concept into its similar and dissimilar characteristics allows officers to understand (and often solve) complex problems by analyzing them in a much simpler way. Instructors can either directly present similarities and differences, accompanied by deep discussion and inquiry, or simply ask officers to identify similarities and differences on their own. Research shows that while instructor-led activities focus on identifying specific items, officer-directed activities encourage variation and broaden understanding. Research also notes that graphic forms are a good way to represent similarities and differences.

2. Summarizing and Note Taking

    These skills promote greater comprehension and transfer by asking officers to analyze a subject, expose what is essential, and then put it in their own words. According to research, this requires substituting, deleting, and keeping some things and having an awareness of the basic structure of the information presented. Research also shows that taking more notes is better than taking fewer notes, though verbatim note taking is ineffective because it does not allow time to process the information. Instructors should encourage and give time for review and revision of notes; notes can be the best study guides for tests.

3. Reinforcing Effort and Providing Recognition

    Effort and recognition speak to the attitudes and beliefs of officers, and instructors must show the connection between effort and achievement. Research shows that although not all officers realize the importance of effort, they can learn to change their beliefs to emphasize effort.

4. Homework and Practice

    Homework provides officers with the opportunity to extend their learning outside the classroom. Instructors should explain the purpose of homework to the officers.

5. Nonlinguistic Representations

    According to research, knowledge is stored in two forms: linguistic and visual. The more officers use both forms in the classroom, the more opportunity they have to achieve. Recently, use of nonlinguistic representation has proven to not only stimulate but also increase brain activity.

6. Cooperative Learning

Organizing officers into cooperative groups yields a positive effect on overall learning. When applying cooperative learning strategies, keep groups small and do not overuse this strategy; be systematic and consistent in your approach.

7. Setting Objectives and Providing Feedback

Setting objectives can provide officers with a direction for their learning. Goals should not be too specific; they should be easily adaptable to the officers' own objectives. Feedback generally produces positive results. Instructors can never give too much; however, they should manage the form that feedback takes.

8. Generating and Testing Hypotheses

A deductive approach (using a general rule to make a prediction) to this strategy works best. Whether a hypothesis is induced or deduced, officers should clearly explain their hypotheses and conclusions.

9. Cues, Questions, and Advance Organizers

Cues, questions, and advance organizers help officers use what they already know about a topic to enhance further learning. These tools should be highly analytical, should focus on what is important, and are most effective when presented before a learning experience.

Classroom Management

A classroom can be anywhere. We typically think of the standard classroom with tables, chairs, whiteboard, projector, turn charts, and so on, but it can be outside, with the instructor teaching by means of stick drawing in the dirt. A good instructor can instruct anywhere. In fact, it is a good idea when qualifying an instructor to turn off the electricity and see how the instructor reacts. If the instructor knows his or her material, he or she can easily adapt to the situation.

If the luxury of a classroom is available, put it to good use for learning. Ensure that the whiteboards are prepared and that there are plenty of different color markers (make sure they have ink in them), turn charts are strategically placed, and tables and chairs are set up for learning.

The following is an example of a classroom arrangement procedure:

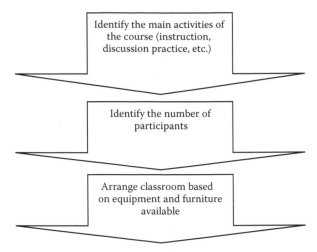

Options for Classroom Management

"CYCLE"

All participants are "equal" and can see each other (Figures 8.6 through 8.8). It is suitable for group discussions and practice with model or real objects. This is the best arrangement for a discussion with 10–12 participants. The instructor is a facilitator (use a table for note taking purposes).

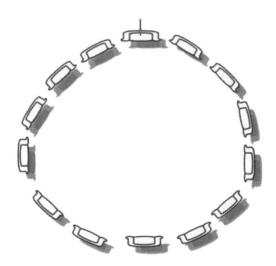

Figure 8.6 Cycle.

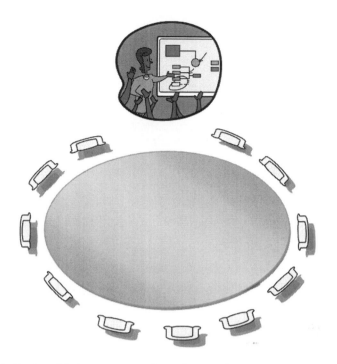

Figure 8.7 Cycle with instructor and teaching aid.

Figure 8.8 Square arrangement.

"FLAT"

This arrangement is usually used in traditional classrooms when teaching and giving lectures. There are blind spots in this arrangement (Figure 8.9).

"CYCLE + FLAT"

Desks are arranged in a U shape. This is good when discussing with the instructor. It is good for microteaching a small group as well (Figure 8.10).

Figure 8.9 Flat arrangement.

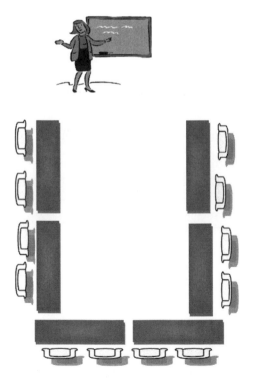

Figure 8.10 Cycle + flat arrangement.

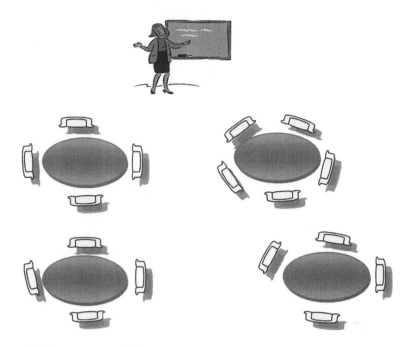

Figure 8.11 Team or collaborative arrangement.

"TEAM" or "COLLABORATIVE"
   The "Team" or "Collaborative" setup is good for team exercises. In this setup, the instructor is more of a facilitator of learning (Figure 8.11).

Managing the Learning Environment

Instructors have an important responsibility to establish and maintain a climate that supports and encourages learning. In order to ensure that the officers have the best possible learning environment, instructors must keep in mind the following during the course duration:

1. Managing group interactions and involving all officers while managing yourself and adapting your delivery to match each officer's needs.
2. Managing time and other environmental issues.
3. Ongoing evaluation of the effectiveness of the instruction.

Strategies to Improve Training Effectiveness with a Focus on Officers

Engagement Strategy

1. Set the tone for training by seizing the officer's attention
   - Provide officers with examples of your own experience.
   - Tell short, interesting stories to boost learning.
   - Introduce relevant facts and statistics that will generate interest and enable you to drive a point home.
   - Ask the officers questions to get them involved and to stimulate interest. Plan these questions, as well as several follow-up questions, in advance.
   - Suggest the benefits officers can expect as a result of the training. Adult learners are more willing to learn and participate when they know what is in it for them.
   - Use props when possible to stir interest and involve more senses (sight, touch, etc.).
   - Lightly use icebreakers to uplift officers, lighten the mood, or help officers get acquainted. Try not to overuse icebreakers; they can wear out quickly.
2. Dealing with difficult officers
   - Remember that prevention is the best cure, so explicitly state your expectations for officer conduct at the beginning of the course or class.
3. Uninvolved officers
   - Ensure you have an environment where everyone feels comfortable in participating.
   - Do not feel as though everyone has to be verbally participating to learn. Some people learn by listening to the experiences and comments of others.
4. Too many questions
   - End a question-and-answer session by stating, "Let's take one more question and move on. If you have more questions, hold them until the end of the class and then see me."
   - Use the turn chart technique (sometimes call the Parking Lot) to write down questions to be addressed later. Tell officers that they can write down more questions during the break.
5. Talking officers
   - Stand close to talkers.
   - Ask them questions.

- Acknowledge their chatter by asking them if they have any questions.
- Shift to an activity that separates the talkers. Approach them during break if the behavior continues; ask them to refrain from talking during class because it is distracting to other officers.
- If all else fails, remove them from the class.

6. Challengers
  - Remember to set expectations up front regarding officer conduct to preempt problems.
  - Clarify and respond to officer challenges regarding why they are there and what they will learn.
  - Approach challengers during a break. Ask them to not disrupt the class and explain that their comments are distracting to other officers. If all else fails, remove them from the class.
  - Do not allow the challenger to frustrate you. You are in control of the class, not them.

7. Know-It-Alls
  - Acknowledge their expertise and ask them to explain concepts or ideas to the group. Make sure their information is accurate; if not, call them on it.
  - Do not allow the know-it-all to prevent other officers from participating. Try to establish a balanced participation.

Effective Questioning Techniques

The use of questions enhances permanent memory retention. It also allows the instructor to assess how much the class is retaining the information. There are two types of questions: open and closed.

Open Questions—these questions have multiple right answers and require more than a short simple answer:

Example: *What are the elements of the Fifth Amendment?*

Closed Questions—these questions have one right answer and can usually be answered with a "yes" or "no" answer.

Example: *Can you unarrest a person?*

There are five forms of questions: overhead, individual, relay, reverse, and rhetorical. Table 8.2 explains each form of questioning and their advantages and disadvantages.

Table 8.2 Effective Questioning Techniques

Type of Question	Explanation of Question Type	Advantages	Disadvantages
Overhead	Question is open for anyone to answer	Full class participation, highest probability of correct answer	Some officers may answer all the questions
Individual	Question is directed at a particular officer	Check for individual understanding, keeps all officers alert	Can place officer on the spot, and if the officer does not know the answer, it can make him or her feel embarrassed
Relay	Question originates from an officer and is relayed to another officer	Great for class participation	Can appear as though the participant does not know the answer
Reverse	Question is thrown back to the asker	Good for "what if" officers	Can appear as though the participant does not know the answer
Rhetorical	Question you do not intend to answer	Gets officers thinking	Can leave some officers confused

Perishable Skills

If you do not use it, you lose it, as the saying goes. All skills delivered in training are perishable to some extent. It depends on how complex the skills are and how often they are used. This is why you will often hear trainers speak of firearms skills as perishable skills; they are not used often and are a complex skill set. These perishable skills need to be kept sharp. Perishable skills are also some of the skills that can get officers into trouble. The following are some key perishable skills officers need to be focused on:

1. Arrest and control techniques
2. Driver training
3. Firearms
4. First responder medical training
5. Legal updates
6. Ethics
7. New procedures or technology (for instance, an agency gets a new communications system)

Creating *Flow* in Training

Mihaly Csíkszentmihályi (1990) developed the concept of *flow* as a state of consciousness where a person performing an activity is fully immersed in the activity and feels energized and focused. This is sometimes referred to by professional athletes as being in the *zone*. Csíkszentmihályi described flow as focused motivation, or as some people call it *hyperfocused*.

The following six factors encompass an experience of flow:

1. Intense and focused concentration on the present moment
2. Merging of action and awareness
3. A loss of reflective *self-consciousness*
4. A sense of personal control or urgency over the situation or activity
5. A distortion of temporal experience; one's subjective experience of time is altered
6. Experience of the activity as intrinsically rewarding, also referred to as autotelic experience (Nakamura and Csíkszentmihályi 2001)

These aspects can appear independently of each other, but only in combination do they constitute a so-called *flow experience*. Additionally, psychology expert Kendra Cherry (2015) has mentioned three other components that Csíkszentmihályi lists as being part of the flow experience:

1. "Immediate feedback"
2. Feeling that you have the potential to succeed
3. Feeling so engrossed in the experience that other needs become negligible

The following are three conditions that have to be met to achieve a flow state:

1. One must be involved in an activity with a clear set of goals and progress. This adds direction and structure to the task.
2. The task at hand must have clear and immediate feedback. This helps officers negotiate any changing demands and allows them to adjust their performance to maintain the flow state.
3. One must have a good balance between the *perceived* challenges of the task at hand and one's own *perceived* skills. One must have confidence in one's ability to complete the task at hand (Csíkszentmihályi et al. 2007).

Figure 8.12 depicts the relationship between the perceived challenges of a task and one's perceived skills. This graph illustrates one further aspect of flow: it is more likely to occur when the activity at hand is a higher-than-average challenge (above the center point) and the officer has above-average skills (to the right of the center point). The center of this graph (where the sectors meet) represents an officer's average levels of challenge and skill across all activities performed by individuals during their daily life. The further

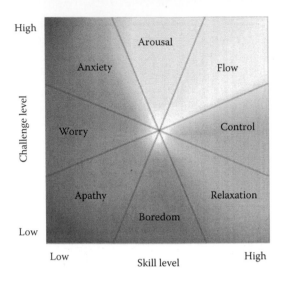

Figure 8.12 Csíkszentmihályi's flow graph. (From Csíkszentmihályi, M., *Finding Flow: The Psychology of Engagement with Everyday Life*. New York: Basic Books, p. 31, 1998. With permission.)

from the center an experience is, the greater the intensity of that state of being (whether it is flow or anxiety or boredom or relaxation).

Conclusion

A lot goes into providing a conducive learning environment for officers, but this does not negate just-in-time learning in the field where the environment may not be the best. Sometimes, you have to work with what you have. What has been illustrated in this chapter is that one should try to optimize and leverage all of the tools necessary to provide a focus on officers and their learning environment.

Field Training and Training Transfer

9

There is a wide array of variables when it comes to training transfer to fieldwork. You may control some of these variables, but for some, you may not have any control over them. This chapter will examine some variables regarding transferring training to the field. This chapter will also look into field training programs (FTPs) and how important they are in enhancing the transfer of training to fieldwork.

All trainers hope their training will transfer to fieldwork, which is the overarching goal of training. However, many trainers will admit it is difficult to achieve this. Why? Training transfer is not simple because of the large amount of variables involved. Some of these variables are outside of the trainer's scope and some are within it (Figure 9.1).

Variables Regarding the Transfer of Training

Performance Self-Efficacy

Self-efficacy could be the most crucial characteristic to an officer's success (Wexley and Latham 2002). Falling under social cognitive theory, self-efficacy can be defined as an officer's belief in his or her ability to achieve under certain situations or, as Bandura (1997) stated, a psychological coping mechanism used to determine how much effort and time will be expended in the face of aversive experiences. Self-efficacy could lead to improved learning and performance (Salas and Cannon-Bowers 2001). The degree of training transfer is higher for officers with high self-efficacy (Merriam and Leahy 2005). Officers who believe they have the capacity to apply training material and skills to their work are more likely to do so.

Studies have supported the importance of officer self-efficacy, including Cannon-Bowers et al. (1995) and their study on US Navy recruit training, which found that recruits who had greater self-efficacy had greater performance than those with lower self-efficacy. Officers with high self-efficacy scored better on both written tests and performance evaluations in a law enforcement training program (Giovengo 2014).

How does self-efficacy develop? These beliefs begin to form in early childhood as children deal with a wide variety of experiences, tasks, and situations. However, the growth of self-efficacy does not end during youth, but

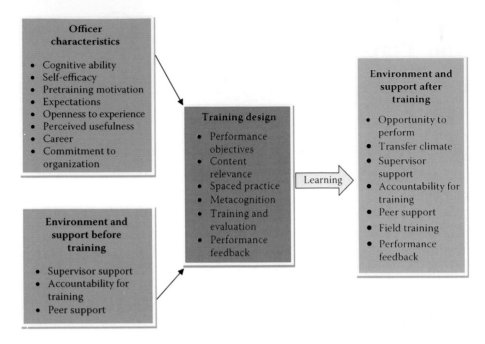

Figure 9.1 Training transfer process.

rather, self-efficacy continues to evolve throughout life as people acquire new skills, experiences, and understanding.

There are four major sources of self-efficacy:

1. **Mastery Experiences**

   "The most effective way of developing a strong sense of efficacy is through mastery experiences," Bandura (1995, p. 3) explained. Performing a task successfully strengthens our sense of self-efficacy. However, failing to adequately deal with a task or challenge can undermine and weaken self-efficacy.

2. **Social Modeling**

   Witnessing other people successfully completing a task is another important source of self-efficacy. According to Bandura (1997), seeing people similar to oneself succeed by sustained effort raises observers' beliefs that they too possess the capabilities of mastering comparable activities to succeed.

3. **Social Persuasion**

   Bandura also asserted that people could be persuaded to believe that they have the skills and capabilities to succeed. Consider a time when someone said something positive and encouraging that helped you achieve a goal. Getting verbal encouragement from others helps people overcome self-doubt and instead focus on giving their best effort to the task at hand.

4. Psychological Responses

Our own responses and emotional reactions to situations also play an important role in self-efficacy. Moods, emotional states, physical reactions, and stress levels can all affect how a person feels about his or her personal abilities in a particular situation. An officer who becomes extremely nervous before speaking in public may develop a weak sense of self-efficacy in these situations. However, Bandura (1997, p. 108) also notes that "it is not the sheer intensity of emotional and physical reactions that is important but rather how they are perceived and interpreted." By learning how to minimize stress and elevate mood when facing difficult or challenging tasks, officers can improve their sense of self-efficacy.

Perceived Utility/Value

Perceived utility or value can influence transfer of training (Burke and Hutchins 2007). Several variables may come into play during an officer's training evaluation:

a. Ease (or difficulty) of skill transfer
b. Belief that the new skills will improve their performance
c. Credibility of the learned skills to improving performance
d. Recognition of the need to improve workplace performance (Burke and Hutchins 2007; Ruona et al. 2002)

To maximize transfer, officers should recognize that newly learned material would improve their work performance. In their meta-analysis of training criteria, Baldwin and Ford (1988) found that trainee *utility* reactions were significant with the transfer of training more so than the trainees' emotional reaction. There is a relationship between motivation to learn and trainee reaction to perceived training transfer, and that motivation to learn is also related to job attitude and improved job competency of perceived training transfer at work (Ng and Ahmad 2012). An officer's perceptions of the value of training, as related to their career goals, were more motivated to learn. Training has an influence over the trainees' goals and expectations of training (Nikandrou et al. 2009).

In contrast, there could be a perceived *barrier* to training transfer. When officers perceive possible barriers, they can become frustrated, thus lowering their motivation to learn and put forth effort, diverging from the perceived value of officers being more motivated (Klein et al. 2006; Mathieu et al. 1992).

Career/Job Variables

Job variables are linked to transfer of training; the greater the task is identified to the job, the higher the motivation to learn. Similarly, Noe and Schmitt (1986) found that officers with high job attachment were more motivated to transfer trained skills to the work environment. The expectancy theory could be utilized in two different levels that are linked to career/job variables. First, if the officer believes his or her efforts will result in learning that can be used for the job, the application of new job skills will have extrinsic or intrinsic rewards. Second, the officer believes that he or she can enhance his or her performance as well as that of the organization (Kontoghiorghes 2004).

Transfer and Organizational Climate

Life outside the training environment is a reality, and research over the last 20 years shows the various factors outside the training environment that have an influence on work performance (Bates and Khasawneh 2005; Kontoghiorghes 2008; Martin 2010; Ruona et al. 2002). Work climate was originally identified by Baldwin and Ford (1988) and then again by Ford and Weissbein (1997) as a factor that influences training transfer. Transfer climate concerns situations in an organization that both enable and hinder what has been learned during training (Rouiller and Goldstein 1993). A supportive work climate is more likely to enhance transfer of training material from the training program to the work environment (Noe and Schmitt 1986). Hedden (2011), in his commentary about law enforcement training, stated that training transfer often fails because of the work environment being inconsistent with training.

Rouiller and Goldstein (1993) identified "situational cues" that served to remind officers of their training, giving the officer an opportunity to utilize their training (p. 383). The cues they identified were goal cues, social cues, and task cues. Goal cues remind officers to use their training in the workplace. Social cues arise from behavioral influences exhibited by peer groups, supervisors, and subordinates. Social cues come from the self-regulation process. Task cues involve the nature and design of the job itself.

Work environment factors are divided into two categories: people-related and work systems factors. Work systems include a change climate, open communications, organization commitment for training transfer, opportunity to use new skills in the workplace, and the match between training and organizational goals (Rouiller and Goldstein 1993). People-related factors include peer support and supervisory support, positive personal outcomes, and mentor availability. This is why FTPs are so important to the transfer of training process.

Organizational culture can predict transfer climates and can affect innovative capacity within an organization (Bates and Khasawneh 2005). Cultural climate can influence self-efficacy beliefs and change attitudes and performance outcomes. Officers observe their work environment and ask whether training really matters to their organization (Tannenbaum et al. 1993).

Opportunity to Perform

Research has strongly supported that a lack of opportunity to perform can be a serious barrier to training transfer. Several factors affect an officer's opportunity to perform on the job, including the opportunity to practice trained tasks on the job (Wexley and Latham 2002). The level of training transfer of officers is greatly affected if they have not been given the opportunity to practice on the job (Yamnill and McLean 2002). Officers using their newly trained skills (vs. those with a lack of opportunity) have the highest form of support (Gilpin-Jackson and Bushe 2007). Another barrier to ability to perform was heavy workload, as identified by Gitonga (2006). The strongest barrier to training transfer was the limited opportunity to utilize training; supervisors need to give officers the opportunity to perform new skills (Clarke 2002).

Agencies have a vested interest that officers transfer their trained knowledge to the workplace. In their study of employees undergoing training, Baldwin and Magjuka (1991) found that accountability in using newly trained skills sends a message to officers that their new skills are valued by the agency. They found accountability to be closely related to rewards or sanctions based on performance. Baldwin and Magjuka (1991) also found many organizations do not hold their officers accountable for their learning. If the training is not evaluated, it could be perceived that it was of low importance to the organization. In her research on training professionals with the American Society of Training and Development, Hutchins (2009) found trainers believed that linking training outcomes to performance appraisals (an accountability measure) is important to training transfer.

Barriers to the Transfer of Training

There can be a multitude of barriers that prevent transfer of training to the job. You may have control over some of these, but not over other barriers. Here are some barriers to the transfer of training outlined by Biech (2005):

1. It is difficult for older officers to change their behavior; thus, they revert to old habits.
2. Peer pressure back at the job may inhibit officers from using their new skills.

3. The officers' supervisors may not understand the new skill set the officers have and, therefore, do not encourage or support them.
4. Further, the supervisors may not agree with the needs or behaviors officers have and, therefore, may try to undermine them.
5. The supervisors may be poor role models for the officers and their new skill set.
6. The culture of the agency may punish the officers with their new skill sets.

This underscores how important the selection and training of field training officers (FTOs) are to the transfer of training.

Tips for Effective Transfer: A Proposed Model

Belair (2012) offers a new model of transfer in light of the difficulties outlined in past research. On the basis of the proposed model of transfer, here are some useful points she recommends for promoting transfer:

- **Extend stakeholders beyond trainers, trainees, and supervisors:** Although peer support has proven in the past to enhance the effects of transfer on officers, new research has shown peer support as being significantly influential on the effects of transfer (Burke and Hutchins 2008). Peer collaboration, networking, and the sharing of ideas relating to the content can act as support for skill transfer in officers (Hawley and Barnard 2005). Further, consider the agency itself as a major stakeholder. The organization's "transfer climate" can directly influence training transfer results. Whether the organization values training can have a direct impact on officer performance (Awoniyi et al. 2004). Many times, the department views training as something an officer has to go through without placing any relevance on the training the officer just received.
- **Extend beyond the classic before, during, and after evaluation of transfer:** It is important to consider that transfer is not necessarily time bound (Burke and Hutchins 2008). Put simply, the transfer problem is not rooted in a specific time phase and, thus, its remedies should not be either. Provide support for transfer throughout the duration of the transfer process and not solely at specific time phases. This can be done by FTO programs.
- **Consider trainer characteristics and evaluation as influential factors:** Officer characteristics, the design and delivery of the training, and the environment all have been considered as influential factors that may inhibit or support transfer. Consider incorporating expressions in the

delivery of the content and ensure that the content is well organized. Further, incorporate assessment of transfer from the perspective of the officer, the trainer, and the organization. This helps create an environment that values and supports learning (Bates 2003).

- **Include moderating variables:** Consider the size (small, medium, or large) of the agency. These factors may have a direct effect on the training department and the way in which transfer is evaluated (Burke and Hutchins 2008). Although the ambition to create a perfect training transfer model is admirable, the fact remains that transfer is nothing short of complex. That said, in order to provide for optimal effectiveness of training for transfer, it is essential that all aspects of training be garnered into a manageable practice.

Field Training Programs

A system in place that enhances training transfer for law enforcement is the FTP. The strength of any agency's training program lies in the FTP. The FTP is an extension of the academy. The FTP is a true measurement of what was actually learned in the academy and an efficient gauge of training transfer. Doerner et al. (2003) have this to say about FTO programs:

> The FTO program represents a critical juncture for both the agency and the incoming personnel. The agency wants to put only well-qualified officers on the streets. As far as the recruits are concerned, this period is an "acid test." It is the first time the aspirant gets to try the job and see if it fits. (p. 209)

Many agencies do not believe they need an FTP because of the "we hire the best" attitude. This is a very wrong assumption. Here is a real example. A law enforcement agency hires another special agent from another well-known agency that has 15 years of experience with the previous agency. The new agency has a field training and evaluation program (FTEP), but the agency is hesitant in placing this 15-year veteran into the FTEP believing he already has "experience." Even the new agent's FTO is expressing doubt in placing this agent into the FTEP, saying that this new agent has more experience than he does. They all fail to realize that this agent's 15 years of experience was with another agency; this new agency has different laws, a different mission, and a different environment in which it works. At the training manager's insistence, they put this 15-year veteran into the FTEP.

Approximately a month into the FTEP, the FTO calls the training manager about a problem with this "experienced" agent. The FTO says this veteran agent has difficulty confronting suspects. He says this agent could not handle face-to-face confrontation. The situation gets so bad that the agency began to take steps to fire this experienced agent for his poor job performance. Eventually, this new agent goes back to his old agency. It was later found out this experienced agent had spent a good majority of his career doing white-collar fraud cases and rarely confronted suspects. The FTEP did its job; it located and documented poor performance and lack of training transfer.

There also should be a modified version of an FTP for newly promoted supervisors. Many times, field officers are promoted to supervisor based on the quality of work they did as a field officer. However, the agency may not provide any supervisor training, or they have supervisor training but fail to monitor how the new supervisor uses his or her new supervisor skill sets. The realization here is being a supervisor requires a different set of skills from a field officer. If no supervisor training or monitoring is provided to new supervisors, then supervisors may tend to believe that *their* way is the only correct way of being a good field officer since they were promoted based on *their* fieldwork. This will lead to a world of trouble to the organization.

There is a need for careful selection and training when it comes to choosing an FTO. It would be best to have your star performers as your FTOs. The FTO is the true introduction to the agency and the culture of the agency.

Models of Field Training

Field Training and Evaluation Program

There are basically two models of FTPs in existence. The most noted is the traditional FTEP, referred to as the San Jose model, since the program originated from the San Jose Police Department in 1970. The impetus of this program grew in the early 1960s when the California Commission on Peace Officer Standards and Training started a training academy that included a new officer-training checklist. San Jose became involved when an incompetent new officer caused a two-car collision where a citizen was killed. The investigation on the accident revealed that the new officer had a record of poor driving habits that went undocumented. Robert Allen, Michael Roberts, and others over time developed a 14-week FTEP, which was to be conducted after an officer graduated from the academy. The new officer is assigned a trained FTO who oversees the daily progression of the new officer on the job. Generally, there are three phases the new officer progresses through. The first phase is like an observation phase where the new officer watches how the FTO performs his or her work. The second phase is more of a blended phase where both the new officer and the FTO perform some work together. In the final phase, the new officer does almost all of the work while the FTO observes the new officer. There are daily observation reports that are completed at the end of each shift by a trained FTO using a 1–7 Likert scale.

This model has withstood many court cases and is considered the gold standard for field training. Here are some solid reasons why an FTEP has to be conducted:

- A court-approved procedure, within Equal Employment Opportunity Commission (EEOC) Guidelines, for dealing with affirmative action issues is provided.
- Increased support for management and administrative policies.
- Negligent hiring and retention, training, and supervision issues are reduced.
- The cost of training is controlled in that nonqualified persons are not retained by the agency.
- Standardization of training and evaluation procedure is established.
- Individual competency is identified for promotional purposes; before getting promoted, line personnel practice supervisory skills.
- Another career path is available to the line officer.
- Line officers become more involved in decision making and work in a participative environment.
- The probationary officer assimilates job skills more rapidly with FTO guidance.
- FTOs become more capable, knowledgeable, and cautious as a result of their role model responsibilities.

Police Training Officer Program

For decades, the San Jose model stood as the only proven model for field training new officers. However, in 2003, a new FTP called the Police Training Officer Program (PTOP), sometimes referred to as the Reno Model, was introduced. The original design of this model makes it one of the newest law enforcement training innovations in decades. This new approach has been regarded as the foundation for lifelong learning that prepares new officers for the complexities of policing.

The PTOP flexibility allows future changes in policing to be easily incorporated. An important long-term benefit to the agency is the further institutionalization of community policing and problem solving. The PTOP was first tested in the Reno Police Department and subsequently tested by several other agencies. The PTOP model was developed to create an FTO program based on Bloom's Taxonomy (Rushing 2010). The PTO is a good fit for Generation X and Millennial police officers (Scott 2010).

As outlined in *A Problem-Based Learning Manual for Training and Evaluating Police Trainees* (Office of Community Oriented Policing Services 2004), a new officer is assigned a trained PTO. There are five phases in the PTOP: an Integration Phase, a Non-Emergency Incident Response Phase, an Emergency Incident Response Phase, a Patrol Activities Phase, and a Criminal Investigation Phase. The trainee has one problem-based learning (PBL) exercise during each phase of training. The PTO and the trainee each keep a daily journal of their activities. At the end of each week, there is a coaching session between the FTO and the new officer and a training report.

What is unique to this program is its use of the adult learning theory of PBL. *The Problem-Based Learning Manual for Training and Evaluating Police Trainees* (Office of Community Oriented Police Services 2004) describes the PTO's objectives:

- To formulate learning opportunities for new officers that meet or exceed the training needs of the policing agency and the expectations of the community.
- To have officers apply their academy learning to the community environment by giving them real-life problem-solving activities.
- To foster the officer's growing independence from the PTO over the course of the program.
- To produce graduates of the training program who are capable of providing responsible, community-focused police services.
- To prepare officers to use a problem-solving approach throughout their careers by employing PBL methods.
- To design fair and consistent evaluations that address an officer's skills, knowledge, and ability to problem solve effectively.

Both of these models have their strengths and weaknesses as outlined below:

FTEP
- Time and court tested
- Strong familiarity in the law enforcement community
- Great documentation system
- Can be somewhat inflexible
- Has not had any modern upgrades since inception
- Is rooted in the behaviorist (Skinner) approach to learning

PTOP
- Not time or court tested, but getting there.
- New officers are better able to think creatively, act autonomously, and solve problems with their communities.
- Linked very closely to community policing, which may not work as well with state or federal law enforcement agencies.

- Officers are empowered to ask questions and search for nontraditional solutions knowing they have the latitude to do so (Rushing 2010).
- Uses a modern adult learning model, which can appear a little too "touchy feely" in the law enforcement environment.
- Is rooted in the constructivist (Piaget) approach to learning.

Obviously, an agency that already has an FTEP would have to retool the entire training program (materials, training, etc.) if it wants to switch from an FTEP to a PTOP. This would entail a high front-end cost to the agency. Either way, there is nothing to lose and a whole lot to gain by having either of these two FTPs.

Conclusion

There are a substantial number of variables when it comes to the actual transfer of training to the workplace. Some of these variables fall outside of the training division. Some of these variables are organizational issues that have to be addressed by the managers of the agency. It is good for a training manager to know these variables when management complains about training not working. Many times, failure of training transfer is linked to other variables outlined in this chapter. Take, for instance, when a new officer meets his FTO for the first time, and the FTO says to the new officer, "Forget all that stuff they taught you at the academy. I'm going to show you how to work in the 'real world.'" That statement causes cognitive dissonance in the new officer. The new officer now starts to question what he or she was taught at the academy. Studies show that the power of an FTO outweighs what the new officer was taught at the academy. Therefore, the FTOs and the academy must be in alignment on what is conveyed to the new officer.

Distance Training 10

Words of Caution

For law enforcement agencies, efficiency and effectiveness are critical, and law enforcement agencies have been slow to embrace technology to maximize both effectiveness and efficiency. There are many ways technology has been introduced to the law enforcement training environment. These may include a combination of different technological methods. First, this chapter will give you some basic ideas and pointers about distance learning. Volumes of books have been written on distance learning alone, and the field is currently evolving. Before embarking on any e-training platform, there are some words of caution that need to be heeded. Many people think e-training is a great way to save money on training. This can be a wrong assumption. E-training can cost more money on the front end than regular training. The cost of design, development, implementation, and evaluation is substantially more than that of regular training. First, you have to have subject-matter experts (SMEs) that have a thorough understanding of the many e-training platforms. These people have distinct skills that are slightly different from your normal curriculum and instruction staff. Putting a PowerPoint on steroids and placing it on the web is *not* e-training. Much more detail is needed in the e-training platform in contrast to the dynamics of classroom learning. Also, forget the assumption that the "younger" generation will fully embrace e-learning because they have been raised around computers. Studies show that unless your e-training is designed to meet the standards of modern-day video games, the younger generation loses interest faster in e-learning platforms.

Technology is changing the face of law enforcement training and instructional practices, ranging from online asynchronous instruction to the use of advanced virtual reality simulations (Pellegrino and Scott 2004). Although there are new instructional practices as a result of technology, there is no guarantee of technology success in the law enforcement training environment (Bonk and Wisher 2000). We have to be cautious when planning instruction solely on technology that we do not ignore the psychology of human learning (Clark 2015). However, there is little doubt that technology is restructuring conceptions on learning and presents new opportunities to provide a complete self-directed learning experience (Knowles et al. 2005).

Stressed training budgets cause a serious examination of converting classroom training to e-training. Training professionals can find improved efficiencies in e-training; they can also find ways to meet other important agency needs such as getting on-demand training to employees or delivering training to widely scattered workforces. What is important is that agencies fully understand the forces driving them to consider the conversion process in the first place, and the factors will likely be different from agency to agency (Osborn 2011). The following are some business reasons for converting from classroom training to e-training:

1. **Costs**—examining travel, facilities, and materials (more on this later in this chapter).
2. **Geographically dispersed workforce** (especially true in state and federal agencies).
3. **Consistent message**—some types of training such as legal updates or new employee orientation can be converted to an e-training format that is consistent every time it is delivered (Osborn 2011).

Today's officers have been conditioned to seek and absorb knowledge in ways that would have seemed impossible just a few years ago. Google, YouTube, Wikipedia, and voice-activated applications, such as Apple's Siri and Microsoft's Cortana, have created a lot of officers who seek information just in time and, very often, in ways that take advantage of social connections. They want information on their own terms, both personally and professionally. Also, more often than not, they do not seek that information via face-to-face interactions—they leverage the electronic media with which they are so comfortable. Training professionals must keep abreast of the needs of today's talent pool or risk falling into irrelevancy in the workplace.

The types of training that can be somewhat easy to convert to e-training are as follows:

- **On-boarding.** New employee on-boarding can be great content to convert into e-learning, because some of the learning is purely cognitive in nature. In other words, you want to know whether the training participant comprehends basic information such as the location of policy manuals on your system, or you want to find out the remaining vacation or personal days on their pay stub. This sort of pure cognitive learning objective is ideally suited to e-learning.
- **New policies or updates.** New policy releases create a range of challenges for officer training. Frequently, new policy launches require many officers to have immediate access to accurate information.

Obviously, waiting for everyone to have the free time to attend a classroom session might not be realistic. Thus, e-training can be an excellent solution for the rapid development and deployment of new training content to large numbers of officers on a short timeline.

- **Compliance.** Training many compliance subjects can be a great blended learning opportunity. For instance, if you have to provide ethics training on a new set of rules and regulations, an e-training course might be a perfect vehicle for teaching large numbers of officers the basics of the rules and regulations. E-training will work very well to deliver this content and allow you an opportunity to test for basic comprehension. You can use platforms such as GoToMeeting to provide opportunities for in-depth group conversations around the complicated changes sometimes associated with new rules and regulations.
- **Safety training.** For most safety training sessions, officers need to leave the classroom with knowledge of some specific equipment or procedures. These types of purely cognitive learning objectives work very well in an e-training course. You can deliver content, provide ongoing access to the materials, and allow officers to print any job aids or written materials they might need or want to reinforce the learning. You can also use tests, assessments, or quizzes to ensure comprehension of the safety rule or equipment.

Cost of Utilizing Technology

The cost design and development of an e-learning platform can be contrasted from design and development times shown in Table 6.11. Kapp and Defelice (2009) also compared traditional training times to distance learning design and development times. The results of their comparison are shown in Table 10.1.

The increase of time for e-training is mainly based on the lack of understanding between SMEs and the design and developers of the e-training platform. Remember the classroom has to be recreated into electronic media. More importantly, lack of understanding or even lack of compatible technology between SMEs, training managers, and instructional system designers (IDSer) is a barrier to e-training. Clear communication with all stakeholders is key to any e-training design and development.

When converting classroom training to an e-training platform, you still have to go through the analysis, design, development, implementation, and evaluation (ADDIE) process. An effective and informative needs analysis requires you to identify several very important pieces of information starting with the primary reason for changing this specific training content from an instructor-led class to an e-training course. For instance, you may be offering leadership development sessions that last 3 days. Your agency is finding the

Table 10.1   Allocation of Training Times for Distance versus Traditional Development

Type of Training (per 1 Hour of Finished Instruction)	Most Experienced Design and Developer (per 1 Hour of Instruction)	Minimum Experienced Design and Developer (per 1 Hour of Instruction)
Traditional Design and Development of Instruction		
Stand-up training	43 hours	70 hours
Self-instructional print	80 hours	125 hours
Instructor-led web-based training delivery	49 hours	89 hours
E-learning *without* a Template		
Text-only; limited interactivity; no animations	93 hours	153 hours
Moderate interactivity; limited animations	122 hours	186 hours
High interactivity; multiple animations	154 hours	243 hours
E-learning *with* a Template (i.e., Lectora, Captivate, WebEx, Storyline)		
Limited interactivity, no animations	118 hours	365 hours
Moderate interactivity; limited animations	90 hours	240 hours
High interactivity; multiple animations	136 hours	324 hours

Source: Reprinted with permission from Kapp, K. M. & Defelice, R. A. (August 31, 2009). *Time to Develop One Hour of Training.* American Society for Training and Development.

disruption to operations to be significant. A very good reason for converting 2 days of the training into an e-learning course could be to minimize the operational disruption by reducing the out-of-office time for the training from 3 days to 1 day.

E-training needs to be performance focused and have a meaningful context to officers. E-training is engagement driven with authentic contexts. E-training needs to provide realistic decision models and individualized challenges. Finally, e-training should be spaced practiced with real-world consequences. Therefore, here are some thoughts about e-training:

1. *Do not assume that e-training is the solution.* Performance issues may be addressed by other means other than e-training.
2. *Provide realistic practice.* Simulations, scenario-based training, and so on need to be incorporated into an e-training platform, and the designs of these training methods are a big cost in e-training.

3. *Provide guidance and feedback.* The e-training officers need guidance and feedback to reinforce their comprehension and develop effective performance skills.
4. *Provide realistic consequences.* During performance feedback, the officers will need a sense of real-world consequences.
5. *Adapt to officers' needs.* Employ the capability of e-training to create a learning environment that is flexible and adaptive to the officers' needs.
6. *Motivate meaningful involvement.* Provide officers with a training experience that is relevant to their goals and motivate them to engage in the process of learning.
7. *Use interactivity to trigger deep engagement.* E-training should support application rehearsal, reflection, debate, synthesis, and evaluation, not just page clicking, rollovers, navigation, and memorization.
8. *Provide support for posttraining evaluation.* Support instruction with the appropriate blend of after-training follow-up, providing venues that reinforce key learning points, collect supervisory support for learning application, and generate mechanisms that enable further on-the-job learning.
9. *Sustain performance preparation.* E-training officers need to be motivated to apply what they have learned, immunized against obstacles, and prepared to deal with specific situations.

Digital Natives versus Digital Immigrants

In Chapter 8, we touched upon training for generational differences. This really becomes an issue when setting up distance training. A "digital native" belongs to the group of officers born during the last 35 years (X'ers and Millennials). Digital Natives identify with, value, and trust technology. These officers are always checking their "wireless" smartphone or tablet for information, social contacts, and so on. On the other hand, a Digital Immigrant (mainly Boomers) has had to adapt to technology as it has evolved into their lives. Digital Immigrants do things like ask people into their office to see a website versus sending them the URL through instant messaging. They tend to print out material to edit it versus just editing it on a screen. Hence, be cautious when you place a Digital Immigrant teaching a Digital Native.

Prensky (2001) reported that Digital Native college graduates have spent less than 5000 hours of their lives reading, but more than 10,000 hours playing video games, excluding 20,000 hours watching TV. That number is probably higher today. Digital Natives prefer graphics over text and are savvy multitaskers. Currently, Millennials are driving the distance training wave.

Guiding Principles

Here are some basic guiding principles when it comes to distance training:

1. **Technology is not the only medium of distance learning.**
   Technology is just one aspect of distance training. You do not want to focus too much on just the technology side of things.

2. **Distance training must match officer needs.**
   Not all officers are suited for distance training. Some officers still prefer traditional forms of training. Further, not all training can be placed into distance training. Psychomotor skills are very difficult to evaluate in a distance learning platform. A brain surgeon still has to perform brain surgery on a real brain.

3. **Instructors are vital to distance training.**
   Very few officers can truly learn with no instructors involved to facilitate the learning process. For distance training, instructors have to be trained on how to deliver instruction via a distance-training format. It is quite different from being in a classroom.

4. **Officer support is critical.**
   This will be touched on more a little later in this chapter, but distance training needs support especially regarding its technical aspects.

5. **Interaction and feedback is essential.**
   Just like traditional training, feedback from instructors is critical to distance training.

6. **A vast amount of planning is required.**
   There are a lot of moving parts in distance training, such as technology, administrative, and support involved in distance training, including infrastructure. Many distance-training programs take a minimum of 6 months to develop, and many times much, much longer.

7. **Instructional design is just as important as it is for traditional training.**
   The design of a distance-training program is critical to success. Instructional designers with subject matter expertise are essential to quality distance training design.

8. **A team approach is necessary.**
   There are many specific tasks and skills necessary to creating a quality distance-training program; thus, a team approach is critical.

9. **Officers must be highly motivated.**
   For officers to succeed in a distance-training program, it is very important that they are highly motivated. As mentioned earlier,

distance training is not for everyone; hence, it is important that your distance-learning officers want to learn from a distance-learning format.

10. **Distance training is complex and difficult.**

It is common to underestimate the difficulty and complexity of developing distance-training programs. It requires not only a high level of commitment but also a considerable amount of expertise that many law enforcement academies just do not have.

Distance Training Models

Bielawski and Metcalf (2003) outlined several different ways technology is used, such as synchronous e-training (which is an instructor-facilitated learning environment conducted in a virtual classroom with all participants present) or asynchronous e-training (meaning the training will be self-paced, with very little instructor involvement) (Table 10.2).

Synchronous Training Model

Benefits
- Humanizes the classroom
- Higher level of motivation
- Sense of immediacy
- Social learning
- More interactive
- Instructional pacing

Disadvantages
- Not flexible in time
- More costly
- More difficult to coordinate

There is also an asynchronous e-learning environment, which is a self-paced non–instructor-led virtual class.

Asynchronous Training Model

Benefits
- Increased flexibility
- Synthesis of concepts

Disadvantages
- Lack of motivation

Table 10.2   Synchronous/Asynchronous E-Training

Synchronous	Asynchronous
• Have an agenda	• Set discussion expectation and guidelines
• Break up the presentation into bite-sized chunks	• Keep it organized using threaded discussions
• Stick to one topic or purpose at a time	• Facilitator summarizes key points and sends them out to the participants
• Summarize key points	

- Less interaction
- Isolation

Finally, there is the blended learning environment, which has both a synchronous and/or an asynchronous e-learning portion and an instructor-led resident portion of the class.

Blended Training

Blended training (BT) is sometimes referred to as "hybrid" or "mixed mode." BT is a learning environment that combines face-to-face instruction or facilitation with synchronous or asynchronous e-learning utilizing many different technologies of delivery (i.e., computer, smartphone, or electronic tablet) (Graham 2006). The contrast between the two modalities can appear somewhat extreme. For instance, face-to-face traditional classroom is an instructor-led, trainee-to-trainee interaction in a live high-fidelity environment, versus distance learning that emphasizes a self-paced, asynchronous, low-fidelity environment (Graham 2006). Many organizations choose a BT format for three reasons: (a) increased access/flexibility, (b) improved androgogy, and (c) increased cost-effectiveness (Graham et al. 2005).

BT may be considered the "best of both worlds"; it can also provide the least of both worlds if not well designed (Graham 2006, p. 9). For example, the online portion can suffer if very large amounts of information are made available for officers to grasp independently (Waddoups and Howell 2002). However, there is some emerging evidence that BT can increase course achievement.

Distance Learning Stages

A good portion of the design and development content is very similar to that of traditional training through the ADDIE process. However, with distance learning, you have other variables to consider:

- What type of hardware or software will be needed to deliver the training? There are a multitude of issues such as processors, graphic cards, Internet speed, bandwidth, and so on that have to be addressed.
- Is your training going to be synchronous (meaning live with an instructor and all officers present at the same time) or asynchronous (meaning the training will be self-paced, with very little instructor involvement)?
- What type of support services is your distance learning going to have in case there is a problem?
- Training needs to be evaluated; how are you going to address online assessments?
- What is your budget?

A comprehensive predesign analysis will reveal details about the audience, performance requirements, tasks, and training requirements. These details are critical for an accurate estimate of level of effort and to ensure the solution meets performance goals. If a contractor is employed, these details are also critical to a quality statement of work.

As you collect predesign analysis data or prepare to begin design, it is important to keep in mind the differences between a physical and a digital environment. The facilitated training environment, like those provided by resident training and on-the-job training, provides adaptive features difficult to replicate in asynchronous instruction. In the facilitated environment, assessments and activities can consider subjective measurements and provide adaptive feedback. This subjective measurement and adaptive feedback are the greatest strengths of the facilitated environment.

The digital environment is not the physical environment. Familiarity with the unique strengths and weaknesses provided by the digital environment can create strong alignments in expectations. These alignments will result in well-defined requirements and accurate objectives. Well-defined requirements and objectives will likely lead to well-designed solutions. The transition from a physical to a digital environment is one of the toughest challenges for a traditional trainer or training designer and the officer. This is the main reason for hiring people, or contracting, with subject matter expertise on designing and developing a distance learning course.

Technical Testing

Technical testing evaluates technical compatibility and function. The following elements will be evaluated during technical testing:

Runtime Functionality

- Does the product meet functionality requirements?
- Does the product load to the learning management system (LMS) and trigger completion?
- Do screens load in a reasonable time and provide load feedback?
- Do all features work?
- Do all links work? (Links have a tendency to break in Internet-based systems, like Microsoft's SharePoint)

Runtime Packaging

- Is the packaging logical?
- Does the package contain very large files?
- Does the package contain redundant or unnecessary files?

The technical test also includes criteria to evaluate the user experience. The following elements will be evaluated during usability testing:

- Clarity of communication
- Logical navigation flow

Can you start to see how the language is different regarding distance learning versus traditional training? To be done correctly, an agency needs to put considerable thought before launching into an e-training venue.

Implementing E-Training

You can build an excellent e-learning course, but if none of the officers access and complete the course, your great work will not have the impact you intended. Adults are generally very receptive to learning on the job, but you have to be able to explain to your officers some fundamental things about the e-training you are asking them to complete. As noted earlier in this book, adults will gravitate to training when they see and appreciate the relevance of the training to the performance of their jobs. Adults also learn best when they exercise autonomy over the pace of their training. Thus, as you plan to implement your course, here are some factors you want to ensure are included:

- Inform officers how successfully completing the training can help them with their jobs.
- Provide clear expectations for completion of the training while providing officers control and substantial choices about how they will manage their schedules to complete the course.
- Articulate the goals of the training.
- Demonstrate respect for your officers in your messaging and expectations.

Generally, you will need to start your internal marketing efforts before you give officers access to the e-learning course. A big part of your challenge is to effectively lead the change from classroom delivery to e-learning. Officers react to change in a variety of ways, and your marketing plans need to take into account the different ways and amount of time officers need to embrace something new. Identify your officers who are most likely to be early adopters of e-learning. Develop messages for these officers that are designed to get them into the course quickly and find ways to capture their feedback and share that information.

Electronic Performance Support Solutions

An Electronic Performance Support Solution (EPSS) is a packaged (self-contained) digital task support resource. The EPSS unifies relevant support and reference information, media, and guidance at a single, accessible point, organized in a logical and consistent structure. The provision of too little or too much information can cause a significant decrease in performance. A well-designed EPSS will provide just enough information to perform the tasks considered.

Who Is the Audience for an EPSS?

EPSS and job aids can successfully span multiple officer states and levels of expertise. Performance support tools are built to increase productivity, improve task accuracy, and enable performance from day 1, with minimal training and regardless of the previous experience of the officer.

EPSS can provide ready task support regardless of formal training availability. EPSS can be a principal complement to a structured field-training program. EPSS will generally have lower sustainment costs than resident training, particularly considering the reach of the EPSS. EPSSs are designed to provide "just enough" orientation and task support to successfully accomplish tasks at the work environment before training. EPSS supports the knowledge and skills gained in training by providing consistent and familiar resources once the officer has returned to work.

Do Performance Support Tools Stand Alone?

Performance support tools can serve as a powerful foundation or complement to a training program and can potentially reduce costs and enable wider exposure to practical activities and coaching opportunities in the classroom. EPSS can also pair well with field training activities and tasks that are not performed frequently.

By design, performance support tools provide a bridge between the technical data that support the system, the concepts that support the application of skills, and the contexts that the officer is likely to encounter when performing a task. The task support and expertise development resources provided by a well-designed EPSS could provide a powerful complement to authoritative guides for field training resources. EPSS is intended to accelerate skill acquisition and expertise development while reducing the demand on the field training officer's time for new or infrequently performed tasks.

Conclusion

Distance training has its advantages and disadvantages. Distance training is a perfect fit for supplementing traditional training. However, distance training can be a very expensive endeavor, if it is going to be designed to have elements of training transfer. EPSS is a great augment to any field training program.

High-Risk Training

11

One of the shortest distances between safety and peril is ignorance.

Ken Murray
Training at the Speed of Life, Volume 1

Introduction

On Friday, October 15, 2010, Petty Officer 3rd Class Shaun Lin, 23, of New York fell from a ladder into the James River while attempting to transfer from a Maritime Safety and Security Team 25-foot small boat to the Coast Guard Cutter Frank Drew during a law enforcement training exercise in the vicinity of the Monitor-Merrimac Bridge Tunnel. His body was recovered the next day in 68°F water near the tunnel. Unfortunately, a story like this one happens much too often. How many times have you heard about an officer shot with a real bullet during a training exercise? These accidents are avoidable with proper screening and precautions.

When it comes to designing and developing high-risk training (HRT), you must realize there are elements of fear an officer may have about the training. As reiterated throughout this book, practicing a skill should consist of allowing the officer to overcome his or her fear by progressive familiarization with the performance. This is especially important in HRT. The training situation should be designed so the officer can perform components of the performance in a relatively risk-free situation, and increase the riskiness of his/her performances as he/her builds confidence.

As the adage goes, "Train how you fight" implies to make training as realistic as possible. The best training is the training that maintains a high level of realism. When an officer's brain has a high level of stimulation, it is when the greatest level of learning occurs. Of course, there are portions of a law enforcement officer's job that are high risk. From the basic traffic stop to high-level SWAT operations, there are degrees of risk involved in training. Obviously, risk cannot be eliminated in HRT, but it can be mitigated. So what determines high risk and HRT?

High Risk—A known or unknown condition or state where an elevated probability of loss of life or property or an increased level of injury is likely or imminent; situations that require special attention or intervention to prevent a potential mishap; or an implication of a dangerous situation.

High-Risk Training—HRT activities and courses expose personnel (officers, instructors, support staff) to a heightened level of risk that will likely result in death, serious bodily injury, or loss of an asset should a mishap occur during training or exercises.

The success and safety of any HRT program or course hinge on the ability of subject-matter experts (SMEs), instructional designers (ISDs), and instructors to identify, evaluate, and mitigate the risks associated with each step of the training. Risks are found in all operational and training environments and are defined as actual or potential conditions where the following can occur as a result of exposure to the condition:

- Injury, illness, or death of personnel
- Damage to or loss of equipment and property
- Mission degradation

A course or program identified as HRT will require the following additional steps during course development:

1. A thorough analysis of prior mishap data for the actual performance involved and performances similar in nature, including the performance of officers, and officers of other organizations, if possible, shall be conducted to identify additional actual and potential training risks.
2. If possible, course developers will consult with a cross section of SMEs and, if available, field personnel to validate risks, identify and describe additional risks, and evaluate the probability and severity of the risks. The risk must be credible in that it must have a reasonable expectation of happening and the consequences must have a measurable impact. Gathering input from a wide array of SMEs, instructors, and field personnel will ensure that one opinion or experience does not unduly influence the risk identification process.
3. After assessing each risk, ISDs and instructors must devise one opinion or experience that does not unduly influence the risk identification process.
4. After assessing each risk, ISDs and instructors must devise one or more potential controls that either eliminate or mitigate the risk or reduce risk (severity/probability/exposure) of a hazardous incident. When developing controls, ISDs and instructors must consider the reason for the risk not just the risk itself.

Types of controls basically fall into three categories:

1. *Equipment Controls*: eliminate or reduce exposure to the risk entirely, such as
   - Automobile airbags
   - Overused equipment (maintain manufacturer guidelines regarding maintenance and replacement of training equipment)
   - Berms behind firing ranges
2. *Administrative Controls*: eliminate or reduce exposure to risks by rules, policy, or training, such as
   - 15 mph speed limit in areas of high pedestrian traffic
   - Fire drills
   - Recurring training requirements
   - Instructor-to-officer ratio
   - EMT/HS on scene for training scenario
3. *Personal Protective Equipment* (PPE): eliminate or reduce exposure to risks by equipment worn or carried by the officer, such as
   - Eye and hearing protection
   - Life vests
   - Ballistic helmet
   - Body armor
   - Protective clothing

Once risk factors have been identified and evaluated and mitigation strategies have been designed, ISDs and instructors must incorporate these considerations into the HRT course curriculum and supplementary materials (officer guide, instructor guide, presentations, lesson plans, etc.). It is imperative that sufficient course preparation and delivery time are devoted to identifying and describing the nature and severity of risks to both instructors and officers. To ensure instructors are informed through course preparation materials and that those instructions are relayed to officers in accordance with agency policy, ISDs must ensure that time is allotted within the course for the following:

- Mitigation strategies.
- Equipment controls.
- Required PPE, including instruction on how to use, inspect, and maintain PPE.
- Administrative controls (might be as straightforward as "Range Safety Rules" for a live fire exercise or performance may be broken down using the "crawl, walk, run" approach into a series of simple exercises, repeated, reinforced, and progressively building toward a highly complex action).

- Officer screening standards (i.e., ensuring prerequisites are met).
- Medical screening. Authorized medical personnel will ensure all physical fitness requirements have been met and that no current medical conditions exist with the officer that will prevent safe performance of the required tasks.

Qualification of HRT Instructors

Without question, the most critical aspect of any HRT course is doing all possible risk assessments and executing all possible risk mitigation tactics to prevent injury to officers or instructors (a sample Operational Risk Form can be downloaded from humanperformance.vpweb.com). All HRT instructors should be qualified instructors before consideration be given to HRT. The instructors need to go through several stages of screening before being selected as an HRT instructor. Much of this can be accomplished by professional certifications through specialized training organizations (i.e., military training, Academi, National Tactical Officers Association, etc.). Medical and physical fitness screenings need to be completed and passed. An oral or a written test regarding policies, procedures, and precautions need to be taken and passed. Instructor evaluations need to be conducted on a more frequent basis for your HRT instructors. Some agencies make an evaluation of HRT instructors on every iteration of an HRT course.

Stage I

Instructor personnel must be scheduled to attend a certified instructor development course, unless they are previously certified within 5 years. There are many different instructor development schools available just in case your agency does not have its own.

Stage II

An HRT mentor instructor shall be assigned to the new instructor during this period. Once the member has graduated from an instructor development course, the prospective instructor should be closely mentored through a qualification process. Prospective instructors should be observed conducting classes based on their assigned courses while working with their mentor instructor. The mentor should oversee that the new HRT instructor completes the required reading and becomes very familiar with any specialized or protective equipment.

Stage III

Before qualifying as an instructor for any HRT, the individual must have substantial knowledge of the material, must have confidence teaching the material, and must have the ability to answer questions completely and with professional bearing. They should be qualified and certified and any training equipment should be utilized in any of the HRT. All of the new HRT training, qualifications, and certification need to be compiled into a qualification folder to be submitted to the training officer or supervisor in charge. New HRT instructors should be able to demonstrate every facet of the HRT they will be instructing and then signed off by senior HRT instructors. Then the new HRT instructor appear before a formal board of senior HRT instructors, the lead training officer, or any other designees, to ask questions of the new instructor. The new instructor should provide a demonstration of any segment of the HRT they will be instructing.

Journeyman High-Risk Instructor

Ongoing evaluations are the primary means of plotting instructor progress during the certification phase. Evaluations are used to ensure that standardized content exists, practices and policies are adhered to, and signs of instructor fatigue are identified. The instructors should be evaluated not only with a regular instructor evaluation form but also with a specialized evaluation regarding the specifics of the HRT.

Maintaining HRT Instructor Status

If the instructor fails the reevaluation attempt, he or she should be immediately pulled out and placed into a remediation program. Failure to pass reevaluation during remediation will result in the HRT instructor losing his or her certification.

It is the responsibility of the lead HRT instructor or training officer to monitor and ensure adherence to the standards in the certification of their course instructors and recurrent efforts to include instructor evaluations. Each instructor shares in the responsibility of maintaining the standards.

HRT Course Officer Screening Process

HRT is not for everyone. Many times, officers can overstate their competencies. There is an old saying that applies to HRT: "If it were easy, everyone would do it"; everyone is not suited for high-risk work or training. Before an officer attends *any* HRT, he or she needs to be properly screened before he or she is allowed to attend HRT. What does that mean? For an officer to undergo any undercover training, he or she needs to pass an advanced psychological assessment beforehand. For an officer to undergo SWAT training, he or she needs to first meet advanced physical fitness requirements. Some officers have died of a heart attack while attending SWAT training because they were not physically fit for the training. Do not allow this to happen to your agency. If an officer wants to attend an HRT, he or she needs to be mentally and physically prepared before being allowed to undergo the HRT. Any course identified as high risk will commence with an officer briefing before any HRT. Included in the briefing to all officers will be a review of the HRT to be conducted over the course, a review of the Officer Statement of Understanding, and the completion of a medical risk factor screening.

Officer Statement of Understanding

Here is an example of an Officer Statement of Understanding, which should be read and signed by the officer attending the training:

> High-Risk Training is voluntary. Accordingly, you have the option to individually request Training Time Out (TTO), or to terminate training by dropping on request (DOR). Any time you make a statement such as "I quit", "DOR" or words of that effect, you shall be immediately removed from the training environment and referred to the appropriate supervisor.

Basic TTO Officer Briefing

The purpose of the Training Time Out (TTO) is to correct the situation of concern, provide clarifying information, or remove the officer from the potentially hazardous environment. Any officer or instructor in any training situation where they are concerned for their own or another's safety may call a TTO or may request clarification of procedures or requirements. TTO is also an appropriate means for one to obtain relief if he or she is experiencing pain, heat stress, or other serious physical discomfort. A TTO may be signaled, by uttering the words "Training Time Out," "Out of Role," crossed hands in a (T), a raised clenched fist, or other specific signals which will be briefed prior to a specific performance test or practical application. If the TTO signal is not acknowledged, the signaler shall shout "Training Time Out" (or other action as required by the training class). The instructor shall attempt to relieve and remove the officer from the training environment. If an adequate number of instructors are available to allow training to continue safely, the lead instructor may elect to do so. However, if this is not practical, training will be stopped until the situation is corrected.

Drop on Request (DOR) Briefing

When a DOR is made, the instructor and lead course or course manager will counsel the officer immediately. If the issues that prevent the officer from continuing with the training cannot be resolved, then the officer is removed from training immediately. All officer training materials and equipment are removed from the officer and accounted for and will not be returned. A request to DOR is a time-sensitive issue, and the officer must be able to decisively wish to return to training or continue the DOR process before the beginning of the next lesson of their course.

After an officer is removed from training, the lead instructor will initiate the DOR paperwork. The instructor will complete the appropriate portion of the DOR paperwork and sign. The officer will be given the DOR paperwork and should submit a written request detailing the reasons for the DOR. The request should clearly indicate that the officer wants to DOR (e.g., I [name], desire to be removed from training in XYZ course for the following reason[s]: XXX). Once the counseling and form are complete, the request shall be submitted directly to the appropriate supervisor. In no case shall an officer be coerced or threatened to induce him or her to return to training after a DOR.

Supervisor Interview

The supervisor shall interview the officer requesting the DOR. During this interview, the supervisor must be able to reasonably determine the following:

a. The real motivation for the request.
b. If the decision to DOR is the result of some training factors that may lead other officers to DOR, can training be changed to alleviate this factor without adversely affecting program objectives?
c. If the officer desires to reenter the program.
d. If officer retention is warranted, are there actions (counseling, change of instructor, or special assistance) that might cause the officer not to DOR? Are such actions justified in view of the impact upon the overall training program and upon other officers?

The interview needs only to be detailed enough to satisfy the supervisor and for the officer to understand the process of the DOR. If the officer still desires a DOR after completion of the interview, then the officer will be directed to the lead instructor for further interview and administrative processing.

General Safety Guidelines

These are just a few general safety guidelines and are in no way to be the only steps for training safely. For deeper safety guidelines covering a wide variety of training venues, Ken Murray's *Training at the Speed of Life, Volume 1*, is a great resource.

Nonlethal Training Areas

1. Follow the instructor and training safety officer's (TSO) guidance and assist as directed.
   - An emergency call box is located...
   - **Safety Equipment:** An Automatic External Defibrillators or AED, first aid kit, and an eye wash station are located...
   - In case of fire...
   - Water coolers are located...
   - Officers shall pick up all expended rounds after conclusion of training.
2. **No Live Firearms/Ammunition/Chemical Irritants/Edged or Impact Weapons Are Permitted in the Training Area. (It is recommended that all officers be warned before entering the nonlethal training area [NLTA].)**
3. Treat the NLTA firearm with the same degree of seriousness and responsibility afforded "live" firearms and ammunition.
4. All firearms to be used in the training scenario will have, at a minimum, the proper firearm conversion kits installed. The firearms will be marked with blue paint on the muzzle, the front of the trigger, and the bottom of the magazine. The TSO will check these firearms before the training evolution.
5. Do not handle any ammunition or load any firearms until directed to do so.
6. Indiscriminate firing and unsafe or frivolous behavior will not be tolerated. Remember firearms awareness and muzzle control. Your finger will remain outside the trigger guard until you are ready to fire the firearm.
7. All participants must wear designated safety equipment and the equipment must remain in place until an instructor ends the exercise.
8. Mandatory safety protective equipment includes, but is not limited to, ODU uniform or coveralls with sleeves rolled down, gloves, hard athletic cup or Redman-style groin protector, approved helmet, and throat protector. There are **NO EXCEPTIONS!**

9. Check helmets before training to ensure that the lens is locked into place and free of cracks. When in doubt, ask an instructor.
10. Upon hearing "CEASE FIRE, CEASE FIRE" or the alarm siren, stop all activity immediately.
11. If a helmet or throat guard becomes dislodged during an exercise, immediately protect yourself by shielding your eyes, face, or throat area and shout "CEASE FIRE, CEASE FIRE."
12. No one will go for your firearm. There are no tricks. (**EXCEPTION:** when the written scenario identifies firearm retention as an objective.)
13. Do not physically fight with, punch, kick, strike, or otherwise abuse the role players. (**EXCEPTION:** when physical interaction is within the identified parameters of the written scenario.)
14. If you think a Deadly Force situation becomes necessary, follow the Use of Force policy for your agency.
15. For safety purposes, do not shoot anyone who is closer than **5 feet away**.
16. Do not give up or quit until stopped by an instructor, with exceptions for injuries or potentially unsafe situations. Each of you is a safety officer. When you perceive an unsafe situation, you can stop the action any time by shouting "CEASE FIRE, CEASE FIRE."
17. Report all injuries to the instructor immediately.

Recommendations for Mat Rooms

1. One instructor is required per eight officers for defensive tactics training.
2. Role players must be present for safety brief.
3. Training Environment Safety Precautions:
    - The instructor must emphasize the importance of safety during the opening actions of the lecture portion and before practical exercises.
    - Ask the officers if anyone has any medical issue or recent injury that needs to be addressed.
    - **"OUT OF ROLE"** will be called out to stop any training where a potential for injury is noted or when an injury occurs. Officers are to stop all activity when this command is given.
    - All injuries will be brought to the attention of the instructor and the injured officer will be sent to the medical facility for assessment and treatment.
    - Officers shall remove all jewelry, writing pens, ID badges, watches, and any other items that might cause physical injury from their uniforms before the training session.

- In case of fire…
- **Safety Equipment:** An AED, first aid kit, and an eye wash station are located…
- Water coolers are located…
- An emergency call box is located…

Conclusion

The more realistic training is, the more it will "stick" with the officers. Learning is linked to emotional states of stimulation; the higher the stimulation, the higher the learning. However, depending on the kind of training being conducted, there can be increased risk involved. There is enough risk involved in being an officer; as trainers, our job is to ensure that officers learn and that officers do not get hurt while learning. Every effort should be made that your training is done safely. This is not to imply that someone will not get hurt during a training exercise but to minimize the probability that someone will get hurt.

Learning Management System—Why It Is Not Enough?

12

An academy manager is responsible for overseeing the academy and ensuring its programs are documented in a systematic process. Training documents can be either in paper or electronic format. Electronic documents tend to be better because they take up less office space and do not get lost in someone's in-basket.

A learning management system (LMS) can maintain records for training programs, such as the following:

- Curriculum content (syllabus, lesson plans, and other training material)
- A listing of all instructors and other instructional personnel indicating the actual class in which each instructor presented
- Inclusive dates the program is conducted and actual dates and time when each block of training occurs
- Rosters of participants in each iteration
- Backup files
- A complete record of the officer training evaluation (grades, scores, final results)
- Documentation that verifies the officer successfully completed the training program
- Training development for new instructors and required certifications for instructors
- Documentation of specialized training for instructors
- Learning analytics
- Ensuring officers are evaluated by each learning objective
- Having multiversions of tests and evaluations that test the same objectives in different ways
- Maintaining secure access of officer records and training material
- An archive of all officer training records

With a sound LMS system, an academy can keep cradle-to-grave records on all officers, instructors, courses, and the academy. This provides a level of assurance in cases such as a civil liability incident. A good LMS allows you to streamline training. It helps you document detailed checklists. An LMS can help you budget and allows you to monitor your resources. A sound LMS raises a law enforcement academy to the platinum standard of training and public confidence.

However, an LMS system for law enforcement needs to be more robust than most LMSs. There are more issues that need to be addressed in a law enforcement system. Most LMSs address just knowledge-based training. Knowledge is only a small facet of the total need to track the high-dose liability skills linked to law enforcement. Not only are there physical fitness standards to attend basic training, there is a physical fitness test after an officer leaves the academy as well; general LMS's do not have this ability. Who is authorized to perform the job, security clearance, and medical clearance? With a law enforcement LMS, especially at an academy, you have to address high-volume capacity planning. The academy needs to answer questions such as "What can we train given the fixed resources versus the variable resources such as instructors and equipment?" The academy needs to concentrate on scheduling, students, resources, housing, and registration from a broad layout. The LMS needs to record not only what happens while a student is at the academy but also his or her training after they leave the academy. Here is a list a law enforcement LMS should be able to provide:

- All the portions of the ADDIE (analysis, design, development, implementation, and evaluation) process
- POST or FLETA accreditation standards
- Testing (both written and practical)
- All legally defensible training and documentation
- FTO (field training officer) and officers going through the FTO program
- Body armor renewal
- All requalification training (firearms, instructors, etc.)
- Undercover operators training and skill sets

Learning Analytics

Learning analytics is extremely important in an LMS. Training without the right analytics is like driving without a map. Learning analytics can provide insightful data, such as the following:

1. Compliance training and safety performance. Are you reducing the number of accidents and issues?
2. Training completion and performance ratings. Are the top performers completing more training or scoring better?

Training departments use ADDIE to clearly define what to train and what is going to be of most value. ADDIE is extremely effective, and with the proper use of learning management and analytics, ADDIE becomes a continuous process, instead of a once-per-curriculum–type event. It has become clear that an LMS should have integrated analytics and metrics to allow continual evaluation of the training's impact. Learning analytics can actively measure key metrics related to a performance problem. The analysis stage helps you determine who should participate and what training should be provided. The design and development phases are up to the training department to define and create. The implementation phase is typically accomplished within the LMS, when training is deployed to the officers identified during the analysis phase. Once the officers have consumed the material, the evaluation phase begins. The effectiveness of the training is measured by looking at the impact on the problems first identified. Agencies can use an analytics package to perform the evaluation phase. More importantly, LMS must be integrated into an agency's full suite of applications, along with workforce analytics, to exactly record what the entire business gains from the investment in training.

To maximize your agency's performance, workforce analytics needs to be integrated into a full suite of applications with both workforce metrics and analytics capability. This is where the true insights will be gained. For example, using analytics with learning strategies, you can determine the following:

- What is the relationship between span of control, training, and performance?
- What is the relationship between training completed and the ratio of high performers? Do units that have completed the training have a higher ratio of high performers? Do these units have lower levels of poor and marginal performers?
- What is the relationship between the types of training and their impact? Does course content training within an agency correlate with higher levels of program outcomes within the community?
- What is the relationship between training completed and career paths? Do units that have completed the entire relevant training have a higher ratio of internal promotions to transfers? If so, do you then reward managers who develop their staff more?

These are just a few examples of how everyone, from line managers to executives, can get up-to-the-minute information on the impact training has across the agency, and not just a status report on how much training was delivered. A successful LMS should help

1. Deliver fact/data-based business cases on what kind of training you provide and the reason behind it.
2. Demonstrate why investing in training program X will help the agency execute its strategy and deliver return on investment through authoritative insight.

3. Engage the leaders, HR, finance, and operations with performance metrics to really show what impact training has and what needs to be measured.

4. Embrace training analytics as an integrated part of decision making and combine multiple data sources from operations to training that allow you to measure the relationship and impact training has on the strategy, alignment, officer performance, and productivity of your agency, thereby linking your training strategy to performance.

5. Proactively engage with the training division and the agency to uncover potential problem areas and ensure that they can quantify the impact of interventions. Ultimately, you will be able to identify the gaps in your workforce's capabilities and bridge them with the right training; performance will improve across the agency.

Conclusion

Today's technology is a great way of addressing all the needs of law enforcement training. A good law enforcement LMS not only can assist in tracking everything regarding basic and advanced law enforcement training but also can provide answers to how well your training is working in the field. Learning analytics can address Kirkpatrick's Level 4—Return on Expectations. What is the ROE or ROI of your training? Big data are the future of law enforcement training.

Glossary

Academy: An organization of people who work to provide training in special subjects or skills. It has classrooms and special facilities to aid in training.

ADDIE: ADDIE (Analysis, Design, Development, Implement, and Evaluation) is one of the most recognized industry standards for designing training programs.

Affective Domain: From Bloom's Taxonomy, it has six levels of organized hierarchies of learning that deal with emotions, attitudes, behaviors, and values.

Analysis: A systematic exploration of the way things are and the way things should be; the difference is the performance gap.

Andragogy: The study of adult learning; it originated in Europe in the 1950s and was then pioneered as a theory and model of adult learning in the 1970s by Malcolm Knowles, an American practitioner and theorist of adult education. The theory is that adults learn by doing.

Angoff Method: A method that test developers use to determine the passing percentage (cut score) for a test. It relies on subject-matter experts (SMEs) who examine the content of each test question (item) and then predict how many minimally qualified candidates would answer the item correctly. The average of the judges' predictions for a test question becomes its *predicted difficulty*. The sum of the predicted difficulty values for each item averaged across the judges and items on a test is the recommended Angoff cut score.

Assessment: Any systematic method of obtaining evidence by posing questions to draw inferences about the knowledge, skill, attitudes, and other characteristics of people for a specific purpose.

Asynchronous Learning: A term used in distance learning, it means no instructor is present; learning is self-paced in a virtual classroom. Other participants are not present.

Behavior: The actual steps an officer takes in performing the tasks. Some of these steps are readily observable (disassembly of a firearm) or not observable (decision making).

Blended Training (Learning): A combination of both distance training and resident training.

Bloom's Taxonomy: The most widely used method for creating learning objectives that measure outcomes.

Boomers: People born between 1943 and 1960 (some say 1964); they are the children of the WWII generation.

Case Study: A learning strategy where officers are given a scenario (generally real-world) that requires officer analysis. It can be done step by step, and twists and turns may be added.

Characteristics: Tools that are required to do the job. These concern safety, speed, frequency, complexity, or consequences during work.

Chunk: Information that is similar to a computer byte: the smallest unit of "memory" needed to encode a single character of text.

Closed Skills: Allow the performance of a fixed, unchanging pattern of movement by an officer.

Cognitive Domain: From Bloom's Taxonomy, it has six levels of organized hierarchies of cognition.

Cognitive Overload: A condition stemming from exceeding the limited capacity of working memory. When overloaded, working memory processing becomes inefficient.

Condition: The elements under which the tasks are performed.

Criteria: The quality or quantity attached to a job.

Cut Score: A cut score is based on the minimal acceptable competence level, which represents the threshold between officers who can do the job and those who cannot. The cut score must be defensible, as the most reasonable person on the job would accept.

Demonstration: Involves an instructor showing officers a process or modeling a behavior.

Design Phase: If the analysis identifies a performance gap, the design phase will outline the performance objectives.

Develop: Creating the performance solution from the information gathered in the analysis and design phases and crafting lesson plans, assessments, and methodology.

Diagnostic: An assessment primarily used to identify the needs and prior knowledge of participants for the purpose of directing them to the most appropriate learning experience.

Distal Goals: Long-term goals.

Distance Training (Learning): Training delivered via electronic media format, such as the Internet, or through a tablet, a computer, or a smartphone.

Electronic Performance Support Solution (EPSS): A packaged (self-contained) digital task support resource. The EPSS unifies relevant support and reference information, media, and guidance at a single, accessible point, organized in a logical and consistent structure.

Enabling Performance Objective (EPO): Describes the steps (thinking, acting) to reach a Terminal Performance Objective.

Evaluate: Measurement of how well the performance solution achieved the objectives of the training program.

Exam: A summative assessment used to measure an officer's knowledge of skills for the purpose of documenting his or her current level of knowledge or skill.

Experiential Learning: An activity that is used to encourage individuals to reflect, describe, analyze, and communicate what they recently experienced.

FEA: Front-End Analysis determines the influences of a performance gap by conducting a series of analyses—performance analysis (which includes organizational and environmental analyses) and cause analysis (which includes the organization's environmental support and the individual's behavioral repertory).

Feedback: Either a form of endorsement of one's behavior or a way to improve one's behavior.

Field Training and Evaluation Program (FTEP): Sometimes referred to as the San Jose model. FTEP originated in 1970 from San Jose, California, where a new officer's skills and abilities are evaluated by a field training officer using a 1–7 Likert scale. It is rooted in the behaviorist approach to learning.

Field Training Officer (FTO): A trained officer who is assigned to a new officer to evaluate the latter's skills and abilities in a field setting.

Fine Motor Skills: Psychomotor learning involving precise control of small muscle groups (i.e., shooting). Fine motor skills generally demand more practice time.

FOR: Frame of Reference training is one of the latest attempts at increasing the accuracy of performance ratings. Participants are given descriptions of each measurement of competence and are then instructed to discuss what qualifications they believe are needed for each measurement and to rate the performance near the same level of competency.

Formal Learning: Learning objectives set up by trainers, which provide a learning product (i.e., training program). Formal learning has structured learning objectives, activities, and feedback.

Formative: An assessment whose primary objective is to provide search and retrieval as well as prescriptive feedback to an officer.

Games: A computer-based or a tangible event that leads to learning or review of material.

Generation X: People born between 1961 (some say 1964) and 1981.

Generation Y: People born between 1982 and 2003 (sometimes referred to as *Millennials*).

Golem Effect: The lower the expectations that are placed on officers, the lower their performance will be.

Gross Motor Skills: Psychomotor learning involving large muscle groups (i.e., running, jumping, punching).

Group Work: A teaching methodology in which the class is broken into smaller groups to discuss and analyze a situation.

Guided Learning: A teaching methodology in which an instructor guides the officers through a situation to which the officers have to provide input.

Hard Skills: Actions, such as shooting a firearm, which are performed as consistently and correctly as possible every time, are hard, high-precision skills.

High Risk: A known or unknown condition or state in which an elevated probability of loss of life or property or an increased level of injury is likely or imminent; situations that require special attention and/or intervention to prevent a potential mishap; or an implication of a dangerous situation.

High-Risk Training (HRT): High-risk training activities and courses expose personnel (officers, instructors, support staff) to a heightened level of risk that will likely result in death, serious bodily injury, or loss of an asset should a mishap occur during training or exercises.

Human Performance Technology (HPT): HPT is a systematic approach to analyzing and diagnosing human performance problems. HPT is a field of practice that has evolved largely as a result of the experience, reflection, and conceptualization of professional practitioners striving to improve human performance in the workplace.

Implement: This stage includes delivery of the performance solution.

Independent Practice: A teaching methodology that may involve a series of questions that an officer has to independently answer on his own.

Informal Learning: The learner sets the goals and objectives of their learning. Learning is not necessarily structured in terms of effort and time (i.e., workplace).

Instructional System Design: A systematic way of designing and developing a course.

JTA: Job Task Analysis examines every aspect of a job to see the actual performance required to do the job.

Law Enforcement: The generic name for the activities of the agencies responsible for maintaining public order and enforcing the law, particularly the activities of prevention, detection, and investigation of crime and the apprehension of criminals.

Law Enforcement Officer: An employee of a law enforcement agency who is an officer sworn to carry out law enforcement duties.

Learning: The activity or process of gaining knowledge or skill by studying, practicing, being taught, or experiencing something.

Learning Management System (LMS): An electronic software package that assists in scheduling instructors and housing training documents and student records.

Learning Transfer System Inventory (LTSI): An alternate form of training assessment and learning transfer based on four domains: motivation, environment, secondary influences, and ability elements.

Lecture: A learning methodology in which an instructor is in front of a class teaching material. It typically takes place in a classroom.

Level 1 Assessment—Reaction: Based on Kirkpatrick's four levels of evaluations, Level 1 is the degree to which a person favorably or unfavorably reacts to a training event.

Level 2 Assessment—Learning: Based on Kirkpatrick's four levels of evaluations, Level 2 is the degree to which a person acquires the intended knowledge, skills, and attitudes based on his or her participation in the training.

Level 3 Assessment—Behavior: Based on Kirkpatrick's four levels of evaluations, Level 3 is the degree to which a person applies the skills acquired during the training when he or she is on the job.

Level 4 Assessment—Results: Based on Kirkpatrick's four levels of evaluations, Level 4 is the degree to which target outcomes occur as a result of the training in contrast to the cost outlay for the training event.

Likert Scale: A method that prompts respondents to express their opinion on a statement being presented. Likert scales are often 4-point scales (strongly agree, agree, disagree, strongly disagree) but can go as far as 10-point scales.

Metacognition: Refers to an individual's self-awareness about what he or she knows and understands, along with ways of processing his or her own cognition through self-control and self-manipulation.

Millennials: See Generation Y.

Myelin: An electrically insulating substance that forms a layer, the myelin sheath, usually around only the axon of a neuron.

Neuroplasticity: Changes in how neurons and synapses interact with each other in our brain, thus affecting our behavior, brain processes, thinking, emotions, and changes resulting from brain damage.

Nonformal learning: Learning from someone in the organization who is not necessarily part of the training department (i.e., FTO, supervisor) and who sets the learning objectives or tasks.

Open Skills: Skills that demand an officer to be adaptable, able to read the situation, and able to anticipate what will happen next.

Performance: The act of doing a job or an activity in accordance with a set standard of completeness and accuracy.

Performer: The person who is actually doing the performance.

Permanent Memory: Memory that organizes ideas, processes information, and contains skills that are in the cognitive domain, also known as *long-term memory.*

Police Training Officer Program (PTOP): Sometimes referred to as the Reno Model, PTOP was introduced in 2003. Its foundation is Problem-Based Learning. It is rooted in the constructivist approach to learning.

Pressure: When an officer is in a situation where the consequences affect the level of success or survival. Pressure is the "do-or-die" situation. Pressure is performance or task related.

Primacy: Officers retain information that they learn for the first time longer than they retain information they must relearn. Unlearning incorrect procedures, or bad habits, is always more difficult than learning correct procedures from the beginning.

Proximal Goals: Short-term goals that are influential in accomplishing distal goals (long-term goals).

Psychomotor Domain: From Bloom's Taxonomy, it has six levels of organized hierarchies of psychomotor learning.

Pygmalion Effect: A phenomenon wherein the greater the expectation placed upon officers, the better they perform.

Quiz: A formative assessment used to measure an officer's knowledge or skills for the purpose of providing feedback to inform the officer of his or her current level of knowledge or skill.

Recency: Officers retain information acquired last the easiest. The longer an officer goes without practicing a new concept, the easier it is for him or her to forget.

Reflection: A teaching methodology that requires officers to invest a large amount of time trying to self-analyze and understand their personal attitudes.

Reliability: A test is reliable if it consistently measures what it claims to measure and has confidence in the scores it produces.

Role Play: Assuming a scripted role to be acted out by an officer with another classmate.

Scaffolding: Guidance included in lessons to reduce officer confusion and make learning more efficient. Scaffolding is especially needed in a scenario-based learning design.

Scenario: Simulated real-life situation using role players and props.

Sensory Memory: Memory based on temporary storage of information from the senses.

Simulation: A teaching methodology involving a scenario that resembles the real work environment an officer may face.

SME: Subject-matter experts are recognized experts on specific subjects.

Soft Skills: High-flexibility skills that have many paths to good results, not just one. These skills aren't about doing the same thing perfectly every time, but rather about being nimble and interactive, and about recognizing patterns as they unfold and making smart, timely choices.

Spiral or Rapid Development: Recognizes that the standard ADDIE process can be slow and allows the development work in later stages to influence reconsideration of the work completed at the early stages. The process shows that work done during implementation and evaluation is fed back into the analysis phase.

Star Performers: Star performers are the best at performing a certain task in the operational setting.

Stress: What an officer distinguishes as the demands of the situation outweigh the officer's ability to respond.

Student Teach Back: A teaching methodology that requires the student to take charge of a class and deliver training material to the class.

Summative: An assessment whose primary purpose is to give a quantitative grade and make a judgment about the participant's achievement. This is typically known as a certification event if the goal is to document that the test taker has specialized expertise.

SWOT: An analysis to determine the strengths, weaknesses, opportunities, and threats to the organization.

Synchronous Learning: A term used in distance learning, meaning an instructor-facilitated learning conducted in a virtual classroom with all participants present online.

Terminal Performance Objective (TPO): Describes tasks the officer will be required to do upon completion of the instruction.

Test: A diagnostic assessment to measure an officer's knowledge or skills for the purpose of informing the officers or their instructor of their current level of knowledge or skill.

Training: The act, process, or method of one that trains; the skill, knowledge, or experience acquired by one that trains.

Validity: A test is valid if it actually measures or assesses what it claims to measure or assess.

Working Memory: Uses information from both permanent and sensory memory; it is information we actively process but for a short period (about 12 seconds).

References

Allen, K. A. and Friedman, B. D. (2010). Affective learning: A taxonomy for teaching social work values. *Journal of Social Work Values and Ethics*, 7(2). Retrieved from: http://www.jswvearchives.com/fall2010/f10neuman.pdf.

Alliger, G. M. and Janak, E. A. (1989). Kirkpatrick's levels of training criteria: Thirty years later. *Personnel Psychology*, 42, 331–342. doi:10.1111/j.1744-6570.1989 .tb00661.x.

Alliger, G. M., Tannenbaum, S. I., Bennett, Jr., W., Traver, H. and Shotland, A. (1997). A meta-analysis of the relations among training criteria. *Personnel Psychology*, 50, 341–358. doi:10.1111/j.1744-6570.1997.tb00911.

American Society of Training and Development (2009). *The Value of Evaluation: Making Training Evaluations More Effective.* Alexandria, VA: ASTD. Retrieved from: http://www.astdalaska.org/outside_files/Evaluation_Value.pdf.

American Society of Training and Development (2008). *Tapping the Potential of Informal Learning. An ASTD Research Study.* Alexandria, VA: ASTD.

Anderson, J. R. (1995). *Learning and Memory: An Integrated Approach.* New York: John Wiley.

Anderson, L. W., Krathwohl, D. R., Airasian, P. W., Cruikshank, K. A., Mayer, R. E., Pintrich, P. R., Raths, J. and Witrock, M. C. (2001a). *A Taxonomy for Learning, Teaching, and Assessing: A Revision of Bloom's Taxonomy of Educational Objectives* (Complete edition). New York: Longman.

Anderson, T., Rourke, L., Garrision, R. and Archer, W. (2001b). Assessing teaching presence in a computer conferencing context. *Journal of Asynchronous Learning Networks*, 5(2), 1–17. Retrieved from: http://www.aln.org/publications/jaln /v5n2/pdf/v5n2_anderson.pdf.

Apking, A. M. and Mooney, T. (2010). Success case methodology in measurement and evaluation. In Moseley, J. L. and Dessinger, J. C. (Eds.), *Handbook of Improving Performance in the Workplace* (Vol. 3), San Francisco: Pfeiffer.

Argyris, C. and Schön, D. (1978). *Organizational Learning: A Theory of Action Perspective.* Reading, MA: Addison Wesley.

Armstrong, J. S. (2012). Natural learning in higher education. *Encyclopedia of the Sciences of Learning.* Heidelberg: Springer.

Artwohl, A. and Christensen, L. (1997). *Deadly Force Encounters: What Cops Need to Know to Mentally and Physically Prepare for and Survive a Gunfight.* Boulder, CO: Paladin Press.

Asken, M. J., Grossman, D. and Christensen, L. W. (2010). *Warrior Mindset.* Millstadt, IL: Human Research Group.

Awoniyi, K., Salas, E. and Garofano, C. (2004). A study of best practices in training transfer and proposed model for transfer. In L. A. Burke and H. M. Hutchins (2008). *Human Resource Development Quarterly*, 19(2), 107–128.

Baldwin, T. T. and Ford, J. K. (1988). Transfer of training: A review and directions for future research. *Personnel Psychology, 41*, 63–105. doi:10.1111/j.1744-6570.1988.tb00632.x.

Baldwin, T. T. and Magjuka, R. J. (1991). Organizational training and signals of importance: Linking pretraining perceptions to intentions to transfer. *Human Resources Development Quarterly, 2*(1), 25–36. doi:10.1002/hrdq.3920020106.

Bandura, A. (1995). *Self-efficacy in Changing Societies.* New York: Cambridge Press.

Bandura, A. (1997). *Self-efficacy: The Exercise of Control.* New York: W. H. Freeman.

Bates, R. (2003). A study of best practices in training transfer and proposed model for transfer. In L. A. Burke and H. M. Hutchens (2008). *Human Resources Development Quarterly, 19*(2), 107–128. doi:10.1002/hrdq.1230.

Bates, R. (2004). A critical analysis of evaluation practice: The Kirkpatrick model and the principles of beneficence. *Evaluation and Program Planning, 27*, 341–347. doi:10.1016/j.evalprogplan.2004.04.011.

Bates, R. and Khasawneh, S. (2005). Organizational learning culture, learning transfer climate and perceived innovation in Jordanian organizations. *International Journal of Training and Development, 9*(2), 96–109. doi:10.1111/j.1468-2419.2005.00224.x.

Belair, A. (April 6, 2012). Transfer of training: Moving beyond the barriers. *Training.* Retrieved from: http://www.trainingmag.com/content/transfer-training-moving-beyond-barriers.

Biech, E. (2005). *Training for Dummies.* Hoboken, NJ: Wiley Publishing.

Bielawski, L. and Metcalf, D. (2003). *Blended eLearning: Integrating Knowledge, Performance, Support, and Online Learning.* Amherst, MA: HRD Press, Inc.

Bloom, B. S. (1956). *Taxonomy of Educational Objectives Handbook 1: Cognitive Domain.* New York: Longman.

Blume, B. D., Ford, J. K., Baldwin, T. T. and Huang, J. L. (2010). Transfer of training: A meta-analytic review. *Journal of Management, 36*(4), 1065–1105. doi:10.1177/0149206309352880.

Bonk, C. J. and Wisher, R. A. (2000). *Applying Collaborative and E-learning Tools to Military Distance Learning: A Research Framework* (Army Project Number 20363007A792). Alexandria, VA: U.S. Army Research Institute for the Behavioral and Social Sciences. Retrieved from: http://www.dtic.mil/cgibin/GetTRDoc?AD=ADA389681.

Bopp, W. and Schultz, D. (1972). *A Short History of American Law Enforcement.* Springfield, IL: Charles C. Thomas.

Bransford, J. D., Brown, A. L. and Cocking, R. R. (2000). *How People Learn: Brain, Mind, Experience, and School.* Washington, DC: National Academy Press.

Brown, T. C. and Warren, A. M. (2009). Distal goal and proximal goal transfer of training interventions in an executive education program. *Human Resource Development Quarterly, 20*(3), 265–284. doi:10.1002/hrdq.20021.

Burke, L. A. and Hutchins, H. M. (2007). Training transfer: An integrative literature review. *Human Resource Development Review, 6*(3), 263–296. doi:10.1177/1534484307303035.

Burke, L. A. and Hutchins, H. M. (2008). A study of best practices in training transfer and proposed model of transfer. *Human Resource Development Quarterly, 19*(2), 107–128. doi:10.1002/hrdq.1230.

Cannon-Bowers, J. A., Salas, E., Tannenbaum, S. I. and Mathieu, J. E. (1995). Toward theoretically based principles of training effectiveness: A model and initial investigation. *Military Psychology, 7*(3), 141–164. doi:10.1207/s15327876mp0703_1.

Carroll, P. (2011). *Win Forever: Live, Work, and Play Like a Champion*. New York: Penguin Group.

Chappell, A. T. (2008). Police academy training: Comparing across curricula. *Policing: An International Journal of Police Strategies and Management, 31*(1), 36–56. doi: 10.1108/13639510810852567.

Cherry, K. (2015). *What Is Flow?* Retrieved from: http://psychology.about.com/od /PositivePsychology/a/flow.htm.

Clark, R. C. (2015). *Evidence-Based Training Methods* (2nd ed.). East Peoria, IL: ASTD DBA Association for Talent Development.

Clark, R. C., Nguyen, F. and Sweller, J. (2005). *Efficiency in Learning: Evidence-Based Guidelines to Manage Cognitive Load*. New York: John Wiley & Sons.

Clark, R. and Wittrock, M. C. (2000). Psychological principles in training. In S. Tobias and J. D. Fletcher (Eds.), *Training and Retraining: A Handbook for Business, Industry, Government, and the Military* (pp. 51–84). New York: Macmillan Reference.

Clarke, N. (2002). Job/work environment factors influencing training transfer within a human service agency: Some indicative support for Baldwin and Ford's transfer climate construct. *International Journal of Training and Development, 6*(3), 146–162. doi:10.1111/1468-2419.00156.

Colquitt, J. A., LePine, J. A. and Noe, R. A. (2000). Toward an integrative theory of training motivation: A meta-analytic path analysis of 20 years of research. *Journal of Applied Psychology, 85*(5), 678–707. doi:10.1037//0021-9010.85.5.678.

Coutinho, S. A. and Neuman, G. (2008). A model of metacognition, achievement goal orientation, learning style and self-efficacy. *Learning Environments Research, 11*, 131–151. doi:10.1007/s10984-008-9042-7.

Coyle, D. (2012). *The Little Book of Talent: 52 Tips for Improving Your Skills*. New York: Bantam.

Csíkszentmihályi, M. (1990). *Flow: The Psychology of Optimal Experience*. New York: Harper and Row.

Csíkszentmihályi, M. (1998). *Finding Flow: The Psychology of Engagement with Everyday Life*. New York: Basic Books.

Csíkszentmihályi, M., Abuhamdeh, S. and Nakamura, J. (2007). Flow. In Elliot, A. and Dweck, C. S. (Eds.), *Handbook of Competence and Motivation* (pp. 598–698). New York: The Guilford Press.

de la Harpe, B., Radloff, A. and Parker, L. (1997). *The relationship between first year university students' use of metacognitive control strategies and academic achievement*. Paper presented at the HERDSA Conference, Adelaide, Australia. Retrieved from: http://www.herdsa.org.au/?page_id=186.

Dehn, M. J. (2011). *Working Memory and Academic Learning: Assessment and Intervention*. New York: John Wiley & Sons.

Dick, W., Carey, L. and Carey, J. O. (2011). *Systematic Design of Instruction* (7th ed.). Upper Saddle River, NJ: Pearson.

Doidge, N. (2007). *The Brain That Changes Itself*. New York: Penguin Publishing.

Doerner, W. G., Horton, C. and Smith, J. L. (2003). The field training officer program: A case study approach. In M. J. Palmiotto (Ed.), *Policing and Training Issues* (pp. 207–234). Upper Saddle River, NJ: Prentice Hall.

Elliott, P. H. and Folsom, A. C. (2013). *Exemplary Performance: Driving Business Results by Benchmarking Your Star Performer*. San Francisco: Jossey-Bass.

Ericsson, K. A. (2006). *Cambridge Handbook of Expertise and Expert Performance.* Charness, N., Feltovich, P. J. and Hoffman, R. R. (Eds.). New York: Cambridge University Press.

Federal Bureau of Investigation (2006). *Violent Encounters.* Washington, DC: U.S. Department of Justice.

FLETC (Federal Law Enforcement Training Center) (2011). *Stress and Decision Making.* Glynco, GA: U.S. Department of Homeland Security.

Fidishun, D. (2000). *Andragogy and technology: Integrating adult learning theory as we teach with technology.* [Conference Paper]: 5th Annual Instructional Technology Conference. Retrieved from: http://www.mtsu.edu/~itconf/proceed00 /fidishun.htm.

Flavell, J. H. (1979). Metacognition and cognitive monitoring: A new area of cognitive development. *American Psychologist, 34*(10), 906–911. doi:10.1037/0003 -066X.34.10.906.

Ford, J. K. and Weissbein, D. A. (1997). Transfer of training: An updated review and analysis. *Performance Improvement Quarterly, 10*(2), 22–41. doi:10.1111/j.1937 -8327.1997.tb00047.x.

Gagne, R. and Medsker, K. L. (1995). *The Conditions of Learning: Training Applications.* Belmont, CA: Wadsworth Publishing Company.

Gagne, R. M., Wager, W. W., Golas, K. C. and Keller, J. M. (2005). *Principles of Instructional Design* (5th ed.). Belmont, CA: Thomsom/Wadsworth.

Gaines, L. and Kappeler, V. E. (2011). *Policing in America.* Los Angeles: Sage Publications.

Gawande, A. (2009). *The Checklist Manifesto—How to Get Things Right.* New York: Metropolitan Books.

Geiwitz, J. (1994). *Training metacognitive skills for problem solving* (ARI Research Note 95-03). Alexandria, VA: U.S. Army Research Institute for the Behavioral and Social Sciences. Retrieved from: http://www.dtic.mil/cgi-bin/GetTRDoc ?AD=ADA290310.

Gilbert, T. (1996). *Human Competence* (2nd ed.). Silver Spring, MD: International Society for Performance Improvement.

Gilpin-Jackson, Y. and Bushe, G. R. (2007). Leadership development training: A case study of post-training determinants. *Journal of Management and Development, 26*(10), 980–1004. doi:10.1108/02621710833423.

Giovengo, R. D. (2014). *Training transfer, metacognition skills, and performance outcomes in blended versus traditional training programs* (Doctoral dissertation, Walden University, 2014).

Gitonga, J. W. (2006). *Work environment factors influencing the transfer of learning for online learners* [Report]. Retrieved from: http://www.eric.ed.gov/content delivery/SERVlet/ERICSerlet?accno=ED492788.

Gottfredson, C. and Mosher, B. (2011). *Innovative Performance Support.* New York: McGraw-Hill.

Graham, C. R. (2006). Blended learning systems: Definitions, current trends, and future directions. In C. J. Bonk and C. R. Graham (Eds.), *Handbook of Blended Learning: Global Perspectives, Local Design* (pp. 3–21). San Francisco: Pfeiffer Publishing.

Graham, C. R., Allen, S. and Ure, D. (2005). Benefits and challenges of blended learning environments. In M. Khosrow-Pour (Ed.), *Encyclopedia of Information Science and Technology* (pp. 253–259). Hershey, PA: Idea Group.

Greenaway, R. (1992). Reviewing by doing. *Journal of Adventure Education and Outdoor Leadership, 7*(2), 8–13.

Grossman, R. and Salas, E. (2011). The transfer of training: What really matters. *International Journal of Training and Development, 15*(2), 103–120. doi:10.1111 /j.1468-2419.2011.00373.x.

Hale, J. (2002). *Performance-Based Evaluation: Tools and Techniques to Measure the Impact of Training.* San Francisco: Jossey-Bass/Pfeiffer.

Hancock, P. A. and Szalma, J. L. (2008). *Performance under Stress.* Burlington, VA: Ashgate Publishing Company.

Harlen, W. and James, M. (1997). Assessment and learning: Differences and relationships. *Assessment in Education: Principles, Policy and Practice, 4*(3), 365–371. doi: 10.1080/0969594970040304.

Harless, J. H. (1973). An analysis of front-end analysis. Improving Human Performance. *Research Quarterly, 4,* 229–244.

Harmon, P. (1984). A hierarchy of performance variables. *Performance and Instruction, 23*(10), 27–28.

Harris, L., Jr., Mulligan, J., and Thetford, R. (2012). *Instructor Development: An Essential Guide for Understanding and Implementing Law Enforcement Training.* North Charleston, SC: CreateSpace Independent Publishing Platform.

Harrow, A. J. (1972). *A Taxonomy of the Psychomotor Domain: A Guide for Developing Behavioral Objectives.* United Kingdom: Longman Group.

Haskell, E. H. (2001). *Transfer of Learning: Cognition, Instruction, and Reasoning.* New York: Academic Press.

Hattie, J. and Yates, G. (2014). *Visible Learning and the Science of How We Learn.* London: Routledge.

Hawley, J. D. and Barnard, J. K. (2005). A study of best practices in training transfer and proposed model for transfer. In L. A. Burke and H. M. Hutchins (2008). *Human Resource Development Quarterly, 19*(2), 107–128.

Hayes, N. (2000). *Foundations of Psychology* (3rd ed.). London: Thomson Learning.

Hedden, H. (Fall, 2011). Supervisors are critical to training transfer. *ILEETA Digest, 9*(3), 6.

Holton III, E. F. (1996). The flawed four-level evaluation model. *Human Resource Development Quarterly, 7*(1), 5–21. doi 10.1080/0969594970040304:10.1002 /hrdq.3920070103.

Holton III, E. F., Bates, R. A. and Ruona, W. E. A. (2000). Development of a generalized Learning Transfer System Inventory. *Human Resource Development Quarterly, 11*(4), 333–360. doi:10.1002/1532-1096(200024).

Holton III, E. F., Chen, H. C. and Naquin, S. S. (2003). An examination of learning transfer system characteristics across organizational settings. *Human Resource Development Quarterly, 14,* 459–482. doi:10.1002/hrdq.1079.

Holton III, E. F., Bates, R. A., Bookter, A. I. and Yamkovenko, V. B. (2007). Convergent and divergent validity of the Learning Transfer System Inventory. *Human Resource Development Quarterly, 18*(3), 358–419. doi:10.1002/hrdq.1210.

Hundersmarck, S. (2009, August). Police recruit training: Facilitating learning between the academy and field training. *FBI Law Enforcement Bulletin.* Quantico, VA.

Hutchins, H. M. (2009). In the trainer's voice: A study of training transfer practices. *Performance Improvement Quarterly, 22*(1), 69–93. doi:10.1002/piq.20046.

Intergovernmental Studies Program, Rockefeller College of Public Affairs and Policy, University of Albany (2006). *A Practitioner Guide to Transfer of Learning and Training*. Retrieved from: www.albany.edu/polis/pdf/transfer%20learning _primer_final.pdf.

Johnson, D. C., Thom, N. J., Stanley, E. A., Haase, L., Simmons, A. N., Shih, P. B., Thompson, W. K., Potterat, E. G., Minor, T. R. and Paulus M. P. (2014). Modifying resilience mechanisms in at-risk individuals: A controlled study of mindfulness training in marines preparing for deployment. *American Journal of Psychiatry, 171*(8), 844–853. doi: 10.1176/appi.ajp.2014.13040502.

Kapp, K. M. and Defelice, R. A. (August 31, 2009). *Time to Develop One Hour of Training*. American Society for Training and Development. Retrieved from: http://www.astd.org/Publications/Newsletters/Learning-Circuits/Learning -Circuits-Archives/2009/08/Time-to-Develop-One-Hour-of-Training.

Karpicke, J. D. and Roediger, H. L. (2008). The critical importance of retrieval for learning. *Science, 15,* 966–968.

Keller, J. A. (1987). Development and use of the ARCS model of motivational design. *Journal of Instructional Development, 10*(3), 2–10.

Kirkpatrick, D. L. (1976). Evaluation of training. In R. L. Craig (Ed.), *Training and Development Handbook: A Guide to Human Resource Development*. New York: McGraw-Hill.

Kirkpatrick, D. L. (1998). *Evaluating Training Programs* (2nd ed.). San Francisco: Berrett-Koehler Publishers, Inc.

Kirkpatrick, J. D. and Kirkpatrick, W. K. (2010). *Training on Trial: How Workplace Learning Must Reinvent Itself to Remain Relevant*. New York: AMACOM.

Kirschner, P. A., Sweller, J. and Clark, R. E. (2006). Why minimal guidance during instruction does not work: An analysis of the failure of constructivist, discovery, problem-based, experiential, and inquiry-based teaching. *Educational Psychologist, 41*(2), 75–86.

Kirwan, C. and Birchall, D. (2006). Transfer of learning from management development programmes: Testing the Holton model. *International Journal of Training and Development, 10*(4), 252–268. doi:10.1111/j.1468-2419.2006.00259.x.

Klein, J. D., Spector, J. M., Grabowski, B. and de la Teja, I. (2004). *Instructor Competencies: Standards for Fact-to-Face, Online, and Blended Settings*. Greenwich, CT: Information Age Publishing.

Klein, H. J., Noe, R. A. and Wang, C. (2006). Motivation to learn and course outcomes: The impact of delivery mode, learning goal orientation, and perceived barriers and enablers. *Personnel Psychology, 59,* 665–702. doi:10.1111 /j.1744-6570.2006.00050.x.

Knowles, M. S., Holton III, E. F. and Swanson, R. A. (2005). *The Adult Learner* (6th ed.). Burlington, MA: Elsevier.

Kolb, D. A. (1984). *Experiential Learning: Experience as the Source of Learning and Development*. Upper Saddle River, NJ: Prentice Hall.

Kontoghiorghes, C. (2001). Factors affecting training effectiveness in the context of the introduction of technology—A US case study. *International Journal of Training and Development, 5*(4), 248–260. doi:10.1111/1468-2419.00137.

Kontoghiorghes, C. (2004). Reconceptualizing the learning transfer conceptual framework: Empirical validation of a new systematic model. *International Journal of Training and Development, 8*(3), 210–221. doi:10.1111/j.1360-3736.2004.00209.x.

Kontoghiorghes, C. (2008). A holistic approach toward motivation to learn in the workplace. *Performance Improvement Quarterly*, *14*(4), 45–59. doi:10.1111/j.1937-8327.2001.tb00229.x.

Krathwohl, D. R., Bloom, B. S. and Masia, B. B. (1964). *Taxonomy of Educational Objectives: The Classification of Educational Goals. Handbook II: The Affective Domain*. New York: Longman, Green.

Kyllonen, P. C. (2000). Training assessment. In S. Tobias and J. D. Fletcher (Eds.), *Training and Retraining: A Handbook for Business, Industry, Government, and the Military* (pp. 525–549). New York: Macmillan Reference.

Leutner, J. (Winter, 2013). Learning enables high performance. *Training Industry Quarterly*, 7.

Lieb, S. (1991). Principles of adult learning. *VISION Journal* [electronic version]. Fall. Retrieved from: http://honolulu.hawaii.edu/intranet/committees/FacDevCom/guidebk/teachtip/adults-2.htm.

Lim, D. H. and Johnson, S. D. (2002). Trainee perceptions of factors that influence learning transfer. *International Journal of Training and Development*, *6*(1), 36–48. doi:10.1111/1468-2419.00148.

Lim, D. H. and Morris, M. L. (2006). Influence of trainee characteristics, instructional satisfaction, and organizational climate on perceived learning and training transfer. *Human Resource Development Quarterly*, *17*(1), 85–115. doi:10.1002/hrdq.1162.

Livingston, J. A. (1997). *Metacognition: An Overview*. Retrieved from: http://gse.buffalo.edu/fas/shuell/cep564/Metacog.htm.

Lombardo, M. M. and Eichinger, R. W. (1996). *The Career Architect Development Planner*. Minneapolis, MN: Lorninger.

Lumley, T. (2002). Assessment criteria in a large-scale writing test: What do they really mean to the raters? *Language Testing*, *19*, 246–277.

Mager, R. F. (1997). *Preparing Instructional Objectives* (3rd ed.). Atlanta, GA: CEP Press.

Marrapodi, J. (2010). Front end analysis: Show me the problem. Presentation at the Learning Solutions Conference, Orlando, FL. Retrieved from: http://www.elearningguild.com/showFile.cfm?id=3895.

Martin, H. J. (2010). Workplace climate and peer support as determinants of training transfer. *Human Resources Development Quarterly*, *21*(1), 87–104. doi:10.1002/hrdq.20038.

Marton, F. and Säljö, R. (1976). On qualitative differences in learning: I—Outcome and process. *British Journal of Educational Psychology*, *46*, 4–11. doi:10.1111/j.2044-8279.1976.tb02980.x.

Marzano, R. J. (1998). *A Theory-Based Meta-Analysis of Research on Instruction*. Aurora, CO: Mid-continent Regional Educational Laboratory. Retrieved from: http://www.mcrel.org/pdf/instruction/5982rr_instructionmeta_analysis.pdf.

Marzano, R. J. and Kendal, J. S. (2007). *The New Taxonomy of Educational Objectives* (2nd ed.). Thousand Oaks, CA: Corwin Press.

Mathieu, J. E., Tannenbaum, S. I. and Salas, E. (1992). Influences of individual and situational characteristics on measures of training effectiveness. *Academy of Management Journal*, *4*, 828–847. doi:10.2307/256317.

Mayer, R. E. (2008). Science of learning. *American Psychologist*, *63*(8), 757–769. doi:10.1037/0003-066X.63.8.757.

Mayer, R. E., Stull, A., DeLeeuw, K., Almeroth, K., Bimber, B., Chun, D., Bulger, M., Campbell, J., Knight, A. and Zhang, H. (2009). Clickers in college classrooms: Fostering learning with questioning methods in large lecture classes. *Contemporary Educational Psychology*, 34(1), 51–57.

McGonigal, K. (2015). *The Upside of Stress*. New York: Avery.

McNamara, M. W. (2006, August 1). Legal corner: Department liability for failure-to-train. Retrieved from: http://www.policeone.com/pc_print.asp?vid=16650045.

Medina, J. (2008). *Brain Rules*. Seattle: WA: Pear Press.

Meichenbaum, D. (2008). Stress inoculation training: A preventative and treatment approach. In P. M. Lehrer, R. L. Woolfolk and W. S. Sime (3rd ed.), *Principles and Practice of Stress Management*. New York: Guilford Press.

Merriam, S. B. and Leahy, B. (2005). Learning transfer: A review of the research in adult education and training. *PAACE Journal of Lifelong Learning*, 14, 1–24. doi:10.1177/0149206309352880.

Merrill, M. D. (2007). A task-centered instructional strategy. *Journal of Research on Technology in Education*, 40(1), 5–22. Retrieved from: http://www.iup.edu /WorkArea/linkit.aspx?LinkIdentifier=idandItemID=18475.

Miller, G. A. (1956). The magical number seven, plus or minus two: Some limits on our capacity for processing information. *Psychological Review*, 63, 81–97.

Miner, J. B. (2005). *Organizational Behavior 1: Essential Theories of Motivation and Leadership*. Armonk, NY: M.E. Sharpe.

Moorhead, G. and Griffin, M. (1992). *Organizational Behavior*. Boston: Houghton Mifflin.

Murphy, E. (2008). A framework for identifying and promoting metacognitive knowledge and control in online discussants. *Canadian Journal of Learning and Technology*, 34(2), 1–27. Retrieved from: http://www.cjlt.ca/index.php/cjlt/rt /printerFriendly/491/222.

Murray, K. R. (2006). *Training at the Speed of Life, Volume 1—The Definitive Textbook for Military and Law Enforcement Reality Based Training*. Gotha, FL: Armiger Publications, Inc.

Nakamura, J. and Csikszentmihalyi, M. (20 December 2001). Flow theory and research. In C. R. S. E. Wright and S. J. Lopez (Eds.), *Handbook of Positive Psychology*. Oxford University Press (pp. 195–206).

Nijveldt, M., Beijaard, D., Brekelmans, M., Wubbels, T. and Verloop, N. (2009). Assessors' perceptions of their judgment processes: Successful strategies and threats underlying valid assessment of student teachers. *Studies in Educational Evaluation*, 35, 29–36.

Nikandrou, I., Vassiliki, B. and Bereri, E. (2009). Trainee perceptions of training transfer: An empirical analysis. *Journal of European Industrial Training*, 33(3), 255–270. doi:10.1108/03090590910950604.

Ng, K. S. and Ahmad, N. (2012). *Impact of Motivation to Learn on Perceived Training Transfer: Empirical Evidence from a Bank*. In: International Conference on Technology Management, Business and Entrepreneurship 2012 (ICTMBE 2012), 18–19 December 2012, Renaissance Melaka Hotel, Melaka.

Noe, R. A. and Schmitt, N. (1986). The influence of trainee attitudes on training effectiveness: Test of a model. *Personnel Psychology*, 39, 497–523. doi:10.1111 /j.1744-6570.1986.tb00950.x.

Office of Community Oriented Policing Services (2004). A problem-based learning manual for training and evaluating police trainees. Retrieved from: http://ric-zai-inc.com/Publications/cops-w0247-pub.pdf.

Osborn, C. (February, 2011). How to convert classroom training into e-learning. A White Paper from BizLibrary. Retrieved from: http://www.bizlibrary.com.

Osman, M. E. and Hannafin, M. J. (1992). Metacognition research and theory: Analysis and implications for instructional design. *Educational Technology Research and Development*, *40*(2), 83–99. doi:10.1007/BF02297053.

Palmiotto, M. J. (2003). An overview of police training through the decades: Current issues and problems. In M. J. Palmiotto (Ed.), *Policing and Training Issues* (pp. 1–24). Upper Saddle River, NJ: Prentice Hall.

Pashler, H., McDaniel, M., Rohrer, D. and Bjork, R. (2008). Learning styles: Concepts and evidence. *Psychological Science in the Public Interest*, *9*(3), 105–119.

Pierce, W. (2003). *Metacognition: Study strategies, monitoring, and motivation.* Text version of a workshop presented November 17, 2004, at Prince George's Community College. Retrieved from: http://academic.pg.cc.md.us/~wpeirce/MCCCTR/metacognition.htm.

Pellegrino, J. and Scott A. (2004). *The transition from simulation to game-based learning.* Paper presented at the Interservice/Industry Training Simulations, and Education Conference, Orlando, FL. Retrieved from: http://www.learningarchitects.net/files/Transition_from_Sims_to_Games.pdf.

Phillips, K. (2012). Developing valid level 3 evaluations: The secrets of survey design. *2012 ASTD-TCC Regional Conference and Expo,* October 24, 2012. Phillips Associates.

Pintrich, P. R. and De Groot, E. V. (1990). Motivational and self-regulated learning components of classroom academic performance. *Journal of Educational Psychology*, *82*(1), 33–40. doi:10.1037/0022-0663.82.1.33.

Prensky, M. (2001). Digital natives, digital immigrants. *On the Horizon*, *9*(5), 1–15. Retrieved from: http://www.nnstoy.org/download/technology/Digital%20Natives%20-%20Digital%20Immigrants.pdf.

President's Task Force on 21st Century Policing (2015). *Interim Report of the President's Task Force on 21st Century Policing.* Washington, DC: Office of Community Oriented Policing Services.

Quinsland, L. K. and Van Ginkel, A. (1984). Processing the experience. *The Journal of Experiential Education*, *7*(2), 8–13.

Reaves, B. A. (Feb. 2009). State and local law enforcement training academies, 2006. *Bureau of Justice Statistics Special Report*. U.S. Department of Justice, Office of Justice Programs. Retrieved from: http://www.bjs.gov/content/pub/pdf/slleta06.pdf.

Rock, D. (2009). *Your Brain at Work*. New York: Harper Business.

Rosenberg, M. (2012, July). Marc my words: Why I hate instructional objectives. *Learning Solutions Magazine*. Retrieved from: http://www.learningsolutionsmag.com/articles/965/marc-my-words-why-i-hate-instructional-objectives.

Rouiller, J. Z. and Goldstein, I. L. (1993). The relationship between organizational transfer climate and positive transfer of training. *Human Resources Development Quarterly*, *4*(4), 377–390. doi:10.1002/hrdq.3920040408.

Rovai, A. P., Wighting, M. J., Baker, J. D. and Grooms, L. D. (2009, January). Development of an instrument to measure perceived cognitive, affective, and psychomotor learning in traditional and virtual higher education classroom settings. *Internet and Higher Education, 121*(1), 7–13.

Ruona, W. E. A., Leimbach, M., Holton III, E. F. and Bates, R. (2002). The relationship between learner utility reactions and predicted learning transfer among trainees. *International Journal of Training and Development, 6*(4), 218–228. doi:10.1111/1468-2419.00160.

Rushing, P. S. (2010, February). A new training strategy for training police officers—The PTP program. *CALEA Update,* 102. Retrieved from: http://www.calea.org/calea-update-magazine/issue-101/police-training-officer-pto-program.

Salas, E. and Cannon-Bowers, J. A. (2001). The science of training: A decade of progress. *Annual Review of Psychology, 52,* 471–499. doi: 10.1146/annurev.psych.52.1.471.

Salas, E., Milham, L. M. and Bowers, C. A. (2009). Training evaluation in the military: Misconceptions, opportunities, and challenges. *Military Psychology, 15*(1), 3–16. doi:10.1207/S15327876MP1501_01.

Sandeen, C. (2008). Boomers, Xers, and millennials: Who are they and what do they really want from continuing higher education? *Continuing Higher Education Review, 72,* 11–31.

Schmitt, M. C. and Newby, T. J. (1986). Metacognition: Relevance to instructional designing. *Journal of Instructional Development, 9*(4), 29–33. doi:10.1007/BF02908316.

Schmidt, R. A. and Wrisberg, C. A. (2008). *Motor Learning and Performance: A Situation-Based Learning Approach* (4th ed.). Champaign, IL: Human Kinetics.

Schraw, G. and Dennison, R. S. (1994). Assessing metacognitive awareness. *Contemporary Educational Psychology, 19,* 460–475. doi.org/10.1016/j.bbr.2011.03.031.

Schraw, G. and Moshman, D. (1995). Metacognitive theories. *Educational Psychology Review, 7*(4), 351–371. doi:10.1007/BF02212307.

Scott, J. (2010, November). The status of field training. *The Police Chief,* p. 66. Retrieved from: http://www.nxtbook.com/nxtbooks/naylor/CPIM1110/#/66.

Secret Service on the Line: Restoring Trust and Confidence: Hearing before the Committee on Homeland Security and Governmental Affairs, United States Senate, 112 Cong. 559 (2012). Retrieved from: http://www.gpo.gov/fdsys/pkg/CHRG-112shrg75215/html/CHRG-112shrg75215.htm.

Seyler, D. L., Holton, III, E. F., Bates, R. A., Burnett, M. F. and Carvalho, M. B. (1998). Factors affecting motivation to transfer training. *International Journal of Training and Development, 2*(1), 2–16.

Shepherd, E. and Godwin, J. (2010). *Assessment through the learning process.* Questionmark White Paper.

Shia, R. M. (2005). *Assessing academic intrinsic motivation: A look at student goals and personal strategy* (Master's thesis, Wheeling Jesuit University, 2005). Retrieved from: http://www.cet.edu/research/PDF/motivation.pdf.

Shrock, S. A. and Coscarelli, W. C. (2007). *Criterion-Referenced Test Development* (3rd ed.). San Francisco: Pfeiffer.

Smith, S. C. and Bost, L. W. (2007). Collecting post-school outcome data: Strategies for increasing response rates. National Post-School Outcomes Center. Retrieved from: http://www.psocenter.org.

Soderstrom, N. C. and Bjork, R. A. (2013). Learning versus performance. In Dunn, D. S. (Ed.), *Oxford Bibliographies Online: Psychology*, New York: Oxford University Press.

Sitzmann, T., Brown, K. G., Casper, W. J., Ely, K. and Zimmerman, R. D. (2008). A review and meta-analysis of the nomological network of trainee reactions. *Journal of Applied Psychology*, 93, 280–295.

Sweller, J. (1988). Cognitive load during problem solving: Effects on Learning. *Cognitive Science*, 12(2), 257–285. doi: 10.1207/s15516709cog1202_4.

Tannenbaum, S. I. and Yukl, G. (1992). Training and development in work organizations. *Annual Review of Psychology*, 43, 399–441. doi:10.1146/annurev.ps.43.020192.002151.

Tannenbaum, S. I., Cannon-Bowers, J. A., Salas, E. and Mathieu, J. E. (1993). *Factors that influence training effectiveness: A conceptual model and longitudinal analysis* (Technical Report 93-011). Orlando, FL: Naval Training Systems Center, Human Systems Integration Division. Retrieved from: www.personal.psu.edu/krm10/Live%20Fire%20Project/effectivness.pdf.

Teodorescu, T. M. and Binder, C. (2004). Getting to the bottom line competence is what matters. *Performance Improvement*, 43(8), 8–12. doi: 10.1002/pfi.4140430805.

Terrace, H. (2001). Chunking and serially organized behavior in pigeons, monkeys and humans. In Cook, R. G. (Ed.), *Avian Visual Cognition*. Medford, MA: Comparative Cognition Press.

Thalheimer, Will (2010). *How much do people forget?* Retrieved from: http://www.willatworklearning.com/2010.12/how-much-do-people-forget.pdf.

Thorndike, E. L. and Woodworth, R. S. (1901). The influence of improvement in one mental function upon the efficiency of other functions. *Psychological Review*, 8, 247–261. Retrieved from: http://psychclassics.yorku.ca/Thorndike/Transfer/transfer1.htm.

Tinsley, H. E. A. and Weiss, D. J. (2000). Interrater reliability and agreement. In H. E. A. Tinsley and S. D. Brown (Eds.), *Handbook of Applied Multivariate Statistics and Mathematical Modeling* (pp. 95–124). New York: Academic Press.

US Copyright Office (2012, June). Copyright—Fair Use. Retrieved from: http://www.copyright.gov/fls/fl102.html.

US House Committee on the Judiciary (1961, July). *Report of the Register of Copyrights on the General Revision of the U.S. Copyright Law*. Washington, DC: U.S. Government Printing Office.

Vanteenkiste, M., Lens, W. and Deci, E. L. (2006). Intrinsic versus extrinsic goal contents in self-determination theory: Another look at the quality of academic motivation. *Educational Psychologist*, 41(1), 19–31. doi:10.1207/s15326985ep4101_4.

Vroom, V. H. (1964). *Work and Motivation*. New York: Wiley.

Waddoups, G. and Howell, S. (2002). Bringing online learning to campus: The hybridization of teaching and learning at Brigham Young University. *International Review of Research in Open and Distance Education*, 2(2). Retrieved from: http://www.irrodl.org/index.php/irrodl/article/view/52/108.

Weisinger, H. (2015). *Performing under Pressure: The Science of Doing Your Best When It Matters Most*. New York: Crown Business.

Weldon, E. (1998). *The effects of proximal and distal goals on strategy development and group performance* (ARI Research Note 98-22). Alexandria, VA: U.S. Army Research Institute for the Behavioral and Social Sciences. Retrieved from: http://www.dtic.mil/cgi-bin/GetTRDoc?AD=ADA349438.

Wexley, K. N. and Latham, G. P. (2002). *Developing and Training Human Resources in Organizations* (3rd ed.). Upper Saddle River, NJ: Pearson Education, Inc.

Wlodkowski, R. J. (2008). *Enhancing Adult Motivation to Learn* (3rd ed.). San Francisco: Jossey-Bass.

Yamnill, S. and McLean, G. N. (2002). Factors affecting transfer of training in Thailand. In Symposium 17 (Ed.), Academy of Human Resource Development Conference Proceedings (p. 23). Bowling Green, OH. doi:10.1002/hrdq.1210.

Zmeyov, S. I. (1998). Andragogy. Origins, developments and trends. *International Review of Education* [electronic version], 44(1) p. 105. Retrieved from: http://www.springerlink.com/content/u6367k2r10218668/fulltext.pdf.

Index

Page numbers followed by f and t indicate figures and tables, respectively.